CUET-UG

Humanities

17
Solved Papers

3 Geography | 5 History | 5 Political Science
2 Psychology | 2 Sociology

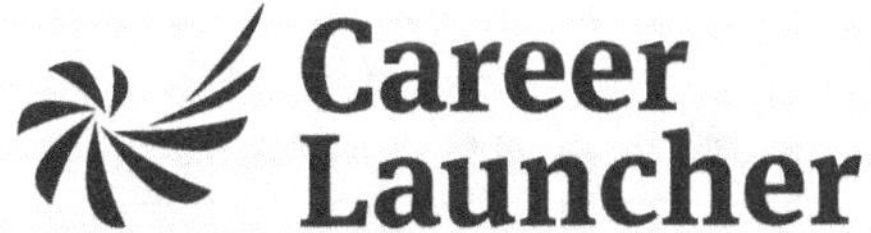

Title   : **CUET - UG :** Humanities - 17 Solved Papers

Language   : English

Editor's Name : AMIT SINGH

Copyright ©   : 2023 CLIP

Typeset & Published by :

Career Launcher Infrastructure (P) Ltd.

A-45, Mohan Cooperative Industrial Area, Near Mohan Estate Metro Station, New Delhi - 110044

Marketed by :

G.K. Publications (P) Ltd.

Plot No. 9A, Sector-27A, Mathura Road, Faridabad, Haryana-121003

ISBN   : **978-93-5681-136-2**

Printer's Details : Printed in India, New Delhi.

For product information :

Visit ***www.gkpublications.com*** or email to ***gkp@gkpublications.com***

Contents

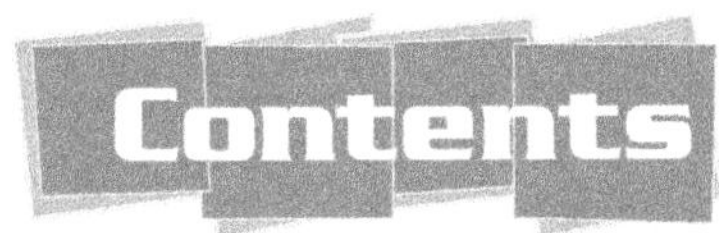

GEOGRAPHY

HISTORY

POLITICAL SCIENCE

PSYCHOLOGY

SOCIOLOGY

CUET EXAM PATTERN 2023

Sections	Subjects/ Tests	No. of Questions	To be Attempted	Duration
Section IA	13 Languages	50	40 in each language	45 minutes for each language
Section IB	19 Languages			
Section II	27 Domain-specific Subjects	50	40	45 minutes for each subject
Section III	General Test	75	60	60 minutes

CUET 2023 EXAM STRUCTURE - SLOT 1

Test/Subjects	No. of questions to be attempted	Marks per question	Total marks	Duration of exam
Language (any one of the 13 languages opted in Section IA)	40 out of 50	5	200	45 minutes per language
Domain Specific Subjects (Max. 2 subjects)	40 out of 50	5	200	45 minutes per subject
General Test	60 out of 75	5	300	60 minutes

CUET TEST STRUCTURE 2023 - SLOT 2

Test/Subjects	No. of questions to be attempted	Marks per question	Total marks	Duration of exam
Language (any one of the remaining 12 languages opted in Section IA (if one already taken in slot 1) and 1 from Section IB - as applicable)	40 out of 50	5	200	45 minutes per language
Domain Specific Subjects (Max. 4 subjects)	40 out of 50	5	200	45 minutes per subject

CUET 2023 MARKING SCHEME

Correct Answer	5 marks will be awarded to students
Incorrect Answer	One mark will be deducted
No Answer	0 marks will be awarded

GEOGRAPHY

1. Out of the given options choose the most appropriate one to define 'Density of Population'.
   (a) Number of live births in a year per thousand of population.
   (b) Change in number of persons of a territory dining a specific period of time.
   (c) Ratio between the number of women and men in the population.
   (d) Number of persons living in per square km of an area.

2. In Indonesia and Malaysia, shifting cultivation is known by which of the following names?
   (a) Jhuming
   (b) Milpa
   (c) Ladang
   (d) Viticulture

3. In which of the following countries. Ruhr industrial region is located?
   (a) France
   (b) Spain
   (c) Germany
   (d) England

4. Industry producing raw materials for other' industries is known by which of the following?
   (a) Basic industry
   (b) Small scale industry
   (c) Cottage industry
   (d) Food processing industry

5. Since which year radio broadcasting started in India for the first time?
   (a) 1920
   (b) 1923
   (c) 1916
   (d) 1925

6. Which of the following is the longest highway in India?
   (a) NH-1
   (b) NH-2
   (c) NH-8
   (d) NH-7

7. Name the telecommunication service4, which is not considered as "Mass Media"?
   (a) Mobile phone
   (b) Radio
   (c) T.V
   (d) Newspaper

8. In which of the following period negative growth rate of population was recorded in India?
   (a) 1901-1911
   (b) 1911-1921
   (c) 1951-1961
   (d) 1971-1981

9. Which one of the following is the length of Panama Canal?
   (a) 160 Km
   (b) 72 Km
   (c) 117 Km
   (d) 195 Km

10. 'Neeru-Meeru' a watershed development and management programme is associated with which of the following?
    (a) Rajasthan
    (b) Andhra Pradesh
    (c) Tamil Nadu
    (d) Haryana

11. The Big Trunk Route runs through which of the following?
    (a) The North Atlantic Ocean
    (b) The Mediterranean - Indian Ocean
    (c) The South Atlantic Ocean
    (d) The South Pacific Ocean

12. A geothermal energy plant has been commissioned at which of the following places?
    (a) Okhla in Delhi
    (b) Tarapur in Maharashtra
    (c) Manikaran in Himachal Pradesh
    (d) Narora in Uttar Pradesh

13. Drought Prone Area Programme was initiated during which five year plan in India?
    (a) Fourth
    (b) Second
    (c) Sixth
    (d) Fifth

14. Who among the following is the author of "The Population Bomb"?
    (a) Peter Hagget
    (b) Ehrlich
    (c) A. N. Strahler
    (d) Thomas Malthus

15. The Swachh Bharat Mission (SBM) launched by the Government of India is a part of-
    (a) Rural renewable mission
    (b) Rural Souchalaya mission
    (c) Urban Souchalaya mission
    (d) Both (b) and (c)

16. Which one of the following state of India has the lowest rank in the human development index according to Indian National Human Development Report 2011?
    (a) Rajasthan
    (b) Bihar
    (c) Chhattisgarh
    (d) Haryana

17. In the production of cotton. India stands at which rank in the world cotton production?
    (a) First
    (b) Second
    (c) Third
    (d) Fourth

18. The important underground railways, 'Channel Tunnel' joins which two cities of Europe?

    (a) Rome - Berlin

    (b) Geneva - Amsterdam

    (c) London - Paris

    (d) Moscow - Stockholm

19. Which of the following is not a metallic mineral?

    (a) Iron

    (b) Mica

    (c) Copper

    (d) Bauxite

20. Name the city where Asia's largest slum Dharavi is located?

    (a) Delhi

    (b) Mumbai

    (c) Kolkata

    (d) Chennai

21. How much world population is estimated to live in urban areas by 2050?

    (a) One-fourth of world population

    (b) Three-fourth of world population

    (c) One-third of world population

    (d) Two-third of world population

22. The level of steady noise is measured by sound level expressed by which one of the following?

    (a) cB

    (b) dB

    (c) aB

    (d) iB

23. Which one of the following is not an approach to human development?

    (a) Basic needs approach

    (b) Capability approach

    (c) Need fulfilment approach

    (d) Welfare approach

24. The nucleus of the Gujarat Industrial region is:

    (a) Vadodara - Jamnagar

    (b) Bharuch - Kojali

    (c) Ahmedabad - Vadodara

    (d) Valsad - Jamnagar

25. Which one of the following cities became the mega city by 1950?

    (a) Paris   (b) New York

    (c) Delhi   (d) Shenzhen

26. Integrated Tribal Development Project in Bharmaur region was notified in which of the following year?

    (a) 1960

    (b) 1980

    (c) 1985

    (d) 1975

27. Match **List I** with **List II**.

List I - Nuclear Power Projects	List II - States of India
A. Tarapur	I. Karnataka
B. Kalpakkam	II. Uttar Pradesh
C. Narora	III. Tamil Nadu
D. Kaiga	IV. Maharashtra

Choose the correct answer from the options given below:

    (a) A-IV, B-III, C-II, D-I

    (b) A-II, B-IV, C-III, D-I

    (c) A-III, B-I, C-IV, D-II

    (d) A-I, B-II, C-III, D-IV

28. Match List I with List II.

List I - Mines Refinery	List II - Centres
A. Iron ore mine	I. Digboi
B. Copper mine	II. Durg
C. Oil refinery	III. Maikala hill
D. Bauxite mine	IV. Khetri

Choose the correct answer from the options given below:

    (a) A-IV, B-II, C-I, D-III

    (b) A-II, B-IV, C-III, D-I

    (c) A-II, B-IV, C-I, D-III

    (d) A-IV, B-II, C-III, D-I

29. Match List I with List II.

List I - Ports	List II - Functions
A. Entrepot ports	I. Tanker port
B. Naval ports	II. Collections Centres
C. Packet station	III. Warships
D. Oil ports	IV. Ferry ports

Choose the correct answer from the options given below:

    (a) A-I, B-IV, C-II, D-III

    (b) A-III, B-I, C-IV, D-II

    (c) A-II, B-III, C-IV, D-I

    (d) A-IV, B-I, C-III, D-II

30. Match List I with List II.

List I - Railway Zone	**List II - Headquarters**
A. Northern	I. Chennai
B. Eastern	II. Mumbai
C. Western	III. Kolkata
D. Southern	IV. New Delhi

Choose the correct answer from the options given below:

(a) A-I, B-IV, C-III, D-II

(b) A-II, B-I, C-IV, D-III

(c) A-IV, B-III, C-II, D-I

(d) A-III, B-II, C-I, D-IV

31. Match **List I** with **List II**.

List I - Oil refineries located	**List II - State of India**
A. Koyali	I. Kerala
B. Barauni	II. Assam
C. Digboi	III. Bihar
D. Kochi	IV. Gujarat

Choose the correct answer from the options given below:

(a) A-III, B-II, C-I, D-IV

(b) A-I, B-II, C-III, D-IV

(c) A-III, B-IV, C-II, D-I

(d) A-IV, B-III, C-II, D-I

32. Identify the characteristics of rural settlements in India.

A. These settlement act as nodes of economic growth

B. People are less mobile in villages

C. Settlements are specialized in agriculture or other primary activities

D. Life is complex and fast and social relations are formal

E. Social relations among people are intimate

Choose the correct answer from the options given below:

(a) A, B and C only

(b) B, C and D Only

(c) C, D and E Only

(d) B, C and E Only

33. Read the following statements care folly concerning Indian Railways.

A. Indian Railways is one of the longest in the world.

B. It is the largest government undertaking in the country.

C. Indian Railway is divided into 20 zones.

D. Indian Railway was introduced in 1853.

Choose the correct answer from the options given below:

(a) A, C and D only

(b) B, C and D Only

(c) A, B and C Only

(d) A, B and D Only

34. Read the following care folly with reference to Human Development in India:

A. Kerala is at the top in human development index.

B. States showing higher total literacy rates have huge gaps between male-female literacy.

C. Odisha is among the top five states in human development category.

D. India has been among the medium HD I category.

Choose the correct answer from the options given below:

(a) A and B Only

(b) A and C Only

(c) A and D Only

(d) B and C Only

35. Identify which is not a feature of nucleated settlements.

A. Communities are closely knit.

B. People share common occupations.

C. Settlements size is relatively large.

D. Economic activities are very specialized.

Choose the correct answer from the options given below:

(a) A and B Only

(b) A and C Only

(c) B and D Only

(d) C and D Only

36. Arrange the following incidents in sequential order according to their developments.

A. Air' transport was nationalized.

B. Air transport was provided by four major companies.

C. Air transport in India was hunched between Allahabad and Naini.

D. Bharat Airways. Himalayan aviation Ltd. joined the services.

Choose the correct answer from the options given below:

(a) D, A, C, B   (b) A, B, C, D

(c) C, B, D, A   (d) B, A, C, D

37. Arrange the following approaches in a sequence according to their periodical development.

 A. Spatial organization

 B. Regional analysis

 C. Humanistic approach

 D. Areal differentiation

 Choose the correct answer from the options given below:

 (a) A, B, D, C

 (b) B, C, A, D

 (c) D, A, C, B

 (d) B, D, A, C

38. Arrange the following agglomerated cities according to their population in descending order.

 A. Delhi

 B. Greater Mumbai

 C. Chennai

 D. Kolkata

 Choose the correct answer from the options given below:

 (a) D, B, A, C

 (b) C, B, A, D

 (c) B, A, D, C

 (d) A, C, D, B

39. Arrange the development of following approaches in geography in chronological order.

 A. Areal differentiation

 B. Post modernism

 C. Regional analysis

 D. Behavioural school

 Choose the correct answer from the options given below:

 (a) C, A, B, D   (b) A, B, C, D

 (c) C, A, D, B   (d) A, D, C, B

40. Arrange the following regions from low to high population density.

 A. Oceania

 B. Africa

 C. North America

 D. Europe

 Choose the correct answer from the options given below:

 (a) A, C, D, B   (b) A, C, B, D

 (c) C, A, D, B   (d) C, A, B, D

Directions for Questions 41 to 45: Read the following information and answer.

Indira Gandhi Canal (Nahar) Command Area

Indira Gandhi Canal, previously known as Rajasthan canal, is one of the largest canal systems in India. The canal originates at Harike barrage in Punjab and runs parallel to Pakistan border at an average distance of 40 km in Thar Desert (Marusthali) of Rajasthan. The construction work of the canal system has been carried out through two stages. The command area of stage-I lies in Ganganagar, Hanumangarh and northern part of Bikaner districts. It has a cultural command area of 5.53 lakh hactares. The command area of stage - II is spread over Bikaner, Jaisalmer, Barmer, Jodhpur, Nagaur and Churu districts covering culturable command area of 14.10 lakh hectares.

The introduction of canal irrigation in this dry land has transformed its ecology, economy and society. It has influenced the environmental conditions of the region both positively as well as negatively, The availability of soil moisture for a longer period of time and various afforestation and pasture development programmes under CAD have resulted in greening the land. This also helped in reducing wind erosion and siltation of canal systems. But the intensive irrigation and excessive use of water has led to the emergence of twin environmental problems of waterlogging and soil salinity. Introduction of canal irrigation has brought about a perceptible transformation in the agricultural economy of the region. Soil moisture has been a limiting factor in a success fill growing of crops in this area, Spread of canal irrigation has led to increase in cultivated area and intensity of cropping. This has also caused waterlogging and soil salinity, arid thus, in the long run, it hampers the sustainability of agriculture.

41. Identify the correct statements.

 A. Canal irrigation has brought a perceptible transformation in the agriculture.

 B. Canal leads to afforestation.

 C. It has also caused water logging and soil salinity.

 D. Spread of canal led to decrease in cultivated area.

 Choose the correct answer from the options given below:

 (a) A, C and D Only   (b) A, B and D Only

 (c) A, B and C Only   (d) B, C and D Only

42. Which one of the followings is the most important effect in Indira Gandhi Canal Command Area?

(a) Agricultural development

(b) Eco-development

(c) Sustainable development

(d) Water transport development

43. Find the difference between the command area of stage-I and stage-II choose the correct answer from the following.

(a) 8.97   (b) 8.87

(c) 8.67   (d) 8.57

44. The canal runs parallel to which neighbouring country?

(a) Bhutan

(b) Bangladesh

(c) Nepal

(d) Pakistan

45. Stage-I of Indira Gandhi Canal lies in which of the following command area?

(a) Nagaur

(b) Ganganagar

(c) Barmer

(d) Jodhpur

Directions for Questions 46 to 50: Read the following information and answer.

Census Years	Total Population	Growth Rate*	
		Absolute Number	% of Growth
1901	238396327	—	—
1911	252093390	(+) 13697063	(+) 5.75
1921	251321213	(–) 772117	(–) 0.31
1931	278977238	(+) 27656025	(+) 11,60
1941	318660580	(+) 39683342	(+) 14.22
1951	361088090	(+) 42420485	(+) 13.31
1961	439234771	(+) 77682873	(+) 21.51
1971	548159652	(+) 108924881	(+) 24.80
1981	683329097	(+) 135169445	(+) 24.66
1991	846302688	(+) 162973591	(+) 23.85
2001	1028610328	(+) 182307640	(+) 21.54
2011	1210193422	(+) 181583094	(+) 17.64

46. During which period, the population percent growth rate was recorded highest in India?

(a) 1951-61   (b) 1961-71

(c) 1971-81   (d) 1981-91

47. Calculate the difference of population growth percent rate from 2001 to 2011.

(a) 3.00%   (b) 3.10%

(c) 3.90%   (d) 3.50%

48. During which one of the following years, the growth rate of population was negative?

(a) 1911-21   (b) 1921-31

(c) 1931-41   (d) 1901-11

49. During which one of the following years, the population growth rate was less in comparison to the previous year?

(a) 1931-41   (b) 1941-51

(c) 1951-61   (d) 1961-71

50. Compute the difference between the population of 1991 and 2001 and choose the correct answer from the given options.

(a) 34, 52, 81, 231

(b) 35, 38, 89, 734

(c) 36, 38, 89, 734

(d) 36, 38, 90, 734

Answer Keys

1. (d)	**2.** (c)	**3.** (c)	**4.** (a)	**5.** (b)	**6.** (d)	**7.** (a)	**8.** (b)	**9.** (b)	**10.** (b)
11. (a)	**12.** (c)	**13.** (a)	**14.** (b)	**15.** (d)	**16.** (c)	**17.** (b)	**18.** (c)	**19.** (b)	**20.** (b)
21. (d)	**22.** (b)	**23.** (c)	**24.** (c)	**25.** (b)	**26.** (d)	**27.** (a)	**28.** (c)	**29.** (c)	**30.** (c)
31. (d)	**32.** (d)	**33.** (d)	**34.** (c)	**35.** (d)	**36.** (c)	**37.** (d)	**38.** (c)	**39.** (c)	**40.** (a)
41. (c)	**42.** (a)	**43.** (d)	**44.** (d)	**45.** (b)	**46.** (a)	**47.** (c)	**48.** (a)	**49.** (b)	**50.** (a)

Explanations

1. (d) The density of population is usually measured in persons per sq. km.

2. (c) Shifting cultivation also known as slash and burn agriculture is prevalent in tropical region in different names, e.g. Jhuming in North eastern states of India, Milpa in Central America and Mexico and Ladang in Indonesia and Malaysia.

3. (c) The Ruhr region is responsible for 80 per cent of Germany's total steel production.

4. (a) The iron and steel industry forms the base of all other industries and, therefore, it is called a basic industry. It is basic because it provides raw material for other industries such as machine tools used for further production.

5. (b) Radio broadcasting started in India in 1923 by the Radio Club of Bombay.

6. (d) In India, there are many highways linking the major towns and cities. For example, National Highway No. 7 (NH 7), connecting Varanasi with Kanya Kumari, is the longest in the country.

7. (a)

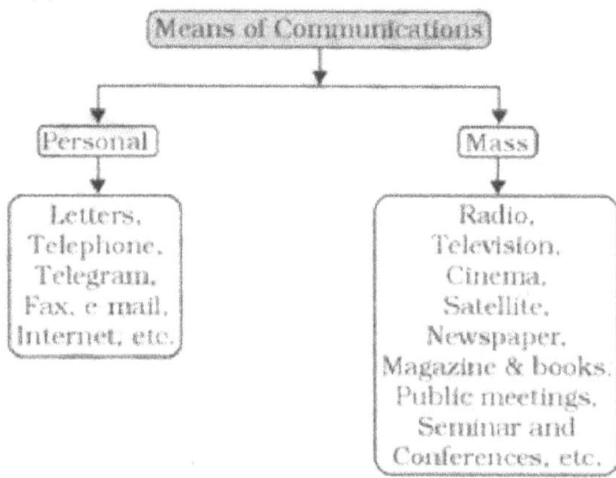

8. (b) **Phase I:** The period from 1901-1921 is referred to as a period of stagnant or stationary phase of growth of India's population, since in this period growth rate was very low, even recording a negative growth rate during 1911-1921. Both the birth rate and death rate were high keeping the rate of increase low. Poor health and medical services, illiteracy of people at large and inefficient distribution system of food and other basic necessities were largely responsible for a high birth and death rates in this period.

9. (b) **The Panama Canal:** This canal connects the Atlantic Ocean in the east to the Pacific Ocean in the west. It has been constructed across the Panama Isthmus between Panama City and Colon by the U.S. government which purchased 8 km of area on either side and named it the Canal Zone. The Canal is about 72 km. long and involves a very deep cutting for a length of 12 km. It has a sixlock system and ships cross the different levels (26 m up and down) through these locks before entering the Gulf of Panama.

10. (b) Neeru-Meeru (Water and You) programme (in Andhra Pradesh) and Arvary Pani Sansad (in Alwar, Rajasthan) have taken up constructions of various water-harvesting structures such as percolation tanks, dug out ponds (Johad), check dams, etc., through people's participation.

11. (a) The Northern Atlantic Sea Route - This links North-eastern U.S.A. and North-western Europe, the two industrially developed regions of the world. The foreign trade over this route is greater than that of the rest of the world combined. One fourth of the world's foreign trade moves on this route. It is, therefore, the busiest in the world and otherwise, called the Big Trunk Route. Both the coasts have highly advanced ports and harbour facilities.

12. (c) In India, a geothermal energy plant has been commissioned at Manikaran in Himachal Pradesh.

13. (a) Drought Prone Area Programme was initiated during the Fourth Five Year Plan with the objectives of providing employment to the people in drought-prone areas and creating productive assets.

14. (b) The notion of sustainable development emerged in the wake of general rise in the awareness of environmental issues in the late 1960s in Western World. It reflected the concern of people about undesirable effects of industrial development on the environment. The publication of 'The Population Bomb' by Ehrlich in 1968 and 'The Limits to Growth' by Meadows and others in 1972 further raised the level of fear among environmentalists in particular and people in general.

15. (d) Swachh Bharat Mission (SBM) aims at a pollution-free environment. Its objectives are :

- making India open defecation-free and achieving 100 per cent scientific management of municipal solid waste, construction of individual household latrines (IHHL), community toilet (CT) seats and public toilet (PT) seats;

- making provisions for the supply of clean energy fuel LPG to all households in rural India to reduce domestic pollution;

- providing potable drinking water to every household to control the spread of water-borne diseases; and

- promoting the use of non-convention energy resources, like wind and solar energy.

16. (c) Chhattisgarh with HDI value of 0.358 has the lowest rank.

17. (b) India ranks second in the world in the production of cotton after China. Cotton occupies about 4.7 per cent of total cropped area in the country.

18. (c) Channel Tunnel, operated by Euro Tunnel Group through England, connects London with Paris.

19. (b) Among the non-metallic minerals produced in India, mica is the important one. The other minerals extracted for local consumption are limestone, dolomite and phosphate.

20. (b) Asia's largest slum Dharavi is located in Mumbai.

21. (d) By 2050, an estimated two-thirds of the world's population will live in urban areas, imposing even more pressure on the space infrastructure and resources of cities, which are manifested in terms of sanitary, health, crime problems and urban poverty.

22. (b) The level of steady noise is measured by sound level expressed in terms of decibels (dB).

23. (c) Some of the important approaches are: (a) The income approach; (b) The welfare approach; (c) Minimum needs approach; and (d) Capabilities approach.

24. (c) Gujarat Industrial Region - The nucleus of this region lies between Ahmedabad and Vadodara but this region extends upto Valsad and Surat in the south and to Jamnagar in the west.

25. (b) New York was the first to attain the status of a mega city by 1950 with a total population of about 12.5 million.

26. (d) Bharmaur tribal area comprises Bharmaur and Holi tehsils of Chamba district of Himachal Pradesh. It is a notified tribal area since 21 November 1975. Bharmaur is inhabited by 'Gaddi', a tribal community who have maintained a distinct identity in the Himalayan region as they practised transhumance and conversed through Gaddiali dialect.

27. (a) The important nuclear power projects are Tarapur (Maharashtra), Rawatbhata near Kota (Rajasthan), Kalpakkam (Tamil Nadu), Narora (Uttar Pradesh), Kaiga (Karnataka) and Kakarapara (Gujarat).

28. (c) Iron Ore Mine-Durg; Copper mine-Khetri; Oil Refinery-Digboi; Bauxite mine-Maikal Hill

29. (c) **Entrepot Ports -** These are collection centres where the goods are brought from different countries for export. **Packet Station -** These are also known as ferry ports. **Naval Ports -** These are ports which have only strategic importance. These ports serve warships and have repair workshops for them. **Oil Ports -** These ports deal in the processing and shipping of oil. Some of these are tanker ports and some are refinery ports.

30. (c)

Indian Railways: Railway Zones and Headquarters	
Railway Zone	**Headquarters**
Central	Mumbai CST
Eastern	Kolkata
East Central	Hajipur
East Coast	Bhubaneswar
Northern	New Delhi
North Central	Allahabad
North Eastern	Gorakhpur
North East Frontier	Maligaon (Guwahati)
North Western	Jaipur
Southern	Chennai
South Central	Secunderabad
South Eastern	Kolkata
South East Central	Bilaspur
South Western	Hubli
Western	Mumbai (Church Gate)
West Central	Jabalpur

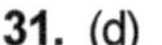

31. (d)

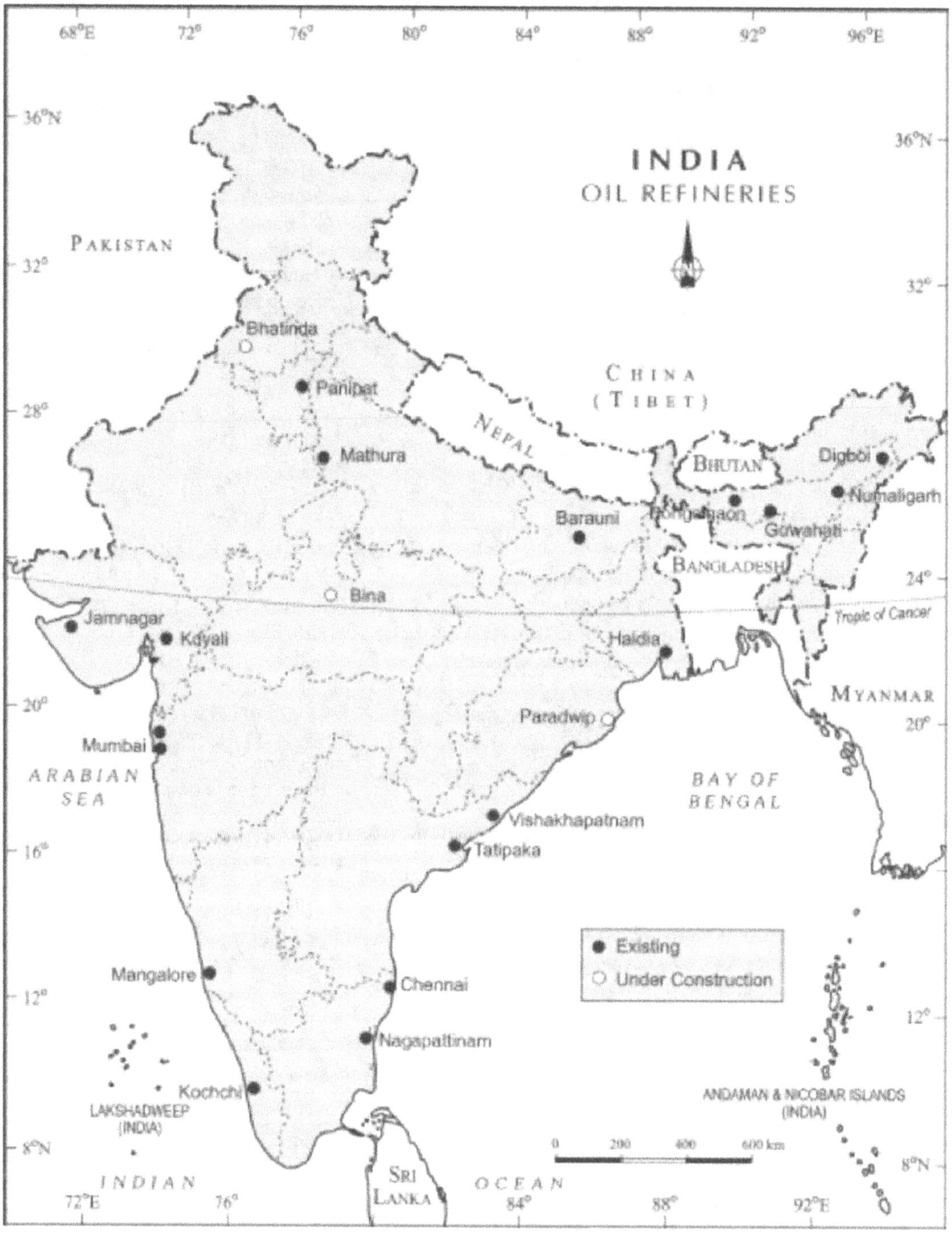

Fig. India - Oil Refineries

32. (d) The rural settlements derive their life support or basic economic needs from land based primary economic activities. Rural people are less mobile and therefore, social relations among them are intimate.

33. (d) Indian Railways, network is one of the longest in the world. It facilitates the movement of both freight and passengers and contributes to the growth of the economy. Indian Railways is the largest government undertaking in the country. The length of Indian Railways network was 67,956 km (Railway yearbook 2019-20). It's very large size puts a lot of pressure on a centralised railway management system. Thus, in India, the railway system has been divided into 16 zones.

34. (c) India has been placed among the countries showing medium human development. Kerala with the composite index value of 0.790 is placed at the top rank followed by Delhi, Himachal Pradesh, Goa and Punjab. As expected, states like Bihar, Odisha and Chhattisgarh are at the bottom among the 23 major states in India.

35. (d) **Compact or Nucleated settlements:** These settlements are those in which large number of houses are built very close to each other. Such settlements develop along river valleys and in fertile plains. Communities are closely knit and share common occupations.

36. (c) **History of Indian Airlines: 1911 -** Air transport in India was launched between Allahabad and Naini. **1947 -** Air transport was provided by four major companies namely Indian National Airways, Tata Sons Limited, Air Services of India and Deccan Airways. **1951 -** Four more companies joined the services, Bharat Airways, Himalayan Aviation Limited, Airways India and Kalinga Airlines. **1953 -** Air transport was nationalised and two Corporations, Air India International and Indian Airlines were formed. Now Indian Airlines is known as 'Indian'.

37. (d)

Broad Stages and Thrust of Human Geography

Period	*Approaches*	*Broad Features*
Early Colonial period	Exploration and description	Imperial and trade interests prompted the discovery and exploration of new areas. An encyclopaedic description of the area formed an important aspect of the geographer's account.
Later Colonial period	Regional analysis	Elaborate description of all aspects of a region were undertaken. The idea was that all the regions were part of a whole, i.e. (the earth): so, understanding the parts in totality would lead to an understanding of the whole.
1930s through the inter-War period	Areal differentiation	The focus was on identifying the uniqueness of any region and understanding how and why it was different from others.
Late 1950s to the late 1960s	Spatial organisation	Marked by the use of computers and sophisticated statistical tools. Laws of physics were often applied to map and analyse human phenomena. This phase was called the quantitative revolution. The main objective was to identify mappable patterns for different human activities.
1970s	Emergence of humanistic. radical and behavioural schools	Discontentment with the quantitative revolution and its dehumanised manner of doing geography led to the emergence of three new schools of thought of human geography in the 1970s. Human geography was made more relevant to the socio-political reality by the emergence of these schools of thought. Consult the box below to know a little bit more about these schools of thought.
1990s	Post-modernism in geography	The grand generalisations and the applicability of universal theories to explain the human conditions were questioned. The importance of understanding each local context in its own right was emphasised.

38. (c) Greater Mumbai (18,414,288), Delhi (16,314,838), Kolkata (14,112,536), Chennai (8,696,010)

39. (c)

Broad Stages and Thrust of Human Geography

Period	Approaches	Broad Features
Early Colonial period	Exploration and description	Imperial and trade interests prompted the discovery and exploration of new areas. An encyclopaedic description of the area formed an important aspect of the geographer's account.
Later Colonial period	Regional analysis	Elaborate description of all aspects of a region were undertaken. The idea was that all the regions were part of a whole, i.e. (the earth): so, understanding the parts in totality would lead to an understanding of the whole.
1930s through the inter-War period	Areal differentiation	The focus was on identifying the uniqueness of any region and understanding how and why it was different from others.
Late 1950s to the late 1960s	Spatial organisation	Marked by the use of computers and sophisticated statistical tools. Laws of physics were often applied to map and analyse human phenomena. This phase was called the quantitative revolution. The main objective was to identify mappable patterns for different human activities.
1970s	Emergence of humanistic. radical and behavioural schools	Discontentment with the quantitative revolution and its dehumanised manner of doing geography led to the emergence of three new schools of thought of human geography in the 1970s. Human geography was made more relevant to the socio-political reality by the emergence of these schools of thought. Consult the box below to know a little bit more about these schools of thought.
1990s	Post-modernism in geography	The grand generalisations and the applicability of universal theories to explain the human conditions were questioned. The importance of understanding each local context in its own right was emphasised.

40. (a)

Region wise Density of Population

Region	Population (2018)	Land Area (Km^2)	Density (P/Km^2)	World Share (in percentage)
Asia	4,545,133,094	31,033,131	146	59.5%
Africa	1,287,920,518	29,648,481	43	16.9%
Europe	742,648,010	22,134,900	34	9.7%
Latin America and the Caribbean	652,012,001	20,139,378	32	8.5%
North America	363,844,490	18,651,660	20	4.8%
Oceania	41,261,212	8,486,460	5	0.5%

41. (c)	**42.** (a)	**43.** (d)	**44.** (d)
45. (b)	**46.** (a)	**47.** (c)	**48.** (a)
49. (b)	**50.** (a)		

1. Which of the following attributes is calculated as persons par unit area?
   (a) Density of population
   (b) Distribution of population
   (c) Growth of population
   (d) Composition of population

2. Which one of the following states has the lowest female literacy rate according to 2011 census?
   (a) Uttar Pradesh   (b) Rajasthan
   (c) Kerala   (d) Haryana

3. "The physical extent of land on which crops are sown and harvested" is known by which one of the following land use categories?
   (a) Net Area Sown
   (b) Current Fallow
   (c) Fallow other than Current Fallow
   (d) Barren and Wastelands

4. Match List I with List II.

List I Basis of classification	List II Types of industries
A. Raw material	I. Metallurgical electronics
B. Ownership	II. Agro, forest, minerals
C. Use of product	III. Public, private
D. Nature of manufactured products	IV. Basic, consumer goods

Choose the correct answer from the options given below:
(a) A-II, B-III, C-IV, D-I   (b) A-I, B-II, C-III, D-IV
(c) A-II, B-I, C-III, D-IV   (d) A-I, B-III, C-IV, D-II

5. Match **List I** with **List II**.

List I Pollution types	List II Sources of Pollution
A. Air Pollution	I. Air craft, automobiles
B. Water Pollution	II. Sewage disposal
C. Land Pollution	III. Combustion of coal
D. Noise Pollution	IV. Improper human activities

Choose the correct answer from the options given below:
(a) A-III, B-I, C-II, D-IV   (b) A-I, B-II, C-III, D-IV
(c) A-II, B-III, C-IV, D-I   (d) A-III, B-II, C-IV, D-I

6. Who among the following scholars proposed the concept of neo-determinism?
   (a) Griffith Taylor   (b) Thomas Malthus
   (c) Ellen C. Semple   (d) Ratzal

7. Which one of the following regions of the world has the highest density of population?
   (a) Europe   (b) Africa
   (c) North America   (d) Oceania

8. Match **List I** with **List II**.

List I Mode of transport	List II Example
A. Pipeline	I. Sadiva-Dhubri
B. Roadways	II. Golden quadrilateral
C. Railways	III. Hazira-Vijaipur
D. Waterways	IV. Konkan

Choose the correct answer from the options given below:
(a) A-III, B-II, C-I, D-IV   (b) A-I, B-II, C-III, D-IV
(c) A-III, B-II, C-IV, D-I   (d) A-II, B-III, C-IV, D-I

9. Which of the following is false regarding increase in population after industrial revolution.
   (a) Technological advancement
   (b) Increase in food supply
   (c) Improvement in medical facilities
   (d) Increase in the percentage of employment

10. Which one of the following countries has the lowest ratio in the world?
    (a) Latvia   (b) Qatar
    (c) France   (d) Japan

11. Arrange the approaches to study human geography in chronological order
    A. Emergence of humanistic school
    B. Exploration and description
    C. Areal differentiation
    D. Regional analysis
    Choose the correct answer from the options given below:
    (a) B, A, D, C   (b) A, C, B, D
    (c) A, C, D, B   (d) B, D, C, A

12. Read the concept of Ageing population carefully
    A. Share of older population becomes proportionally larger
    B. It is a result of higher life expectancy
    C. The proportion of children in the population is high
    D. More expenditure on health care facilities
    Choose the correct answer from the options given below:
    (a) A, B, and D, only   (b) A, C, and D, only
    (c) B, C and D only   (d) A, B, C and D only

13. Choose the correct sequence as per stages of demographic cycle from the below given features.

   A. Both fertility and mortality rate decline considerably

   B. The population growth is slow with agrarian economy

   C. Per capita income becomes high with low population growth

   D. Fertility remains high but declines with time

Choose the correct answer from the options given below:

(a) A, C, D, B   (b) B, C, D, A

(c) B, A, D, C   (d) B, D, A, C

14. Which one of the following concepts of human development is associated with equal access of opportunities?

(a) Empowerment   (b) Sustainability

(c) Equity   (d) Productivity

15. Read the following statements regarding ports.

   A. Oil ports deal with processing and shipping of oil.

   B. Packet stations are concerned with passenger transport covering long distance.

   C. At Entrepot ports goods are brought from different countries for export.

   D. Naval ports are of strategic importance.

Choose the correct answer from the options given below:

(a) A, B and D only   (b) A, B and C only

(c) A, C and D only   (d) B, C and D only

16. Which one of the following materials is transported through Big Inch in U.S.A?

(a) Milk   (b) Petroleum

(c) Water   (d) Cooking gas or LPG

17. Match List I with List II

List I Types of farming	List II Countries
A. Jhumming	I. Central America
B. Milpa	II. Brazil
C. Ladang	III. North Eastern India
D. Coffee fazendas	IV. Malaysia

Choose the correct answer from the options given below:

(a) A-II, B-IV, C-I, D-III   (b) A-III, B-IV, C-II, D-I

(c) A-III, B-I, C-IV, D-II   (d) A-IV, B-I, C-III, D-II

18. Arun moved from Chicago to Mumbai last year in June 2021. By which one following term he will be known in India

(a) Emigrant   (b) Imigrant

(c) Refugee   (d) Domicile

19. High technology industry is characterized by which one of the following?

(a) High chimneys producing industries

(b) High level of transport facility

(c) High-rise building in industry

(d) High level of research and development in industries

20. Which one of the following factors attract outsourcing in a country?

(a) Industries

(b) Cheap and skilled workers availability

(c) High level of professionals availability

(d) Well established infrastructure

21. Read the following statements about tourism carefully

   A. Tourism cultural segregation

   B. Tourism helps to earn foreign exchange

   C. Tourism promotes the growth of infrastructure

   D. Tourism promotes level economy

Choose the correct answer from the options given below:

(a) A, B and C only   (b) B, C and D only

(c) A, B and D only   (d) A, C and D only

22. Arrange the following organisation in order of their establishment.

   A. National Highways Authority of India

   B. Akashvani

   C. Doordarshan

   D. Inland waterway Authority of India

Choose the correct answer from the options given below:

(a) A, B, C, D   (b) D, A, C, B

(c) B, C, D, A   (d) C, B, A, D

23. Match List I with List II.

List I Phases of population growth	List II Features
A. 1901-1921	I. steady population growth
B. 1921-1951	II. population explosion
C. 1951-1881	III. Stagnant population
D. post 1981	IV. Slowing down population growth

Choose the correct answer from the options given below:

(a) A-IV, B-I, C-III, D-II

(b) A-I, B-II, C-III, D-IV

(c) A-II, B-I, C-III, D-IV

(d) A-III, B-I, C-II, D-IV

24. Which one of the following is the main reason of steep increase in import of petroleum in India?

    (a) Expansion of agriculture

    (b) Green Revolution

    (c) Rapid industrialisation and better standard of living

    (d) High growth of non-conventional energy

25. Which one of the following is terminating points of North-South corridor?

    (a) Silchar - porbander

    (b) Chennai - Mumbai

    (c) Delhi - Bangalore

    (d) Srinagar - Kanyakumari

26. Which one of the following is the push factor for migration?

    (a) Employment opportunity

    (b) Education and health facility

    (c) Political stability

    (d) Poor living conditions

27. Nagla, Dhani, Para, Palli are local names of

    (a) Dispersed settlements

    (b) Hamleted settlements

    (c) Agglomerated settlements

    (d) Nucleated settlements

28. Which one of the following is an impact of un regulated migration in metropolitan cities?

    (a) Remittance

    (b) Social change

    (c) Slums development

    (d) Re-distribution of population

29. Which one of the following states has the highest ground water utilisation?

    (a) Kerala   (b) Odisha

    (c) Punjab   (d) Bihar

30. During which one of the following census years the migration was recorded for the first time in India?

    (a) 1862   (b) 1872

    (c) 1881   (d) 1901

31. Which of the following is characteristic of foot loose industry?

    (a) They are set up cooperative sector

    (b) They cause air pollution

    (c) They are generally non polluting in nature

    (d) They depend heavily on raw material

32. Arrange the following ports of India located on the eastern Coast from North to south direction.

    A. Chennai

    B. Paradwip

    C. Vishakhapatnam

    D. Kolkata

    Choose the correct answer from the options given below:

    (a) D, B, C, A   (b) D, B, A, C

    (c) D, A, C, B   (d) D, A, B, C

33. Terminal stations of Trans-Canadian Railways are.

    (a) Halifax to calgory

    (b) Halifax to Vancouver

    (c) Winnipeg to calgery

    (d) Monteral to Vancouver

34. Due to the which one of the following reasons some ships prefer to go via cape route rather than Suez Canal?

    (a) Scenery of cape route is better

    (b) Cape rout is more fuel efficient

    (c) Tolls are heavy in Suez Canal

    (d) Suez canal route takes more time

35. People engaged in primary activities are called

    (a) Green collar workers

    (b) Red collar workers

    (c) Open collar workers

    (d) Gold collar workers

36. 'Kund' or 'Tank' are used to store rainwater in which one of the following states of India?

    (a) Bihar   (b) Andhra Pradesh

    (c) Uttar Pradesh   (d) Rajasthan

37. Arrange the following River Basins of India from South to North.

    A. Godavari Basin

    B. Kaveri Basin

    C. Mahanadi Basin

    D. Ganga Basin

    Choose the correct answer from the options given below:

    (a) A, B, C, D   (b) B, A, C, D

    (c) B, A, D, C   (d) A, C, B, D

38. Which of the following programme was initiated by government of India to Clean Ganga?

    (a) Namami Gange Programme

    (b) Ganga action plan

    (c) Rejuvinate Ganga plain

    (d) Clean Ganga programme

39. Which one of the following is the most popular tourist region of the world?

(a) Mountainous areas of Kashmir

(b) Nile Valley of Africa

(c) Warmer places around Mediterranean coast

(d) Colder areas of Alps

40. Which one of the following activities is **NOT** outsourced to an outside agency?

(a) Information technology

(b) Customer support

(c) Call center service

(d) Whole sale marketing

Directions for Questions 41 to 45: Read the following passage very carefully and answer the questions on the basis of it:

Supply of water to rural settlements in developing countries is not adequate. People in villages, particularly in mountainous and arid areas have to walk long distances to fetch drinking water. Water home diseases such as cholera and jaundice tend to be a common problem. The countries of South Asia face conditions of drought and flood very often. Crop cultivation sequences, in the absence of irrigation, also suffer.

The general absence of toilet and garbage disposal facilities cause health related problems.

The design and use of building materians of houses vary from one ecological region to another.

The houses made up of mud, wood and thatch, remain susceptible to damage during heavy rains and floods, and require proper maintenance every year. Most house designs are typically deficient in proper ventilation. Besides, the design of a house includes the animal shed along with its fodder-store within it. This is purposely done to keep the domestic animals and their food properly protected from wild animals.

41. As per the given paragraph people of which areas in developing countries have to walk for miles for fetching water?

(a) Coastal areas   (b) Riverine plains

(c) Mountainous areas   (d) Deltaic Plains

42. Which of the following poses health related problems in rural areas?

(a) Farm work   (b) Air pollution

(c) Noise pollution   (d) Absence of toilet

43. Which one of the following causes damage to mud built houses in rural areas?

(a) Strong wind   (b) Dust storm

(c) Heavy rain   (d) Drought

44. Why does the design of a rural house include animal shed with fodder house?

(a) Due to lack of space

(b) Due to ritual and tradition

(c) Due to accessibility of food for animals

(d) Due to safety of both animals and their food

45. Which of the following is an effect of drought?

(a) Good harvest

(b) Crop failure

(c) Excess produce of crops

(d) Cheap price of food grains

Directions for Questions 46 to 50: Read the following passage very carefully and answer the questions on the basis of it:

Only one main road traverses the slum, the miscalled 'ninety-foot road', which has been reduced to less than half of that for most of its length. Some of the side alleys and lanes are so narrow that not even a bicycle can pass. The whole neighbourhood consists to temporary buildings, two or three storeyed high with rusty iron stairways to the upper part, where a single room is rented by a whole family, sometimes accommodating twelve or more people.

But Dharavi is a keeper of more sombre secrets than the repulsion it inspires in the rich; a revulsion, moreover, that is, in direct proportion to the role it serves in the creation of the wealth of Bombay. In this place of shadowless, tressless sunlight, uncollected garbage, stagnant pools of foul water, where the only non-human creatures are the shining black crows and long grey rats, some of the most beautiful, valuable and useful articles in India are made. From Dharavi come delicate ceramics and pottery, exquisite embroidery and Zari work, sophisticated leather goods, high-fashion garments, finely - wrought metal work, delicate jewellery settings, wood carvings and furniture that would find its way into the richest houses, both in India and abroad...

Dharavi was an arm of the sea, that was filled by waste, largely produced by the people have come to live there: Scheduled Castes and poor Muslims. It comprises rambling buildings of corrugated metal, 20 metal high in places, used for the treatment of hides and tanning. There are pleasant parts, but rotting garbage is everywhere...."

46. On which of the following areas Dharavi is located?

(a) On Island near Bombay

(b) Off share of Mumbai

(c) Landfill area on the arm of the sea

(d) Central Business District (CBD) of Mumbai

47. Which of the following items is produced in Dharavi?

(a) Iron and steel

(b) Sophisticated leather goods

(c) Cars

(d) Two-wheelers

48. Which one of the following is the reason for miss-called "Ninety foot road" of Dharavi?

(a) It is a metalled ninety-food road

(b) It is very wider and more than ninety-foot road

(c) It is very narrow and less than ninety-foot road

(d) It is an unmetalled ninety-foot road

49. Which one of the Following types of houses are found in Dharavi?

(a) Well ventilated

(b) Well planned

(c) Well constructed

(d) Temporary and congested

50. Which one of the Following describes the narrow lanes found in Dharavi?

(a) A truck can pass easily

(b) A three-wheeler can pass easily

(c) A cycle can not pass easily

(d) A car can pass easily

Answer Keys

1. (a)	**2.** (b)	**3.** (a)	**4.** (a)	**5.** (d)	**6.** (a)	**7.** (b)	**8.** (c)	**9.** (b)	**10.** (b)
11. (d)	**12.** (a)	**13.** (d)	**14.** (c)	**15.** (c)	**16.** (b)	**17.** (c)	**18.** (b)	**19.** (d)	**20.** (b)
21. (b)	**22.** (c)	**23.** (d)	**24.** (c)	**25.** (d)	**26.** (d)	**27.** (b)	**28.** (c)	**29.** (c)	**30.** (c)
31. (c)	**32.** (a)	**33.** (b)	**34.** (c)	**35.** (b)	**36.** (d)	**37.** (b)	**38.** (a)	**39.** (c)	**40.** (d)
41. (c)	**42.** (d)	**43.** (c)	**44.** (d)	**45.** (b)	**46.** (c)	**47.** (b)	**48.** (c)	**49.** (d)	**50.** (c)

Explanations

1. (a) Density of population is expressed as number of persons per unit area.

2. (b) Rajasthan with female literacy rate of 52.66 has lowest female literacy in India.

3. (a) **Net Area Sown:** The physical extent of land on which crops are sown and harvested is known as net sown area.

4. (a) Raw materials-Agro, forest, minerals; Ownership-Public, private; Use of products-Basic, consumer goods; Nature of the manufactured products-Metallurgical, Electronics

5. (d)

Types and Sources of Pollution

Pollution Types	Pollution Involved	Sources of Pollution
Air Pollution	Oxides of sulphur (SO_2, SO_3). Oxides of nitrogen, carbon monoxide, hydro-carbon, ammonia, lead, aldehydes asbestos and beryllium.	Combustion of coal, petrol and diesel. industrial processes, solid waste disposal, sewage disposal, etc.
Water Pollution	Odour, dissolved and suspended solids. ammonia and urea, nitrate and nitrites, chloride, fluoride, carbonates, oil and grease. insecticide and pesticide residue, tannin. coliform MPM (bacterial count) sulphates and sulphides, heavy metals e.g. lead, aresenic, mercury, manganese, etc., radioactive substances.	Sewage disposal, urban run-off, toxic effluents from industries, run-off over cultivated lands and nuclear power plants.
Land Pollution	Human and animal excreta viruses and bacteria, garbage and vectors therein. pesticides and fertiliser-residue alkalinity, fluorides, radio-active substances.	Improper human activities, disposal of untreated industrial waste, use of pesticides and fertilisers.
Noise Pollution	High level of noise above tolerance level.	Aircrafts, automobiles, trains, industrial processing and advertising media.

6. (a) A geographer, Griffith Taylor introduced another concept which reflects a middle path (Madhyam Marg) between the two ideas of environmental determinism and possibilism. He termed it as Neodeterminism or stop and go determinism.

7. (b) Region wise Density of Population

Region	Population (2018)	Land Area (km^2)	Density (P/km^2)	World Share (in percentage)
Asia	4,545,133,094	31,033,131	146	59.50%
Africa	1,287,920,518	29,648,481	43	16.90%
Europe	742,648,010	22,134,900	34	9.70%
Latin America and the Caribbean	652,012,001	20,139,378	32	8.50%
Northern America	363,844,490	18,651,660	20	4.80%
Oceania	41,261,212	8,486,460	5	0.50%

8. (c) Pipeline-Hazira-Vijaypur; Roadways-Golden Quadrilateral; Railways-Konkan; Waterways-Sadiya-Dhubari

9. (b) The expanding world trade during the sixteenth and seventeenth century, set the stage for rapid population growth. Around 1750, at the dawn of the Industrial Revolution, the world population was 550 million. World population exploded in the eighteenth century after the Industrial Revolution. Technological advancement achieved so far helped in the reduction of death rate and provided a stage for accelerated population growth.

10. (b) On an average, the world population reflects a sex ratio of 102 males per 100 females. The highest sex ratio in the world has been recorded in Latvia where there are 85 males per 100 females. In contrast, in Qatar there are 311 males per 100 females.

11. (d)

Broad Stages and Thrust of Human Geography

Period	Approaches	Broad Features
Early Colonial period	Exploration and description	Imperial and trade interests prompted the discovery and exploration of new areas. An encyclopaedic description of the area formed an important aspect of the geographer's account.
Later Colonial period	Regional analysis	Elaborate description of all aspects of a region were undertaken. The idea was that all the regions were part of a whole, i.e. (the earth); so, understanding the parts in totality would lead to an understanding of the whole.
1930s through the inter-War period	Areal differentiation	The focus was on identifying the uniqueness of any region and understanding how and why it was different from others.
Late 1950s to the late 1960s	Spatial organisation	Marked by the use of computers and sophisticated statistical tools. Laws of physics were often applied to map and analyse human phenomena. This phase was called the quantitative revolution. The main objective was to identify mappable patterns for different human activities.
1970s	Emergence of humanistic, radical and behavioural schools	Discontentment with the quantitative revolution and its dehumanised manner of doing geography led to the emergence of three new schools of thought of human geography in the 1970s. Human geography was made more relevant to the socio-political reality by the emergence of these schools of thought. Consult the box below to know a little bit more about these schools of thought.
1990s	Post-modernism in geography	The grand generalisations and the applicability of universal theories to explain the human conditions were questioned. The importance of understanding each local context in its own right was emphasised.

12. (a) **Ageing Population:** Population ageing is the process by which the share of the older population becomes proportionally larger. This is a new phenomenon of the twentieth century. In most of the developed countries of the world, population in higher age groups has increased due to increased life expectancy. With a reduction in birth rates, the proportion of children in the population has declined.

13. (d) The first stage has high fertility and high mortality because people reproduce more to compensate for the deaths due to epidemics and variable food supply. The population growth is slow and most of the people are engaged in agriculture where large families are an asset. Life expectancy is low, people are mostly illiterate and have low levels of technology. Two hundred years ago all the countries of the world were in this stage. Fertility remains high in the beginning of second stage but it declines with time. This is accompanied by reduced mortality rate. Improvements in sanitation and health conditions lead to decline in mortality. Because of this gap the net addition to population is high. In the last stage, both fertility and mortality decline considerably. The population is either stable or grows slowly. The population becomes urbanised, literate and has high technical know-how and deliberately controls the family size.

14. (c) Equity refers to making equal access to opportunities available to everybody. The opportunities available to people must be equal irrespective of their gender, race, income and in the Indian case, caste. Yet this is very often not the case and happens in almost every society.

15. (c) Oil Ports deal in the processing and shipping of oil. Packet Station is also known as ferry ports. These packet stations are exclusively concerned with the transportation of passengers and mail across water bodies covering short distances. Entrepot Ports are collection centres where the goods are brought from different countries for export. Naval Ports are ports which have only strategic importance. These ports serve warships and have repair workshops for them.

16. (b) Big Inch carries petroleum from the oil wells of the Gulf of Mexico to the North-eastern States.

17. (c) Primitive subsistence agriculture or shifting cultivation is prevalent in tropical region in different names, e.g. Jhuming in North eastern states of India, Milpa in Central America and Mexico and Ladang in Indonesia and Malaysia. Some coffee fazendas (large plantations) in Brazil are still managed by Europeans.

18. (b) Immigration: Migrants who move into a new place are called Immigrants.

19. (d) High technology, or simply high-tech, is the latest generation of manufacturing activities. It is best understood as the application of intensive research and development (R and D) efforts leading to the manufacture of products of an advanced scientific and engineering character. Professional (white collar) workers make up a large share of the total workforce.

20. (b) Outsourcing has resulted in the opening up of a large number of call centres in India, China, Eastern Europe, Israel, Philippines and Costa Rica. It has created new jobs in these countries. Outsourcing is coming to those countries where cheap and skilled workers are available. These are also out-migrating countries.

21. (b) Tourism is travel undertaken for purposes of recreation rather than business. It has become the world's single largest tertiary activity in total registered jobs (250 million) and total revenue (40 per cent of the total GDP). Besides, many local persons are employed to provide services like accommodation, meals, transport, entertainment and special shops serving the tourists. Tourism fosters the growth of infrastructure industries, retail trading, and craft industries (souvenirs). In some regions, tourism is seasonal because the vacation period is dependent on favourable weather conditions, but many regions attract visitors all the year round.

22. (c) The National Highways Authority of India (NHAI) was operationalised in 1995. Radio broadcasting started in India in 1923 by the Radio Club of Bombay. Since then, it gained immense popularity and changed the sociocultural life of people. Within no time, it made a place in every household of the country. Government took this opportunity and brought this popular mode of communication under its control in 1930 under the Indian Broadcasting System. It was changed to All India Radio in 1936 and to Akashwani in 1957. Television broadcasting has emerged as the most effective audio-visual medium for disseminating information and educating masses. Initially, the T.V. services were limited only to the National Capital where it began in 1959. After 1972, several other centres became operational. In 1976, TV was delinked from All India Radio (AIR) and got a separate identity as Doordarshan (DD). For the development, maintenance and regulation of national waterways in the country, the Inland Waterways Authority was set up in 1986.

23. (d) **Phase I:** The period from 1901-1921 is referred to as a period of stagnant or stationary phase of growth of India's population, since in this period growth rate was very low, even recording a negative growth rate during 1911-1921.

Phase II: The decades 1921-1951 are referred to as the period of steady population growth.

Phase III: The decades 1951-1981 are referred to as the period of population explosion in India, which was caused by a rapid fall in the mortality rate but a high fertility rate of population in the country.

Phase IV: In the post 1981 till present, the growth rate of country's population though remained high, has started slowing down gradually.

24. (c) There is a steep rise in the import of petroleum products. It is used not only as a fuel but also as an industrial raw material. It indicates the tempo of rising industrialisation and better standard of living.

25. (d) **North-South and East-West Corridors:** North-South corridor aims at connecting Srinagar in Jammu and Kashmir with Kanniyakumari in Tamil Nadu (including Kochchi-Salem Spur) with 4,076-km long road. The East-West Corridor has been planned to connect Silchar in Assam with the port town of Porbandar in Gujarat with 3,640- km of road length.

26. (d) In India people migrate from rural to urban areas mainly due to poverty, high population pressure on the land, lack of basic infrastructural facilities like health care, education, etc. Apart from these factors, natural disasters such as, flood, drought, cyclonic storms, earthquake, tsunami, wars and local conflicts also give extra push to migrate.

27. (b) Hamleted Settlements - Sometimes settlement is fragmented into several units physically separated from each other bearing a common name. These units are locally called panna, para, palli, nagla, dhani, etc. in various parts of the country. This segmentation of a large village is often motivated by social and ethnic factors. Such villages are more frequently found in the middle and lower Ganga plain, Chhattisgarh and lower valleys of the Himalayas.

28. (c) Unregulated migration to the metropolitan cities of India has caused overcrowding.

29. (c) The groundwater utilisation is very high in the states of Punjab, Haryana, Rajasthan, and Tamil Nadu.

30. (c) Actually migration was recorded beginning from the first Census of India conducted in 1881. This data were recorded on the basis of place of birth.

31. (c) Foot loose industries can be located in a wide variety of places. They are not dependent on any specific raw material, weight losing or otherwise. They largely depend on component parts which can be obtained anywhere. They produce in small quantity and also employ a small labour force. These are generally not polluting industries. The important factor in their location is accessibility by road network.

32. (a) Kolkata Port is located on the Hugli river, 128 km inland from the Bay of Bengal. Paradwip Port is situated in the Mahanadi delta, about 100 km from Cuttack. Visakhapatnam Port in Andhra Pradesh is a land-locked harbour, connected to the sea by a channel cut through solid rock and sand. Chennai Port is one of the oldest ports on the eastern coast. It is an artificial harbour built in 1859.

33. (b) Trans–Canadian Railways - This 7,050 km long rail-line in Canada runs from Halifax in the east to Vancouver on the Pacific Coast passing through Montreal, Ottawa, Winnipeg and Calgary.

34. (c) The tolls are so heavy in Suez Canal that some find it cheaper to go by the longer Cape Route whenever the consequent delay is not important.

35. (b) People engaged in primary activities are called red collar workers due to the outdoor nature of their work.

36. (d) In Rajasthan, rainwater harvesting structures locally known as Kund or Tanka (a covered underground tank) are constructed near or in the house or village to store harvested rainwater.

37. (b)

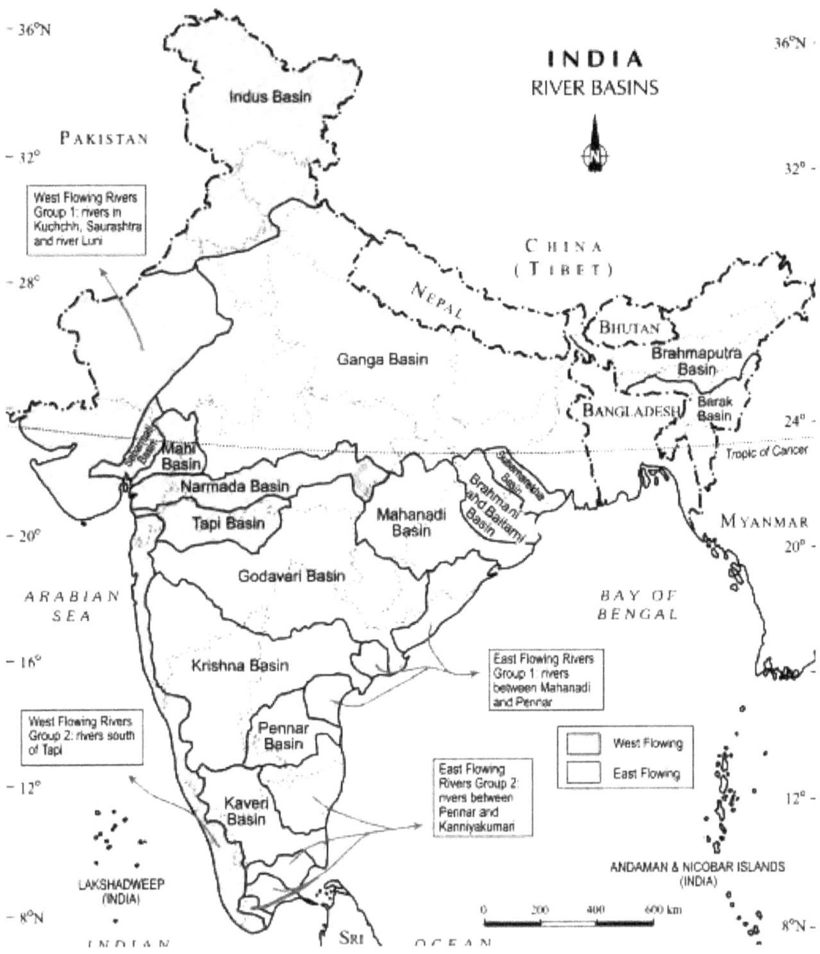

38. (a) **Namami Gange Programme:** Ganga, as a river, has national importance but the river requires cleaning by effectively controlling the pollution for its water. The Union Government has launched the *'Namami Gange Programme'* with the following objectives:

- developing sewerage treatment systems in towns,
- monitoring of industrial effluents,
- development of river front,
- afforestation along the bank of increase biodiversity,
- cleaning of the river surface,
- development of 'Ganga Grams' in Uttarakhand, UP, Bihar, Jharkhand and West Bengal, and
- creating public awareness to avoid adding pollutants in to the river even in the form of rituals.

39. (c) The warmer places around the Mediterranean Coast and the West Coast of India are some of the popular tourist destinations in the world.

40. (d) Business activities that are outsourced include information technology (IT), human resources, customer support and call centre services and at times also manufacturing and engineering.

41. (c)

42. (d)

43. (c)

44. (d)

45. (b)

46. (c)

47. (b)

48. (c)

49. (d)

50. (c)

1. Which one of the foil owing factors is not responsible for the land degradation?
   (a) Soil erosion   (b) Salinity
   (c) Afforestation   (d) Alkalinity

2. What is the total size of population of India as per the 2011 census?
   (a) 1110 million   (b) 1210 million
   (c) 1310 million   (d) 1410 million

3. Which among the following is an Entrepot port for Asia?
   (a) Mumbai   (b) Singapore
   (c) Tokyo   (d) Karachi

4. Identify the ancient town of India from among the given urban centres,
   (a) Kanpur   (b) Chennai
   (c) Chandigarh   (d) Madurai

5. Who introduced the concept of Neo determinism or stop and go determinism in Geography?
   (a) Ratzel
   (b) Griffith Taylor
   (c) Paul Vidal de la blache
   (d) Ellen C Semple

6. Arrange the following conventional energy resource centres of India from North to South direction.
   A. Korba
   B. Neyveli
   C. Singarauli
   D. Singareni
   Choose the correct answer from the option given below:
   (a) A, B, C, D   (b) C, D, B, A
   (c) C, A, B, D   (d) C, A, D, B

7. Arrange the following census years based on the parcentage of population growth rate of India from highest to lowest.
   A. 1911
   B. 1941
   C. 1971
   D. 2001
   Choose the correct answer from the option given below:
   (a) C, D, B, A   (b) C, A, B, D
   (c) C, D, A, B   (d) A, B, C, D

8. Arrange the folio wing continents in order of their respective density of population (persons km^2) from hightest to lowest.
   A. Africa   B. Oceania
   C. Asia   D. Europe
   Choose the correct answer from the option given below:
   (a) B, C, D, A   (b) A, C, D, B
   (c) C, D, A, B   (d) C, A, D, B

9. Arrange the following broad features of different approaches of Human Geography in order to it's evolution from oldest to latest.
   A. Imperial and trade interests prompted the discovery and exploration of new areas.
   B. Discontentment with the quantitative revolution
   C. Identifying mappable patterns for different human activities
   D. Focus on identifying the uniqueness of any region
   E. Elaborate description of all aspects of a region were undertaken
   Choose the correct answer from the option given below:
   (a) A, E, C, B, D   (b) A, E, D, C, B
   (c) A, D, B, C, E   (d) A, D, B, E, C

10. Rain water harvesting has been practiced through various methods. Identify the correct set of statements.
    A. Harvesting through watershed management
    B. Harvesting through used water at domestic level
    C. Harvesting through wells
    D. Harvesting through recharge wells
    Choose the correct answer from the option given below:
    (a) A, B, C   (b) B, C, D
    (c) A, B, D   (d) A, C, D

11. Select the industries which uses weight loosing raw material
    A. Electronic industry
    B. Iron & Steel industry
    C. Sugar industry
    D. Petrochemical industry
    Cheese the correct answer from the option given below:
    (a) B and C only   (b) A and D only
    (c) A and C only   (d) B and D only

12. Which one of the following set of pairs are correctly matched

A. Shipbuilding industry - Lusaka

B. Aircraft industry - Edinburg

C. Automobile industry - Detroit

D. Iron and steel industry - Chicago-Gary

Choose the correct answer from the option given below:

(a) A and B only
(b) A and C only
(c) A & D only
(d) C & D only

13. Read the following statements about primitive subsistence farming and identify the correct statements.

A. Jhumming is practiced in north eastern India

B. Ladang is practiced in Indonesia

C. Ladang is practiced in Malaysia

D. Milpa is practiced in Brazil

Choose the correct answer from the option given below:

(a) B, C, D only
(b) A, C, D only
(c) A, B, C only
(d) A, B, D only

14. Which of the following set of statements are correct about urban settlements?

A. They have municipality corporation and Cantonment board.

B. 50% of the male wokers are engaged in non-agri cultural pursuits.

C. 400 persons per sq. km of density

D. Minimum population of 5000 persons

Choose the correct answer from the option given below:

(a) A, B, C only
(b) B, C, D only
(c) A, C, D only
(d) A, B, D only

15. Match List I with List II

List I Crops	List II Largest producing states
A. Rice	I. Gujarat
B. Wheat	II. West Bengal
C. Maize	III. Uttar Pradesh
D. Groundnut	IV. Karnataka

Choose the correct answer from the option given below:

(a) A-II, B-I, C-IV, D-III
(b) A-III, B-II, C-I, D-IV
(c) A-III, B-II, C-IV, D-I
(d) A-II, B-III, C-IV, D-I,

16. Match List I with List II

List I Group of Towns/cities	List II Types
A. Varanasi, Prayag, Patliputra, Madurai	I. Modern
B. Goa, Mumbai, Kolkata, Chennai	II. Ancient
C. Delhi, Lucknow, Hyderabad	III. Mining
D. Jharia, Digboi, Sitigarauli	IV. Medieval

Choose the correct answer from the option given below:

(a) A-II, B-I, C-IV, D-III
(b) A-IV, B-III, C-II, D-I
(c) A-I, B-II, C-III, D-IV
(d) A-II, B-IV, C-I, D-III

17. Match List I with List II

Match the following with the type of transportation

List I Routes	List II Transport
A. Big Trunk Route	I. Inland waterways
B. The Rhine waterway	II. Trans - Continental Railways
C. Big Inch	III. North Atlantic sea route
D. Trans-Siberian	IV. Pipeline

Choose the correct answer from the option given below:

(a) A-III, B-IV, C-II, D-I
(b) A-IV, B-III, C-I, D-II
(c) A-III, B-I, C-IV, D-II
(d) A-IV, B-III, C-II, D-I

18. Match List I with List II

List I Town	List II Function of the town
A. Gandhinagar	I. Mining
B. Kozhikode	II. Administration
C. Raniganj	III. Garrisson
D. Ambala	IV. Transportation

Choose the correct answer from the option given below:

(a) A-IV, B-II, C-III, D-I
(b) A-IV, B-II, C-I, D-III
(c) A-II, B-IV, C-L D-III
(d) A-II, B-IV, C-III, D-I

19. Which one of the following continents is bestowed with maximum number of countries with very high human evelopment index?

(a) Africa
(b) South America
(c) Asia
(d) Europe

20. Determine the reason why developed economies are retreating from mining, refining and processing of minerals?

(a) Output is low
(b) High labour cost
(c) lack of capital
(d) lack of technology

21. Which of the following formulas is correct for calculating Actual growth of population of any country?
    (a) Births – Deaths
    (b) Births + Deaths
    (c) Births – Deaths + In migration – Out Migration
    (d) Births + Deaths – In migration + Out Migration

22. Which cities from Europe is linked by channel tunnel operated by Euro runnel Group?
    (a) London and Paris
    (b) Berlin and Paris
    (c) London and Amsterdam
    (d) Barcelona and Paris

23. Which of the following factor determines the mineral resource base and topographical differences of any region and ensure diversity, of crops and animals raised.
    (a) Mineral resources
    (b) Climate
    (c) Geological structure
    (d) Size of population

24. Population increased by difference between births and deaths in a particular region between two points of time is known as-
    (a) Growth of population size
    (b) Growth rate of population
    (c) Natural Growth of population
    (d) Natural Growth rate of population

25. Which one of the following characteristics is not a feature of intensive subsistence agriculture?
    (a) Per capita high labour productivity
    (b) Small farm size
    (c) Mostly agricultural activities done by manual labour
    (d) To maintain soil fertility farm yard manure is being used

26. Crude birth rate (CBR) is expressed as number of live births in a year per:
    (a) 1000 population
    (b) 10000 population
    (c) 100000 population
    (d) 100 population

27. Which one of the following rivers is recorded as highly polluted?
    (a) Ganga
    (b) Narmada
    (c) Brahmaputra
    (d) Jhelum

28. Which of the following is not a sustainable energy resource?
    (a) Solar
    (b) Wind
    (c) Biogas
    (d) Natural gas

29. The combustion of fossil fuels, industrial process, solid waste disposal and sewage disposal are sources of:
    (a) Water pollution
    (b) Land pollution
    (c) Air pollution
    (d) Noise pollution

30. Which of the following report defines sustainable development as a "Development that meets the needs of the present without compromising the ability of future generation to meet their own need"?
    (a) "The population Bomb" by Ehrlich
    (b) "The limits to Growth" by Meadows
    (c) Brundtland report "Our common future"
    (d) Capability Approach by Amartya sen

31. Most of the steel plants of India are located in which part of India?
    (a) Northern
    (b) Eastern
    (c) Southern
    (d) Western

32. The land which is left without cultivation for one or less than one agricultural year is known as-
    (a) Fallow other than current fallow
    (b) Current fallow
    (c) Culturable wasteland
    (d) Barren and Wastelands

33. Which one of the following states of India has the highest female literacy rate as per 2011 census?
    (a) Mizoram
    (b) Tripura
    (c) Kerala
    (d) Goa

34. Which one of following inter-state migration streams is dominated by male migrants in India?
    (a) Rural - rural
    (b) Rural - urban
    (c) Urban - rural
    (d) Urban - urban

35. Sustainability of human development is best explained by which one of the following properties.
    (a) Increase in income of the country
    (b) Building up financial capability in people
    (c) Enhanced standard of living
    (d) Continuity in the availability of opportunities to each generation

36. Which of the following is a mining town?
    (a) Durgapur
    (b) Bhilai
    (c) Jharia
    (d) Jabalpur

37. India is the second largest producer in the world of which of the following set of crops.
    (a) Sugarcane and Jute
    (b) Cotton and Sugarcane
    (c) Jute and Cotton
    (d) Coffee and Tea

38. Identify the type of ports that handle bulk and general cargo in large volumes from the following options.

(a) Oil ports

(b) Naval ports

(c) Industrial ports

(d) Comprehensive ports

39. Which of the following form of agriculture is found in the highly developed part of the world?

(a) Dairy farming

(b) Mixed farming

(c) Subsistence farming

(d) Commercial grain farming

40. What is the HDI (Human Development Index) rank of India published in UNDP Human Development report 2020?

(a) 121   (b) 131

(c) 141   (d) 151

Directions for Questions 41 to 45: Read the following passage very carefully and answer the questions on the basis of it:

Iron and steel Industry

The Iron and steel industry forms the base of all other industries and, therefore, it is called a basic industry. It is basic because it provides raw material for other industries such as machine tools used for further production. It may also be called a heavy industry because it uses large quantities of bulky raw materials and its products are also heavy.

Iron is extracted from iron ore by smelting in a blast furnace with carbon (coke) and limestone. The molten iron is cooled and moulded to form pig iron which is used for converting into steel by adding strengthening materials like manganese. The large integrated steel industry is traditionally located close to the sources of raw materials - iron ore, coal, manganese and limestone - or at places where these could be easily brought, e.g. near ports. But in mini steel mills access to market is more important than inputs. These are less expensive to build and operate and can be located near markets because of the abundance of scrap metal, which is the main input. Traditionally, most of the steel was produced at large integrated plants, but mini mills are limited to just one-step process – steel making-and are gaining ground.

Distribution: The industry is one of the most complex and capital-intensive industries and is concentrated in the advanced countries of North America, Europe and Asia. In U.S.A, most of the production comes from the north Appalachian region (Pittsburgh), Great Lake region (Chicago-Gary, Erie, Cleveland, Lorain, Buffalo and Duluth) and the Atlantic Coast (Sparrows point and Morisville). The industry has also moved towards the southern state of Alabama. Pittsburg area is now losing ground. It has now become the "rust bowl" of U.S.A. In Europe, U.K., Germany, France, Belgium, Luxembourg, the Netherlands and Russia are the leading producer's. The important steel centres are Scun Thorpe, Port Talbot, Birmingham and Sheffield in the U.K; Duisburg, Dortmund, Dusseldorf and Essen in Germany; Le Creusot arid st. Ettienne in France; and Moscow, St. Petersburgh, Lipetsk, Tula, in Russia and Krivoi Rog and Donetsk in Ukraine. In Asia, the important centres include Nagasaki and Tokyo-Yokohama in Japan; Shanghai, Tienstin and Wuhan in China; and Jamshedpur, Kulti-Bumpur, Durgapur, Rourkela, Bhilai, Bokaro, Salem, Visakhapatnam and Bhadravati in India.

41. Match the List I with List II

List I centers Iron steel industry	List II Countries
A. Pittsburgh	I. United Kingdom
B. Sheffield	II. USA
C. Duisburg	III. Ukraine
D. Krivoi Rog	IV. Germany

Choose the correct answer from the options given below:

(a) A-I, B-II, C-III, D-IV

(b) A-IV, B-III, C-II, D-I

(c) A-II, B-I, C-IV, D-III

(d) A-II, B-I, C-III, D-IV

42. Arrange the following statements related to manufacturing of steel in proper sequence.

A. Smelting is done in a blast furnace with carbon and limestone

B. Which is then used for converting into steel by adding strengthening material Like manganese

C. Iron is extracted from iron ore

D. The molten iron then is cooled and moulded to form pig iron

Choose the correct answer from the options given below:

(a) C, A, D, B   (b) A, B, C, D

(c) B, A, D, C   (d) D, A, B, C

43. The iron and steel industry forms the base of all other industries and provides raw material therefore it is called as:

(a) Light industry

(b) Agro industry

(c) Small scale industry

(d) Basic industry

44. Identify the incorrect statement about iron and steel industry,

   (a) It is basic industry because it provides raw material for other industries

   (b) It uses large quantities of bulky raw materials

   (c) Iron is extracted from iron ore by smelting

   (d) The industry requires less capital investment

45. One of the important centre of steel industry in Asian continent is _______.

   (a) Tokyo   (b) Bangkok

   (c) Dhaka   (d) Kolkata

Directions for Questions 46 to 50: Read the following passage very carefully and answer the questions on the basis of it:

Buses merely skirt the periphery. Autorickshaws cannot go there. Dharavi is part of central Bombay where three wheelers are banned.

Only one main road traverses the slum, the miscalled 'ninety-foot road', which has been reduced to less than half of that for most of its length. Some of the side alleys and lanes are so narrow that not even a bicycle can pass. The whole neighbourhood consists of temporary buddings, two or three storeyed high with rusty iron stairways to the upper part, where a single room is rented by a whole family, sometimes accommodating twelve or more people; it is a land of tropical versions of the industrial dwelling of Victorian London's East end.

But Dharavi is a keeper of more sombre secrets than the revulsion it inspires in the rich; a revulsion, moreover, that is, in direct proportion to the role it serves in the creation of the wealth of Bombay. In this place of shadowless, tressless sunlight, uncollected garbage, stagnant pools of foul water, where the only non-human creatures are the shining black crows and long grey rats, some of the most beautiful, valuable and useful articles in India are made. From Dharavi come delicate ceramics and pottery, exquisite embroidery and Zari work, sophisticated leather goods, high-fashion garments, finely- wrought metal work, delicate jewellery settings, wood carvings and furniture that would find its way into the richest houses, both in India and abroad...

Dharavi was an arm of the sea, that was filled by waste, largely produced by the people have come to live there: Scheduled Castes and poor Muslims. It comprises rambling buildings of corrugated metal, 20 meter high in places, used for the treatment of hides and tanning. There are pleasant parts, but rotting garbage is everywhere...."

46. Dharavi was an arm of the sea. it was filled by: _______.

   (a) Forests   (b) Cargo

   (c) Waste   (d) Population

47. Dharavi slum habitation is a part of ________.

   (a) Central Bombay

   (b) New Mumbai

   (c) South Bombay

   (d) East Bombay

48. People who live in Dharavi are:

   (a) Educated and industrialist

   (b) Scheduled castes and poor Muslims

   (c) Rich and poor of Mumbai

   (d) Migrants who are rich

49. The building structures of Dharavi is the kind of tropical version of the.

   (a) Central Bombay

   (b) Central Australia

   (c) Victorian London's East End

   (d) East End of Bombay

50. Dharavi is known to manufacture certain specific products.

   (a) Ceramic, Jewellery and wood carving

   (b) Information technology and services

   (c) Books and newspapers

   (d) Fans, electric bulbs and TVs

Answer Keys

1. (c)	**2.** (b)	**3.** (b)	**4.** (d)	**5.** (b)	**6.** (d)	**7.** (a)	**8.** (d)	**9.** (b)	**10.** (d)
11. (a)	**12.** (d)	**13.** (c)	**14.** (c)	**15.** (d)	**16.** (a)	**17.** (c)	**18.** (c)	**19.** (d)	**20.** (b)
21. (c)	**22.** (a)	**23.** (c)	**24.** (c)	**25.** (a)	**26.** (a)	**27.** (a)	**28.** (d)	**29.** (c)	**30.** (c)
31. (b)	**32.** (b)	**33.** (c)	**34.** (b)	**35.** (d)	**36.** (c)	**37.** (b)	**38.** (d)	**39.** (b)	**40.** (b)
41. (c)	**42.** (a)	**43.** (d)	**44.** (d)	**45.** (a)	**46.** (c)	**47.** (a)	**48.** (b)	**49.** (c)	**50.** (a)

Explanations

1. (c) The pressure on agricultural land increases not only due to the limited availability but also by deterioration of quality of agricultural land. Soil erosion, waterlogging, salinisation and alkalinisation of land lead to land degradation.

2. (b) India is the second most populous country after China in the world with its total population of 1,210 million (2011).

3. (b) Entrepot Ports: These are collection centres where the goods are brought from different countries for export. Singapore is an entrepot for Asia. Rotterdam for Europe and Copenhagen for the Baltic region.

4. (d) **Ancient Towns:** There are number of towns in India having historical background spanning over 2000 years. Most of them developed as religious and cultural centres. Varanasi is one of the important towns among these. Prayag (Allahabad), Pataliputra (Patna), Madurai are some other examples of ancient towns in the country.

5. (b) A geographer, Griffith Taylor introduced another concept which reflects a middle path (Madhyam Marg) between the two ideas of environmental determinism and possibilism. He termed it as Neodeterminism or stop and go determinism.

6. (d)

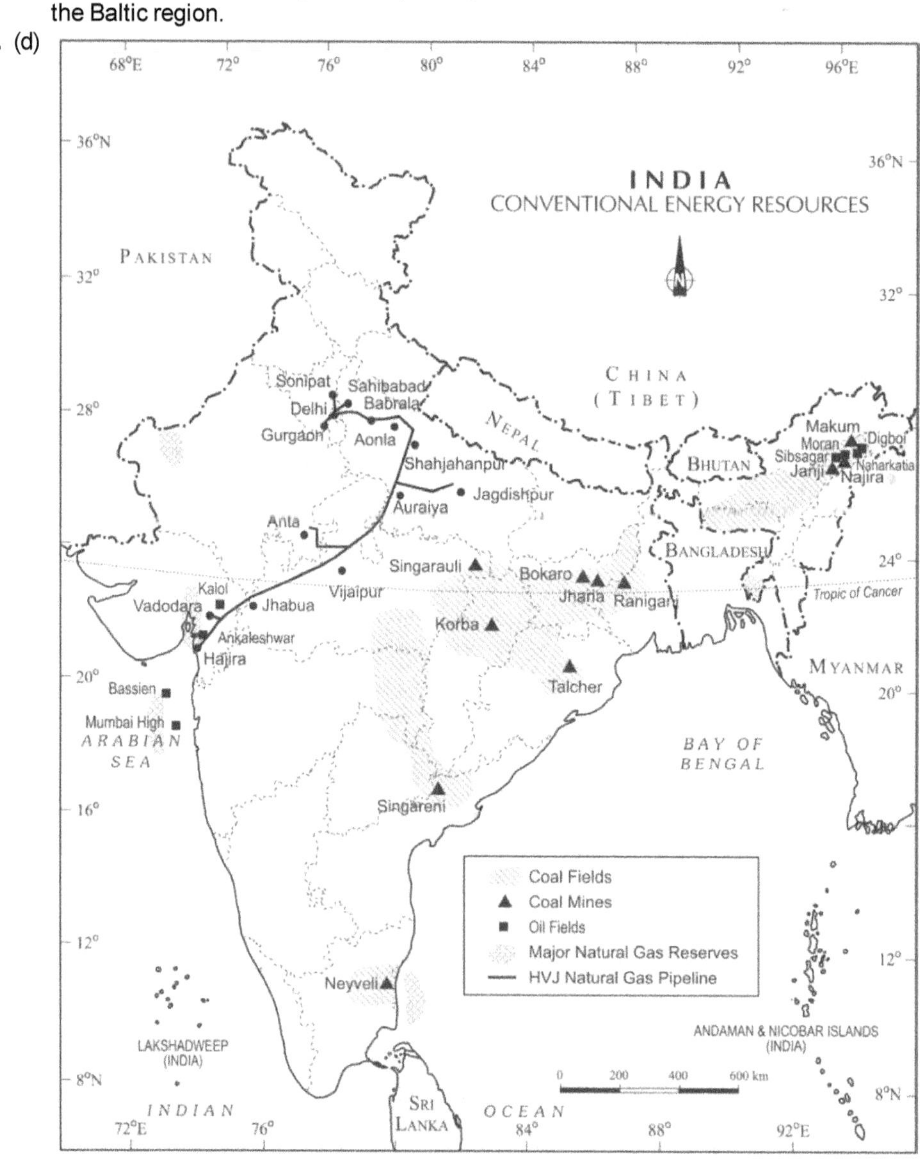

7. (a)

Census Year	Total Population	Growth Rate*	
		Absolute Number	% of Growth
1901	238396327	—	—
1911	252093390	(+) 13697063	(+) 5.75
1921	251321213	(–) 772117	(–) 0.31
1931	278977238	(+) 27656025	(+) 11.6
1941	318660580	(+) 39683342	(+) 14.22
1951	361088090	(+) 42420485	(+) 13.31
1961	439234771	(+) 77682873	(+) 21.51
1971	548159652	(+) 108924881	(+) 24.8
1981	683329097	(+) 135169445	(+) 24.66
1991	846302688	(+) 162973591	(+) 23.85
2001	1028610328	(+) 182307640	(+) 21.54
2011**	1210193422	(+) 181583094	(+) 17.64

8. (d) Region wise Density of Population

Region	Population (2018)	Land Area (km^2)	Density (P/km^2)	World Share (in percentage)
Asia	4,545,133,094	31,033,131	146	59.50%
Africa	1,287,920,518	29,648,481	43	16.90%
Europe	742,648,010	22,134,900	34	9.70%
Latin America and the Caribbean	652,012,001	20,139,378	32	8.50%
Northern America	363,844,490	18,651,660	20	4.80%
Oceania	41,261,212	8,486,460	5	0.50%

9. (b)

Broad Stages and Thrust of Human Geography

Period	Approaches	Broad Features
Early Colonial period	Exploration and description	Imperial and trade interests prompted the discovery and exploration of new areas. An encyclopaedic description of the area formed an important aspect of the geographer's account.
Later Colonial period	Regional analysis	Elaborate description of all aspects of a region were undertaken. The idea was that all the regions were part of a whole, i.e. (the earth); so, understanding the parts in totality would lead to an understanding of the whole.
1930s through the inter-War period	Areal differentiation	The focus was on identifying the uniqueness of any region and understanding how and why it was different from others.
Late 1950s to the late 1960s	Spatial organisation	Marked by the use of computers and sophisticated statistical tools. Laws of physics were often applied to map and analyse human phenomena. This phase was called the quantitative revolution. The main objective was to identify mappable patterns for different human activities.
1970s	Emergence of humanistic, radical and behavioural schools	Discontentment with the quantitative revolution and its dehumanised manner of doing geography led to the emergence of three new schools of thought of human geography in the 1970s. Human geography was made more relevant to the socio-political reality by the emergence of these schools of thought. Consult the box below to know a little bit more about these schools of thought.
1990s	Post-modernism in geography	The grand generalisations and the applicability of universal theories to explain the human conditions were questioned. The importance of understanding each local context in its own right was emphasised.

10. (d) Rainwater harvesting has been practised through various methods by different communities in the country for a long time. Traditional rainwater harvesting in rural areas is done by using surface storage bodies, like lakes, ponds, irrigation tanks, etc. In Rajasthan, rainwater harvesting structures locally known as Kund or Tanka (a covered underground tank) are constructed near or in the house or village to store harvested rainwater (see Fig. 6.3 to understand various ways of rainwater harvesting). There is a wide scope to use rainwater harvesting technique to conserve precious water resource. It can be done by harvesting rainwater on rooftops and open spaces.

11. (a) Sugarcane is a weight-losing crop. The ratio of sugar to sugarcane varies between 9 to 12 per cent depending on its variety. In iron and steel industries, iron ore and coal both are weight-losing raw materials. Therefore, an optimum location for iron and steel industries should be near raw material sources.

12. (d) The Iron and Steel industry is one of the most complex and capital-intensive industries and is concentrated in the advanced countries of North America, Europe and Asia. In U.S.A, most of the production comes from the north Appalachian region (Pittsburgh), Great Lake region (Chicago-Gary, Erie, Cleveland, Lorain, Buffalo and Duluth) and the Atlantic Coast (Sparrows Point and Morisville). Automobile industry is the most prominent industry in Detroit.

13. (c) Primitive subsistence agriculture or shifting cultivation is prevalent in tropical region in different names, e.g. Jhuming in North eastern states of India, Milpa in Central America and Mexico and Ladang in Indonesia and Malaysia. Some coffee fazendas (large plantations) in Brazil are still managed by Europeans.

14. (c) The census of India, 1991 defines urban settlements as "All places which have municipality, corporation, cantonment board or notified town area committee and have a minimum population of 5000 persons, at least 75 per cent of male workers are engaged in non-agricultural pursuits and a density of population of at least 400 persons per square kilometers are urban.

15. (d) India contributes 22.07 per cent of rice production in the world and ranked second after China in 2018. About one-fourth of the total cropped area in the country is under rice cultivation. West Bengal, Uttar Pradesh, and Punjab are the leading rice producing states in the country. About 14 per cent of the total cropped area in the country is under wheat cultivation. Uttar Pradesh, Madhya Pradesh, Punjab, Haryana and Rajasthan are leading wheat producing states. The leading producers of maize are the states of Karnataka, Madhya Pradesh, Bihar, Andhra Pradesh, Telangana, Rajasthan and Uttar Pradesh. Gujarat, Rajasthan, Tamil Nadu, Telangana, Andhra Pradesh, Karnataka and Maharashtra are the leading producers of groundnut.

16. (a) Varanasi, Prayag (Allahabad), Pataliputra (Patna), Madurai are some other examples of ancient towns in the country. Important Medieval towns are Delhi, Hyderabad, Jaipur, Lucknow, Agra and Nagpur. Modern Towns - The British and other Europeans have developed a number of towns in India. Starting their foothold on coastal locations, they first developed some trading ports such as Surat, Daman, Goa, Pondicherry, etc. The British later consolidated their hold around three principal nodes – Mumbai (Bombay), Chennai (Madras), and Kolkata (Calcutta) – and built them in the British style. Mining towns have developed in mineral rich areas such as Raniganj, Jharia, Digboi, Ankaleshwar, Singrauli, etc.

17. (c) The Northern Atlantic Sea Route - This links North-eastern U.S.A. and North-western Europe, the two industrially developed regions of the world. The foreign trade over this route is greater than that of the rest of the world combined. One fourth of the world's foreign trade moves on this route. It is, therefore, the busiest in the world and otherwise, called the Big Trunk Route. The Rhine flows through Germany and the Netherlands. It is navigable for 700 km from Rotterdam, at its mouth in the Netherlands to Basel in Switzerland. Big Inch is one such famous pipeline, which carries petroleum from the oil wells of the Gulf of Mexico to the North-eastern States. About 17 per cent of all freight per tonne-km. is carried through pipelines in U.S.A. Trans–Siberian Railway - This is a trans–siberian Railways major rail route of Russia runs from St. Petersburg in the west to Vladivostok on the Pacific Coast in the east passing through Moscow, Ufa, Novosibirsk, Irkutsk, Chita and Khabarovsk.

18. (c) Mining towns have developed in mineral rich areas such as Raniganj, Jharia, Digboi, Ankaleshwar, Singrauli, etc. Towns supporting administrative headquarters of higher order are administrative towns, such as Chandigarh, New Delhi, Bhopal, Shillong, Guwahati, Imphal, Srinagar, Gandhinagar, Jaipur, Chennai, etc. These towns emerged as garrisson towns such as Ambala, Jalandhar, Mhow, Babina, Udhampur, etc. Transport Cities may be ports primarily engaged in export and import activities such as Kandla, Kochchi, Kozhikode, Vishakhapatnam, etc., or hubs of inland transport, such as Agra, Dhulia, Mughalsarai, Itarsi, Katni, etc.

19. (d) Top Ten Ranked Countries with High Value Index

Rank	Country	Rank	Country
1.	Norway	6.	Germany
2.	Ireland	7.	Sweden
3.	Switzerland	8.	Australia
4.	Hongkong, China (SAR)	9.	Netherlands
5.	Iceland	10.	Denmark

20. (b) The developed economies are retreating from mining, processing and refining stages of production due to high labour costs, while the developing countries with large labour force and striving for higher standard of living are becoming more important.

21. (c) Actual Growth of Population = Births – Deaths + In Migration – Out Migration

22. (a) Channel Tunnel, operated by Euro Tunnel Group through England, connects London with Paris.

23. (c) Geological structure determines the mineral resource base and topographical differences of any region and ensures diversity of crops and animal raised.

24. (c) **Natural Growth of Population:** This is the population increased by difference between births and deaths in a particular region between two points of time.

25. (a) **Intensive Subsistence Agriculture:** This type of agriculture is largely found in densely populated regions of monsoon Asia. Basically, there are two types of intensive subsistence agriculture.

(i) **Intensive subsistence agriculture dominated by wet paddy cultivation:** This type of agriculture is characterised by dominance of the rice crop. Land holdings are very small due to the high density of population. Farmers work with the help of family labour leading to intensive use of land. Use of machinery is limited and most of the agricultural operations are done by manual labour. Farm yard manure is used to maintain the fertility of the soil. In this type of agriculture, the yield per unit area is high but per labour productivity is low.

(ii) **Intensive subsidence agriculture dominated by crops other than paddy:** Due to the difference in relief, climate, soil and some of the other geographical factors, it is not practical to grow paddy in many parts of monsoon Asia. Wheat, soyabean, barley and sorghum are grown in northern China, Manchuria, North Korea and North Japan. In India wheat is grown in western parts of the Indo-Gangetic plains and millets are grown in dry parts of western and southern India. Most of the characteristics of this type of agriculture are similar to those dominated by wet paddy except that irrigation is often used.

26. (a) The crude birth rate (CBR) is expressed as number of live births in a year per thousand of population.

27. (a) The Ganga and the Yamuna are the two highly polluted rivers in the country.

28. (d) Sustainable energy resources are only the renewable energy sources like solar, wind, hydrogeothermal and biomass. These energy sources are more equitably distributed and environment-friendly.

29. (c)

Types and Sources of Pollution

Pollution Types	Pollution Involved	Sources of Pollution
Air Pollution	Oxides of sulphur (SO_2, SO_3). Oxides of nitrogen, carbon monoxide, hydro-carbon, ammonia, lead, aldehydes asbestos and beryllium.	Combustion of coal, petrol and diesel. industrial processes, solid waste disposal, sewage disposal, etc.
Water Pollution	Odour, dissolved and suspended solids. ammonia and urea, nitrate and nitrites, chloride, fluoride, carbonates, oil and grease. insecticide and pesticide residue, tannin. coliform MPM (bacterial count) sulphates and sulphides, heavy metals e.g. lead, aresenic, mercury, manganese, etc., radioactive substances.	Sewage disposal, urban run-off, toxic effluents from industries, run-off over cultivated lands and nuclear power plants.
Land Pollution	Human and animal excreta viruses and bacteria, garbage and vectors therein. pesticides and fertiliser-residue alkalinity, fluorides, radio-active substances.	Improper human activities, disposal of untreated industrial waste, use of pesticides and fertilisers.
Noise Pollution	High level of noise above tolerance level.	Aircrafts, automobiles, trains, industrial processing and advertising media.

30. (c) Concerned with the growing opinion of world community on the environmental issues, the United Nations established a World Commission on Environment and Development (WCED) headed by the Norwegian Prime Minister Gro Harlem Brundtland. The Commission gave its report (also known as Brundtland Report) entitled 'Our Common Future' in 1987. The report defines sustainable development as a "development that meets the needs of the present without compromising the ability of future generations to meet their own needs."

31. (b) Most of the iron and steel industry in India is located in eastern and southern India. In India, there is a crescent shaped region comprising parts of Chhattisgarh, Northern Odisha, Jharkhand and western West Bengal, which is extremely rich in high grade iron ore, good quality coking coal and other supplementing raw materials.

32. (b) Current Fallow is the land which left without cultivation for one or less than one agricultural year. Fallowing is a cultural practice adopted for giving the land rest. The land recoups the lost fertility through natural processes.

33. (c) Kerala has the highest female literacy rate of 91.98%.

34. (b) Females predominate the streams of short distance rural to rural migration in both types of migration. Contrary to this, men predominate the rural to urban stream of inter-state migration due to economic reasons.

35. (d) Sustainability means continuity in the availability of opportunities. To have sustainable human development, each generation must have the same opportunities. All environmental, financial and human resources must be used keeping in mind the future. Misuse of any of these resources will lead to fewer opportunities for future generations.

36. (c) Mining towns have developed in mineral rich areas such as Raniganj, Jharia, Digboi, Ankaleshwar, Singrauli, etc.

37. (b) India ranks second in the world in the production of cotton after China. India was the second largest producer of sugarcane after Brazil in 2018.

38. (d) Comprehensive Ports: Such ports handle bulk and general cargo in large volumes. Most of the world's great ports are classified as comprehensive ports.

39. (b) Mixed Farming: This form of agriculture is found in the highly developed parts of the world, e.g. North-western Europe, Eastern North America, parts of Eurasia and the temperate latitudes of Southern continents.

40. (b) Human Development Index Values of India and some other countires

Country	HDI value	Rank
Norway	0.957	1
Germany	0.947	6
USA	0.926	17
UK	0.932	13
Russian Fed	0.824	52
Malaysia	0.81	62
Sri Lanka	0.782	72
Brazil	0.765	84
China	0.761	85
Egypt	0.707	116
Indonesia	0.718	107
South Africa	0.709	114
India	0.645	131
Bangladesh	0.632	133
Pakistan	0.557	154

41. (c)
42. (a)
43. (d)
44. (d)
45. (a)
46. (c)
47. (a)
48. (b)
49. (c)
50. (a)

HISTORY

1. Match list I with list II

List I – Name of Archaeologists/person	List II - Known for
A. Alexander Cunningham	I. The Story of Indian Archaeology
B. S. N. Roy	II. Ignored the stratigraphy
C. John Marshall	III. An Ex-Army Brigadier
D. R. E. M. Wheeler	IV. First Director General of the Archaeological Survey of India

Choose the correct answer from the options given below:

(a) A-IV, B-I, C-II, D-III

(b) A-I, B-II, C-III, D-IV

(c) A-IV, B-II, C-I, D-III

(d) A-III, B-I, C-II, D-IV

2. Which one of the following pairs is correctly matched?

(a) Banawali - Rajasthan

(b) Lothal - Gujarat

(c) Kalibangan - Punjab

(d) Harappa - Baluchistan

3.

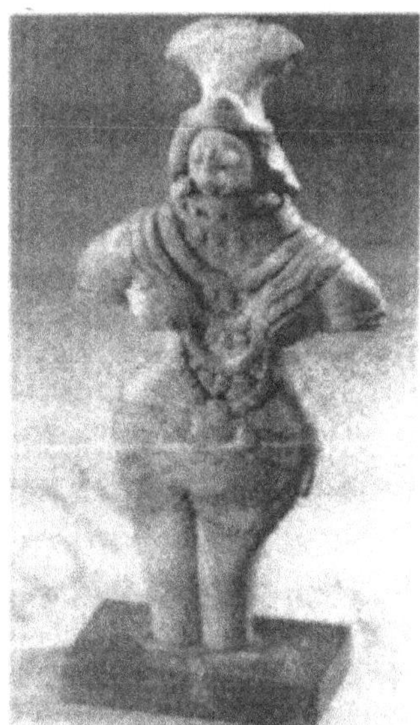

Identify this picture related to Harappan Civilization and choose the correct option.

(a) Priest King   (b) Proto Shiva

(c) Gamesmen   (d) Mother Goddess

4. The initial capital of Magadha was at __________.

(a) Rajgir

(b) Pataliputra

(c) Taxila

(d) Ujjayini

5. Who deciphered Brahmi and Kharosti script?

(a) A. H. Wheeler

(b) John Marshall

(c) James Prinsep

(d) A. Cunningham

6. Harshacharita was written by __________.

(a) Megasthenes

(b) Kautilya

(c) Ravikirti

(d) Banabhatta

7. Identify the correct options from below

A. Ashtadhyayi was written by Panini

B. Tripitakas are associated with Buddhism

C. Mahabharata and Ramayana were written in Sanskrit

D. Puranas were written in Pali language

E. Dharmashastras were written in Brahmi script

Choose the correct answer from the options given below:

(a) A, B and D

(b) A, B and C

(c) C, D and E

(d) A, B and E

8. Match **List - I** with **List - II**.

List I - Types of marriages	List II - Explanation
A. Endogamy	I. Marriage outside the unit
B. Exogamy	II. Practice of women having several husbands
C. Polygyny	III. Marriage within a unit
D. Polyandry	IV. Practice of man having several wives

Choose the correct answer from the options given below:

(a) A-III, B-I, C-IV, D-II

(b) A-I, B-II, C-III, D-IV

(c) A- I, B-IV, C-III, D-II

(d) A-II, B-III, C-IV, D-I

9. The lineage of the family in which a person is born is traced from which of the following?

   (a) Jati   (b) Kula

   (c) Varna   (d) Gotra

10. Which of the following deities is not mentioned hi the Rig Veda?

   (a) Agni

   (b) Soma

   (c) India

   (d) Durga

11. Which of the following is not considered to be the three jewels or 'triratna' of Jainism?

   (a) Right knowledge

   (b) Right faith

   (c) Right livelihood

   (d) Right action

12. The Sangha in Buddhist tradition are associated with __________.

   (a) Merchants

   (b) Traders

   (c) Bhikkus and Bhikkunis

   (d) Dancers

13. Choose the correct sequence of the arrival of foreign travelers to medieval India.

   A. Marco Polo

   B. Ibn Battuta

   C. Duarte Barbosa

   D. Al-Biruni

   E. Francois Bernier

   Choose the correct answer from the options given below:

   (a) A, D, B, C, E   (b) D, A, B, C, E

   (c) A, B, D, E, C   (d) D, A, C, E, B

14. Match both the lists correctly.

List I - Bhakti Saints/Sects	List II - Type of worship
A. Alvars	I. Nirgum Bhakti
B. Guru Nanak	II. Worshipper of Shiva
C. Nayanars	III. Sagun Bhakti
D. Meerabai	IV. Worshipper of Vishnu

   Choose the correct answer from the options given below:

   (a) A-I, B-II, C-III, D-IV

   (b) A-III, B-IV, C-I, D-II

   (c) A-II, B-III, C-IV, D-I

   (d) A-IV, B-I, C-II, D-III

15. Match both the lists correctly.

List I - Sufi Saints	List II - Location
A. Khwaja Qutubuddin Bakhtiyar Kaki	I. Ajodhan
B. Shaikh Muinuddin Sijzi	II. Lahore
C. Shaikh Fariduddin Ganj-i-Shakar	III. Ajmer
D. Abul Hasan Al Hujwiri	IV. Delhi

Choose the correct answer from the options given below:

   (a) A-IV, B-III, C-II, D-I

   (b) A-IV, B-III, C-I, D- II

   (c) A-II, B-III, C-II, D-IV

   (d) A-III, B-IV, C-I, D-II

16. Adi Granth Sahib is a collection of hymns.

   A. It was composed by the tenth Guru Govind Singh

   B. It included hymns composed by Guru Nanak and his four successors

   C. Compositions of poets like Baba Farid, Ravidas and Kabir too were part of it

   D. It was compiled by Guru Tegh Bahadur

   E. These hymns called "Gurbani", are composed in various languages

Choose the correct answer from the options given below:

   (a) A, B and C only

   (b) B, C and E only

   (c) C, D and E only

   (d) A, B and E only

17. Arrange the below given information in chronological order.

   A. Conservation of Hampi begins wider John Marshall

   B. Alexander Greenlaw takes the first detailed photographs of Hampi

   C. Colin Mackenzie visits Hampi

   D. Hampi recognized as a site of National importance

   E. Hampi declared as World Heritage Site by UNESCO

Choose the correct answer from the options given below:

   (a) A, B, C, D, E

   (b) B, C, D, E, A

   (c) C, D, E, A, B

   (d) C, B, A, D, E

18. Krishnadeva Raya, the famous ruler of Vijayanagara Empire belonged to which of the following dynasty?

    (a) Sangama dynasty

    (b) Aravidu dynasty

    (c) Tuluva dynasty

    (d) Suluva dynasty

19. The Vijayanagara Empire was described by the contemporaries as:

    (a) Karnataka Samrajyamu

    (b) Gajapats

    (c) Bahamani

    (d) Ashwapati

20. The Jati Panchayat in Rajasthan performed a number of functions, choose the odd one among the given options.

    (a) Settled civil disputes between members of different castes

    (b) Settled matters related to criminal justice

    (c) Mediated in contested claims on land

    (d) Decided whether marriages were performed according to the norms laid down by a particular caste group

21. Choose the correct option which describes meaning of Imperial Kitabkhana.

    (a) A place where books were lent to nobles

    (b) A place where manuscripts were kept and new manuscripts were produced

    (c) A place where people came and read books

    (d) A place where all writers met and discussions were held

22. The enormous arched gateway - Buland Darwaza was meant to remind visitors of the Mughal Victory over ____________.

    (a) Delhi

    (b) Ajmer

    (c) Fatehpur Sikiri

    (d) Gujarat

23. Consider the statements related to Mansabdari system under Akbar's rule and find the correct option.

    A. All Mansabdars held two numerical designations namely Zat and Sawar

    B. They met the ruler in Diwan-i-am

    C. They participated in military campaigns

    D. They were powerful but not well paid

    E. Mansabdars of 1000 zat or above were ranked as nobles (Umra/amir)

Choose the correct answer from the options given below:

    (a) A, C and D only

    (b) A, C and E only

    (c) B, D and E only

    (d) B, C and E only

24. Qandahar was a bone of contention between the Safavids and the Mughals. In the light of above statement choose the correct option.

    A. The fortress town was initially in the possession of Humayun

    B. It was reconquered in 1595 by Akbar

    C. In 1613 Shah Jahan sent a diplomatic envoy to the court of Shah Abbas

    D. The Safavid court retained diplomatic relations with the Mughals

    E. In the winter of 1622 Mughal army besieged Qandahar

Choose the correct answer from the options given below:

    (a) A, B and D only

    (b) A, B and C only

    (c) B, C and D only

    (d) A, D and E only

25. The great chronicles were written in Mughal Empire which depict the glory of Mughals. Arrange them in chronological order'.

    A. Alamgir Nama

    B. Badshah Nama

    C. Akbar Nama

    D. Humayun Nama

    E. Babur Nama

Choose the correct answer from the options given below:

    (a) E, D, C, B, A   (b) E, D, C, A, B

    (c) A, B, D, C, E   (d) B, C, A, D, E

26. Consider the ways that helped the Zamindars in Bengal to survive under various kinds of pressure. Choose the incorrect one.

    (a) Transferred land in name of their mother to avoid auction

    (b) His agents manipulated the auction

    (c) They used to establish matrimonial alliance with the Britishers

    (d) At times, Lathyals of the former zamindars would not allow an outsider to take possession of the auctioned land

27. The leader of the Santhal Rebellion was:

   (a) Gonoo

   (b) Sidhu Manjhi

   (c) Shah Mai

   (d) Danka Shah

28. The Governor General of Bengal who introduced the Permanent Settlement in 1793 was:

   (a) Lord Clive

   (b) Lord Wellesley

   (c) Lord Cornwallis

   (d) Lord William Bentinck

29. Consider the settlements related to the Santhal Rebellion. Which one is not true.

   (a) The rebellion took place in 1850-51

   (b) The state was levying heavy taxes on land

   (c) Money lenders were charging high interest rates

   (d) Zamindars were asserting control over Damin-i-Koh

30. The Permanent Settlement was rarely extended to any region beyond Bengal, because:

   (a) The peasants wanted to discourage investment in agriculture

   (b) The colonial state wanted to claim its share on the enhanced income of zamindars

   (c) The colonial state did not want to have a class who would be loyal to the company

   (d) They wanted the revenue demand to be permanent

31. Who among the following were not associated with the revolt of 1857?

   A. Maulvi Ahmadullah Shah

   B. Nana Sahib

   C. C. R. Das

   D. Shah Mai

   E. S. N. Sen

   Choose the correct answer from the options given below:

   (a) A and B only

   (b) B and D only

   (c) D and E only

   (d) C and E only

32. In 1864 the Viceroy John Lawrence officially moved his council to this hill station, which also became the official residence of the Commander-in-Chief of the Indian Army. Name the above mentioned hill station.

   (a) Mount Abu

   (b) Dalhousie

   (c) Shimla

   (d) Darjeeling

33. Arrange the following important events in the history of the nationalist movement of India in chronological order.

   A. Proclamation of commitment to "Purna Swaraj"

   B. All India campaign against all - white Simon Commission

   C. "Independence Day" was observed for the first time on 26 January 1930

   D. Champaran Satyagraha

   E. Gandhiji began the Salt March

   Choose the correct answer from the option given below:

   (a) D, B, A, E, C

   (b) D, A, B, C, E

   (c) D, B, A, C, E

   (d) B, A, E, D, C

34. Dr. Khushdeva Singh's book "Love is stronger than Hate..." is about:

   (a) Non-Cooperation Movement

   (b) Swadeshi Movement

   (c) Noakhali Massacre

   (d) Relief work after partition of India

35. Who coined the term 'Pakistan'?

   (a) M. A. Jinnah

   (b) Rehmat Ali

   (c) Mohammad Iqbal

   (d) Mohammad Ali

36. The resolution proposing that the National Flag of India be a "horizontal tricolor of saffron, white and dark green in equal proportion" was moved by:

   (a) Sardar Patel

   (b) Dr. Rajendra Prasad

   (c) Dr. B. R. Ambedkar

   (d) Jawaharlal Nehru

37. Some maharajas now began "to luxuriate in wild dreams of independent power in an India of many partitions". This remark indicated the problem of:

   (a) Violence relating to the partition of India

   (b) Rehabilitation of refugees

   (c) Integration of the Princely States

   (d) Reorganisation of States

38.

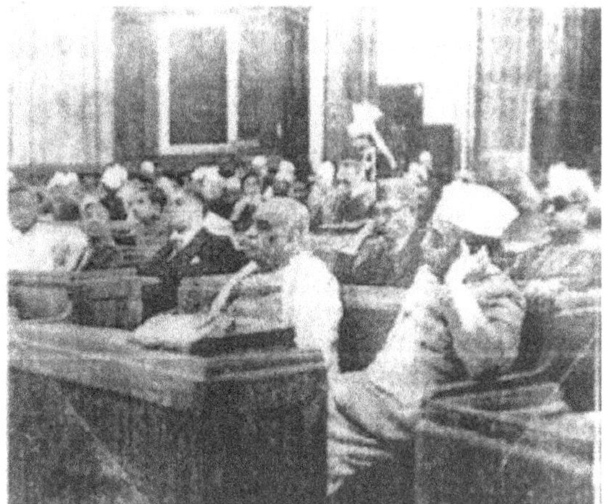

Identify the person in the picture who is known as 'Iron Man' of India.

(a) Mahatma Gandhi

(b) Dr. B. R. Ambedkar

(c) Sardar Vallabhbhai Patel

(d) Sardar Udham Singh

39. Match list I with list II

List - I : Leaders	List - II : Events/Profession Responsibility
A. S. N. Mukherjee	I. Lawyer giving crucial inputs for constitution
B. B. N. Rau	II. Chairman of Drafting Committee
C. B. R. Ambedkar	III. Chief Draughtsman of Constitution
D. K. M. Munshi	IV. Constitutional Advisor to Government of India

Choose the correct answer from the options given below:

(a) A-I, B-IV, C-II, D-III

(b) A-IV, B-I, C-II, D-III

(c) A-III, B-IV, C-II, D-I

(d) A-II, B-III, C-IV, D-I

40. Who among the following were the members of the Constituent Assembly?

A. Rajendra Prasad

B. Somnath Lahiri

C. Subhash Chandra Bose

D. Jyotiba Phule

E. B. Pocker Bahadur

Choose the correct answer from, the options given below:

(a) A, B and C   (b) B, C and D

(c) A, D and E   (d) A, B and E

Directions for Questions 41 to 45:

Please read the passage and answer the question that follow:

Passage

Why was salt the symbol of protest? This is what Mahatma Gandhi wrote:

The volume of information being gained daily show's how wickedly the salt tax has been designed. In order to prevent the use of salt that has not paid the tax which is at times even fourteen times its value, the Government destroys the salt it cannot sell profitably. Thus it taxes the nation's vital necessity; it prevents the public from manufacturing it and destroys what nature manufactures without effort. No adjective is strong enough for characterizing the wicked dog-in-the-manger policy. From various sources I hear tales of such wanton destruction of the nation's property in all parts of India. Maunds if not tons of salt are said to be destroyed on the Konkan coast. The same tale comes from Dandi. Wherever there is likelihood of natural salt being taken away by the people living in the neighbourhood of such areas for their personal use, salt officers are posted for the sole purpose of carrying on destruction. Thus valuable national property is destroyed at national expense and salt taken out of the mouths of the people.

The salt monopoly is thus a fourfold curse. It deprives tire people of a valuable easy village industry, involves wanton destruction of property that nature produces in abundance, the destruction itself means more national expenditure, and fourthly, to crown this folly, an unheard of tax of more than 1,000 per cent is exacted from a. starving people.

This tax has remained so long because of the apathy of the general public. Now that it is sufficiently roused, the tax has to go. How soon it will be abolished depends upon tire strength the people.

41. What did the Government use to do with the salt it could not sell?

(a) Export the salt

(b) Destroy the salt

(c) Ration the salt

(d) Hoard the salt

42. M. K. Gandhi had heard that salt was destroyed by the Government in large quantities in which of the following region?

(a) Malabar coast

(b) Coromandal coast

(c) Konkan coast

(d) Northern Sircar coast

43. Salt officers were posted at various places to:

(a) Distribute the salt among people

(b) Protect the salt from destruction

(c) Carrying the salt to the railways

(d) Destroying the salt

44. Which one of the following statements is incorrect?

(a) The salt monopoly deprived people of an easy village industry

(b) Salt was exported in large quantity to Britain

(c) Salt was destroyed at national expense

(d) A tax of more than 1000 percent was exacted from a poor population

45. The attitude of the general public of India towards the salt tax was:

(a) Submissive

(b) Dissatisfaction

(c) Apathy

(d) Enthusiasm

Directions for Questions 46 to 50:

Please read the passage and answer the questions that follow:

Passage

British pictures offer a variety of images that were meant to provoke a range of different emotions and reactions. Some of them commemorate the British heroes who saved the English and repressed the rebels. "Relief of Lucknow", painted by Thomas Jones Barker in 1859, is an example of this type. When the rebel forces besieged Lucknow, Henry Lawrence, the Commissioner of Lucknow, collected the Christian population and took refuge in the heavily fortified Residency.

Lawrence was killed but the Residency continued to be defended under the command of Colonel Inglis. On 25 September James Outram and Henry Havelock arrived, cut through the rebel forces, and reinforced the British garrisons. Twenty days later Colin Campbell, who was appointed as the new Commander of British forces in India, came with his forces and rescued the besieged British garrison. In British accounts the siege of Lucknow became a story of survival, heroic resistance and the ultimate triumph of British power. Barker's painting celebrated the moment of Campbell's entry. At the centre of the canvas are the British heroes - Campbell, Outram and Havelock. The gestures of the hands of those around lead the spectator's eyes towards the centre. The heroes stand on a ground that is well lit, with shadows in the foreground and tire damaged Residency in the background.

Tire dead and injured in the foreground are testimony to the suffering during the siege, while the triumphant figures of horses in the middle ground emphasise the fact that British power and control had been re-established. To the British public such paintings were reassuring. They created a sense that the time of trouble was past and the rebellion was over; the British were the victors.

46. Thomas Jones Barker painted which famous painting?

(a) "In Memoriam"

(b) "Justice"

(c) "Relief of Lucknow"

(d) "Miss Wheeler"

47. Henry Laurence along with the Christian population took refuge in the heavily fortified Residency because:

(a) The rebel forces besieged Lucknow and the British were in danger

(b) The residency was a comfortable and luxurious place

(c) Henry Lawrence wanted to have rest for some time

(d) The rebels ordered Henry Lawrence to take refuge in the Residency

48. After the death of Lawrence, the Residency was defended under the command of:

(a) Henry Havelock

(b) James Outram

(c) Colonel Inglis

(d) Colin Campbell

49. British accounts saw the siege of Lucknow as:

(a) A horror story

(b) A story of defeat and sorrow

(c) A story of survival, heroic resistance and the ultimate triumph of British power

(d) A story of repentance

50. In the painting "Relief of Lucknow", the figures of horses in the middle ground emphasise the fact that:

(a) The British were ready to fight

(b) The war is still on

(c) British power and control had been re-established

(d) The British were yet to become victors

Answer Keys

1. (a)	**2.** (b)	**3.** (d)	**4.** (a)	**5.** (c)	**6.** (d)	**7.** (b)	**8.** (a)	**9.** (b)	**10.** (d)
11. (c)	**12.** (c)	**13.** (b)	**14.** (d)	**15.** (a)	**16.** (b)	**17.** (d)	**18.** (c)	**19.** (a)	**20.** (b)
21. (b)	**22.** (d)	**23.** (b)	**24.** (a)	**25.** (a)	**26.** (c)	**27.** (b)	**28.** (c)	**29.** (a)	**30.** (b)
31. (d)	**32.** (c)	**33.** (c)	**34.** (d)	**35.** (b)	**36.** (d)	**37.** (c)	**38.** (c)	**39.** (c)	**40.** (c)
41. (b)	**42.** (c)	**43.** (d)	**44.** (b)	**45.** (c)	**46.** (c)	**47.** (a)	**48.** (c)	**49.** (c)	**50.** (c)

Explanations

1. (a) • Alexander Cunningham, the first Director-General of the Archaeological Survey of India (ASI), often called the father of Indian archaeology

  • S.N. Roy wrote *The Story of Indian Archaeology*

  • John Marshall, Director-General of the ASI

  • R.E.M. Wheeler, as an ex-army brigadier, he brought with him a military precision to the practice of archaeology.

2. (b) • Banawali (Haryana).

  • Kalibangan (Rajasthan)

3. (d) Early archaeologists thought that certain objects which seemed unusual or unfamiliar may have had a religious significance. These included terracotta figurines of women, heavily jewelled, some with elaborate head-dresses. These were regarded as mother goddesses.

4. (a) Rajgir

5. (c) James Prinsep deciphered it

6. (d) Banabhatta was a 7th-century Sanskrit prose writer and poet of India. He was the Asthana Kavi in the court of the emperor Harsha,

7. (b)

Major Textual Traditions

c. 500 BCE	*Ashtadhyayi* of Panini, a work on Sanskrit grammar
c. 500-200 BCE	Major Dharmasutras (in Sanskrit)
c. 500-100 BCE	Early Buddhist texts including the *Tripitaka* (in Pali)
c. 500 BCE-400 CE	*Ramayana* and *Mahabharata* (in Sanskrit)
c. 200 BCE-200 CE	*Manusmriti* (in Sanskrit); composition and compilation of Tamil Sangam literature
c. 100 CE	*Charaka* and *Sushruta* Samhitas, works on medicine (in Sanskrit)
c. 200 CE onwards	Compilation of the *Puranas* (in Sanskrit)
c. 300 CE	*Natyashastra* of Bharata, a work on dramaturgy (in Sanskrit)
c. 300-600 CE	Other Dharmashastras (in Sanskrit)

8. (a) **Types of marriages:** *Endogamy* refers to marriage within a unit – this could be a kin group, caste, or a group living in the same locality.

Exogamy refers to marriage outside the unit.

Polygyny is the practice of a man having several wives.

Polyandry is the practice of a woman having several husbands.

9. (b) Sanskrit texts use the term kula to designate families and jnati for the larger network of kinfolk. The term vamsha is used for lineage.

10. (d) The *Rigveda* consists of hymns in praise of a variety of deities, especially Agni, Indra and Soma.

11. (c) In Jainism the three jewels (also referred to as ratnatraya) are understood as samyagdarshana ("right faith"), samyagjnana ("right knowledge"), and samyakcharitra ("right conduct").

12. (c) Buddha founded a *sangha*, an organisation of monks who too became teachers of *dhamma*.

13. (b)

Some travellers who left accounts	
Tenth-eleventh centuries 973-1048	Muhammad ibn Ahmad Abu Raihan al-Biruni (from Uzbekistan)
Thirteenth century 1254-1323	Marco Polo (from Italy)
Fourteenth century 1304-77	Ibn Battuta (from Morocco)
Fifteenth century 1413-82	Abd al-Razzaq Kamal al-Din ibn Ishaq al-Samarqandi (from Samarqand)
1466-72 (years spent in India)	Afanasii Nikitich Nikitin (fifteenth century, from Russia)
Sixteenth century 1518 (visit to India)	Duarte Barbosa, d.1521 (from Portugal)
1562 (year of death)	Seydi Ali Reis (from Turkey)

14. (d) Some of the earliest bhakti movements (c. sixth century) were led by the Alvars (literally, those who are "immersed" in devotion to Vishnu) and Nayanars (literally, leaders who were devotees of Shiva).

15. (a)

Major Teachers of the Chishti Silsila		
Sufi teachers	Year of death	Location of Dargah
Shaikh Muinuddin Sijzi	1235	Ajmer (Rajasthan)
Khwaja Qutbuddin Bakhtiyar Kaki	1235	Delhi
Shaikh Fariduddin Ganj-i- Shakar	1265	Ajodhan (Pakistan)
Shaikh Nizamuddin Auliya	1325	Delhi
Shaikh Nasiruddin Chiragh-i Delhi	1356	Delhi

16. (b) • Adi Granth: literally means "the first book." This is the early compilation of the Sikh Scriptures by Guru Arjan Dev Ji, the fifth Sikh Guru, in 1604.

• This Granth (Book) is the Holy Scripture of the Sikhs.

• The tenth Sikh Guru, Guru Gobind Singh Ji added further holy Shabads to this Granth during the period of 1704 to 1706.

17. (d)

Landmarks in the discovery and conservation of Vijayanagara	
1800	Colin Mackenzie visits Vijayanagara
1856	Alexander Greenlaw takes the first detailed photographs of archaeological remains at Hampi
1876	J.F.Fleet begins documenting the inscriptions on the temple walls at the site
1902	Conservation begins under John Marshall
1986	Hampi declared a world Heritage site by UNESCO

18. (c) Krishnadeva Raya belonged to the Tuluva dynasty.

19. (a) Historians use the term Vijayanagara Empire, contemporaries described it as the karnataka samrajyamu.

20. (b) In Rajasthan jati panchayats arbitrated civil disputes between members of different castes. They mediated in contested claims on land, decided whether marriages were performed according to the norms laid down by a particular caste group, determined who had ritual precedence in village functions, and so on. In most cases, except in matters of criminal justice, the state respected the decisions of jati panchayats.

21. (b) All books in Mughal India were manuscripts, that is, they were handwritten. The centre of manuscript production was the imperial kitabkhana.

22. (d) The enormous arched gateway (Buland Darwaza) was meant to remind visitors of the Mughal victory in Gujarat.

23. (b) • All holders of government offices held ranks (*mansabs*) comprising two numerical designations: *zat* which was an indicator of position in the imperial hierarchy and the salary of the official (*mansabdar*), and *sawar* which indicated the number of horsemen he was required to maintain in service. In the seventeenth century, *mansabdars* of 1,000 *zat* or above ranked as nobles (*umara*, which is the plural of *amir*).

• The nobles participated in military campaigns with their armies and also served as officers of the empire in the provinces.

24. (a) • In 1613 Jahangir sent a diplomatic envoy to the court of Shah Abbas to plead the Mughal case for retaining Qandahar, but the mission failed.

- In the winter of 1622 a Persian army besieged Qandahar. The ill-prepared Mughal garrison was defeated and had to surrender the fortress and the city to the Safavids.

25. (a)

Some Major Mughal Chronicles and Memoirs	
c. 1530	Manuscript of Babur' memoirs in Turkish – saved from a storm – becomes part of the family collection of the Timurids
c. 1587	Gulbadan Begum begins to write the *Humayun Nama*
1589	Babur's memoirs translated into Persian as *Babur Nama*
1589-1602	Abu'l Fazl works on the *Akbar Nama*
1605-22	Jahangir writes his memoirs, the *Jahangir Nama*
1639-47	Lahori composes the first two *daftars* of the *Badshah Nama*
c.1650	Muhammad Waris begins to chronicle the third decade of Shah Jahan's reign
1668	*Alamgir Nama*, a history of the first ten years of Aurangzeb's reign compiled by Muhammad Kazim

26. (c) Zamindars never established matrimonial alliance with the Britishers

27. (b) The leader of the Santhal Rebellion was Sidhu Manjhi

28. (c) Lord Cornwallis proposed the Permanent Settlement system in 1786. This came into effect in 1793, by the Permanent Settlement Act of 1793.

29. (a) The **Santhal Revolt** took place in 1855-56

30. (b) After 1810, agricultural prices rose, increasing the value of harvest produce, and enlarging the income of the Bengal zamindars. Since the revenue demand was fixed under the Permanent Settlement, the colonial state could not claim any share of this enhanced income. Keen on expanding its financial resources, the colonial government had to think of ways to maximise its land revenue. So in territories annexed in the nineteenth century, temporary revenue settlements were made.

31. (d) Elsewhere, local leaders emerged, urging peasants, zamindars and tribals to revolt. Shah Mal mobilised the villagers of pargana Barout in Uttar Pradesh

32. (c) In 1864 the Viceroy John Lawrence officially moved his council to Simla, setting seal to the practice of shifting capitals during the hot season.

33. (c)

Timeline	
1915	Mahatma Gandhi returns from South Africa
1917	Champaran movement
1918	Peasant movements in Kheda (Gujarat), and worker's movement in Ahmedabad
1919	Rowlatt Satyagraha (March-April)
1919	Jallianwala Bagh massacre (April)
1921	Non-cooperation and Khilafat Movements
1928	Peasant movement in Bardoli
1929	"Purna Swaraj" accepted as Congress goal at the Lahore Congress (December)
1930	Civil Disobedience Movement begins; Dandi March (March-April)
1931	Gandhi-Irwin Pact (March); Second Round Table Conference (December)
1935	Government of India Act promises some form of representative government
1939	Congress ministries resign
1942	Quit India Movement begins (August)
1946	Mahatma Gandhi visits Noakhali and other riot-torn areas to stop communal violence

34. (d) Khushdeva Singh wrote about the gruelling relief work of doctor from a memoir he entitled *Love is Stronger than Hate: A Remembrance of 1947*.

35. (b) The name Pakistan or Pak-stan (from Punjab, Afghan, Kashmir, Sind and Baluchistan) was coined by a Punjabi Muslim student at Cambridge, Choudhry Rehmat Ali

36. (d) It was Nehru who moved the crucial "Objectives Resolution", as well as the resolution proposing that the National Flag of India be a "horizontal tricolour of saffron, white and dark green in equal proportion", with a wheel in navy blue at the centre.

37. (c) Integration of Princely states

38. (c) Sardar Vallabhbhai Patel

39. (c) • These six members were given vital assistance by two civil servants. One was B. N. Rau, Constitutional Advisor to the Government of India, who prepared a series of background papers based on a close study of the political systems obtaining in other countries.

- The other was the Chief Draughtsman, S. N. Mukherjee, who had the ability to put complex proposals in clear legal language.

40. (c) A Communist member, Somnath Lahiri saw the dark hand of British imperialism hanging over the deliberations of the Constituent Assembly. He thus urged the members, and Indians in general, to fully free themselves from the influences of imperial rule. In the winter of 1946-47, as the Assembly deliberated, the British were still in India. An interim administration headed by Jawaharlal Nehru was in place, but it could only operate under the directions of the Viceroy and the British Government in London. Lahiri exhorted his colleagues to realise that the Constituent Assembly was British-made and was "working the British plans as the British should like it to be worked out".

41. (b)

42. (c)

43. (d)

44. (b)

45. (c)

46. (c)

47. (a)

48. (c)

49. (c)

50. (c)

1. The first Director-General of the Archaeological survey of India was __________.
   (a) Jim Cook
   (b) Alexander Cunningham
   (c) Ernest Mackay
   (d) Lord Mountbatten

2. Identify the feature which is incorrect about the Harappan script:
   (a) Harrapan script has been deciphered by Ernest Mackay.
   (b) Harappan scripts is pictographic and not alphabetical.
   (c) It has too many signs - some where between 375 - 400.
   (d) The Harappan script was written from right to left.

3. Arrange the following stages of human history in India in chronological order.
   (A) Mesolithic
   (B) Early iron, megalithic burials
   (C) Neolithic
   (D) Chalcolithic
   (E) Lower Paleolithic
   Choose the **correct** answer from the options given below :
   (a) (E), (D), (A), (C), (B)
   (b) (A), (E), (D), (C), (B)
   (c) (E), (A), (D), (B), (C)
   (d) (E), (A), (C), (D), (B)

4. Select the correct information regarding the Mauryan Empire :
   (A) The name of the ruler, Ashok, is not mentioned in every incriptions issued by him.
   (B) Information about Chandragupta can be found in the account of Megasthenes.
   (C) Most of the Ashokan inscriptions were written in the Pali language.
   (D) Taxila was the capital city of the Mauryan Empire.
   (E) Ujjayini, Tosali and Suvarngiri were also important political centres in die empire.
   Choose the **correct** answer from die options given below :
   (a) (A), (B) and (E) only
   (b) (A), (C) and (D) only
   (c) (B), (D) and (E) only
   (d) (A), (C) and (E) only

5. During ancient period Indian spices were transported:
   (a) To the Roman Empire across the Arabian Sea and the Mediterranean.
   (b) To Britain through the Cape of Good Hope and the Atlantic.
   (c) To Japan through the Pacific and the South China Sea.
   (d) To Australia through the Pacific and the Botany Bay.

6. Match List - I with List - II.

List - I (Texts)		List - II (Authors)
(A) Arthashastra	(I)	Harishena
(B) Prayaga Prashasti	(II)	Unknown author
(C) Harshacharita	(III)	Kautilya
(D) Periplus of the Erythraean sea	(IV)	Banabhatta

   Choose the **correct** answer from the options given below :
   (a) (A)-(III), (B)-(IV), (C)-(II), (D)-(I)
   (b) (A)-(IV), (B)-(III), (C)-(I), (D)-(II)
   (c) (A)-(III), (B)-(I), (C)-(IV), (D)-(II)
   (d) (A)-(III), (B)-(II), (C)-(IV), (D)-(I)

7. Match List - I with List - II.

List - I		List - II
(A) Suvamakara	(I)	Charioteer - bards
(B) Maha Sammata	(II)	Guilds
(C) Sutas	(III)	Goldsmith
(D) Shrenis	(IV)	Great Elect

   Choose the **correct** answer from the options given below :
   (a) (A)-(I), (B)-(II), (C)-(III), (D)-(IV)
   (b) (A)-(III), (B)-(IV), (C)-(I), (D)-(II)
   (c) (A)-(II), (B)-(I), (C)-(III), (D)-(IV)
   (d) (A)-(IV), (B)-(III), (C)-(II), (D)-(I)

8. Which of the following rulers followed endogamy ?
   (a) Pandavas
   (b) Satavahanas
   (c) Mauryas
   (d) Guptas

9. Ekalavya, an important character in the Mahabharata, belonged to the following caste :

  (a) Chandala   (b) Sutradhara

  (c) Nishada   (d) Sarthavaha

10. Rajasuya and Ashvamedha were :

  (a) Elaborate sacrificial traditions performed by chiefs and kings.

  (b) The rituals performed by the military chief at the battlefield.

  (c) The rituals performed by the queen longing for a male child.

  (d) Rituals performed when the princes reached adulthood.

11. One can find the conversation between Ajatasattu and the Buddha in __________.

  (a) Jatakas   (b) Vinaya Patika

  (c) Sutta Pitaka   (d) Abhidhamma Pitaka

12. Match List - I with List - II.

List - I (Thinkers)	**List - II (Their Country)**
(A) Zarathustra	(I) Greece
(B) Kong zi	(II) Iran
(C) Plato	(III) China
(D) Mahavira	(IV) India

Choose the **correct** answer from the options given below :

  (a) (A)-(II), (B)-(III), (C)-(I), (D)-(IV)

  (b) (A)-(I), (B)-(II), (C)-(III), (D)-(IV)

  (c) (A)-(IV), (B)-(III), (C)-(II), (D)-(I)

  (d) (A)-(III), (B)-(IV), (C)-(I), (D)-(II)

13. Rihla was authored by __________.

  (a) Ibn Battuta   (b) Al-Biruni

  (c) Abul Fazl   (d) Seydi Ali Reis

14. Lingayats believe that after death, the devotee will be united with __________ and will not return to this world.

  (a) Shiva   (b) Vishnu

  (c) Durga   (d) Lord Rama

15. Identify the correct feature associated with Tantric practices during eighth to eighteenth century :

  (a) The source of knowledge were the Indian Vedas.

  (b) Many ideas of Tantricism influenced Shaivism as well as Buddhism.

  (c) Close association with Jainism and Buddhism.

  (d) Tantric practices were not open to women and lower caste people.

16. Read the given information and identify the personality :

  (A) He rejected sacrifices, ritual baths, image worship and austerities.

  (B) He organised his followers into a community.

  (C) He advocated nirguna bhakti.

  (D) He proposed a simple way to connect to the Divine through "shabad".

  (a) Guru Nanak   (b) Guru Arjan Dev

  (c) Chaitanya   (d) Tulsidas

17. Select the correct information on sufism from :

  (A) Sufism evolved into a well - developed movement by the eleventh century.

  (B) The word silsila means the lineage of spiritual leader to whom the sufis showed loyalty.

  (C) Ziyarat means pilgrimage to the grave of the shaikh.

  (D) The sufis devoutly followed all the rituals of Islam.

  (E) Shaikh Nizamuddin Auliya lived during the rule of Gayasuddin Tuglaq.

Choose the **correct** answer from the options given below :

  (a) (A), (B) and (D) only

  (b) (B), (C) and (D) only

  (c) (A), (C) and (E) only

  (d) (A), (B), (C) and (E) only

18. Temples in the past were not built __________.

  (a) as a means of associating king with the divine.

  (b) as centres of learning.

  (c) to win the support and recognition for king's power.

  (d) as administrative centres.

19. The Religious literature of Lingayats is known as :

  (a) Agrahara   (b) Vachana

  (c) Hadith   (d) Qiyas

20. Whose name was associated with the foundation of the Vijayanagara Empire ?

  (a) Virupaksha   (b) Krishna Devaraya

  (c) Harihara   (d) Gajapati

21. During the seventeenth century several new crops from different parts of the world reached the Indian subcontinent. One of them was __________, which was introduced to India via Africa and Spain.

  (a) Sugarcane   (b) Cotton

  (c) Rice   (d) Maize

22. Arrange the following Mughal chronicles, starting from the one written at the earliest to the one written in tire last:

(A) Abul Fazl works on the Akbar nama

(B) Muhammad Waris begins his chronicle in tire third decade of Shall Jahan's reign.

(C) Gulbadan Begum begins to write the Humayan Nama.

(D) Lahori composes the first two daftars of the Badshah Nama.

(E) Babur's memoirs translated into Persian as Babur Nama.

Choose the **correct** answer from the options given below :

(a) (A), (B), (C), (E), (D)   (b) (B), (D), (E), (C), (A)

(c) (C), (E), (A), (D), (B)   (d) (A), (C), (B), (D), (E)

23. Select the correct information on the Mughals from below.

(A) Zahiruddin Babur hailed from Farghana in Central Asia.

(B) Nasiruddin Humayun defeated Sher Shah Suri in 1540.

(C) Jalaluddin Akbar extended the frontiers of the Mughal Empire to the Hindukush mountains.

(D) Delhi, Agra and Lahore were the different capital cities of the Mughals.

(E) Shah Alam II was the last Mughal Emperor.

Choose the **correct** answer from the options given below :

(a) (A), (B) and (C) only (b) (A), (C) and (D) only

(c) (C), (D) and (E) only (d) (A), (C) and (E) only

24. Arrange tire following events in chronological order :

(A) Santhals began to come to the Rajmahal hills

(B) Permanent Settlement in Bengal

(C) East India Company acquired Diwani of Bengal

(D) Regulating Act passed by tire British Parliament

(E) Ryots in Deccan villages rebel

Choose the **correct** answer from the options given below :

(a) (C), (D), (B), (A), (E) (b) (A), (B), (C), (D), (E)

(c) (C), (E), (A), (D), (B) (d) (C), (B), (E), (A), (D)

25. Match List - I with List - II.

List - I	List - II
(A) Marco Polo	(I) Uzbekistan
(B) Ibn Battuta	(II) Italy
(C) Peter Mundy	(III) England
(D) Al-Biruni	(IV) Morocco

Choose the **correct** answer from the options given below :

(a) (A)-(II), (B)-(IV), (C)-(III), (D)-(I)

(b) (A)-(I), (B)-(II), (C)-(III), (D)-(IV)

(c) (A)-(III), (B)-(II), (C)-(I), (D)-(IV)

(d) (A)-(IV), (B)-(III), (C)-(II), (D)-(I)

26. Arrange the following events from the one that took place first to the one that happened in the late :

(A) The British arrive in Madras.

(B) Portuguese trading companies' arrival in Panaji.

(C) French arrival in Pondicherry.

(D) Dutch trading companies' arrival in Masulipatanam

Choose the **correct** answer from the options given below :

(a) (B), (D), (A), (C)   (b) (A), (D), (C), (B)

(c) (B), (A), (D), (C)   (d) (C), (B), (A), (D)

27. A series of Praja Mandals were established to promote the nationalist ideas in the __________.

(a) Harijans   (b) Arya Samaj

(c) Indigo Planters   (d) Princely States

28. Which was the earliest movement led by Mahatma Gandhi in India ?

(a) Khilafat Movement

(b) Champaran Satyagrah

(c) Amhadabad Mill Strike

(d) Dandi March

29. Identify the correct statements :

(A) Mahatma Gandhi attended the Second Round Table Conference.

(B) Mahatma Gandhi opposed the demand for separate electorate for "lower castes".

(C) Mahatma Gandhi was given sentence of 8 years for violation of law during Non- Cooperation Movement.

(D) Mahatma Gandhi was released from the prison in 1949.

(E) On Gokhle's advice, Gandhiji spent a year travelling around British India, getting to know the land and its people.

Choose the **correct** answer from the options given below :

(a) (A), (B) and (C) only

(b) (B), (C) and (D) only

(c) (A), (B) and (E) only

(d) (C), (D) and (E) only

30. The Lahore session of Congress in the year 1929 was presided by __________.
- (a) Jawaharlal Nehru
- (b) Mahatma Gandhi
- (c) Sardar Vallabh Bhai Patel
- (d) Mohammad Ali Jinnah

31. Subsidiary Alliance was a system devised by __________ in 1798.
- (a) Lord Wellesley
- (b) Lord Dalhousie
- (c) Lord Canning
- (d) Warren Hasting

32. Choose the correct options :
- (A) Bengali Muslims rejected Jinnah's two nation theory and later created Bangladesh in 1971-72.
- (B) Muslim League demanded Pakistan in 1940.
- (C) Cabinet Mission came to India in March 1946.
- (D) "Direct Action Day" was in January 1947.
- (E) In 1935, elections to the provincial legislatures were held for the first time.

Choose the **correct** answer from the options given below :
- (a) (A), (B) and (D) only
- (b) (B), (C) and (E) only
- (c) (C), (D) and (E) only
- (d) (A), (B) and (C) only

33. The Indian National movement which withnessed the women participation in large number for the first time was :
- (a) Quit India Movement
- (b) Champaran Movement
- (c) Non-Cooperation Movement
- (d) Civil Disobediance Movement

34. The "Objectives Resolution" was introduced in the Constituent Assembly by :
- (a) Dr. Rajender Prasad on 26 November 1949.
- (b) Dr. B.R. Ambedkar on 15 August 1947.
- (c) Jawahar Lal Nehru on 13 December 1946.
- (d) Sardar Patel on 26 January 1950.

35. Thomas Roe, tire English envoy of James I, came to the court of :
- (a) Akbar
- (b) Aurangzeb
- (c) Jahangir
- (d) Shah Jahan

36. Income tax falls under the purview of :
- (a) Union list
- (b) State list
- (c) Concurrent list
- (d) Residuary list

37. Match List - I with List - II.

List - I (Leaders)		List - II (Issues)
(A) N.G. Ranga	(I)	Problems of untouchables
(B) Jaipal Singh	(II)	Term minorities to be interpreted in economic terms
(C) J. Nagappa	(III)	Protection of Tribes
(D) Hansa Mehta	(IV)	Justice for women

Choose the **correct** answer from the options given below :
- (a) (A)-(I), (B)-(II), (C)-(III), (D)-(IV)
- (b) (A)-(III), (B)-(II), (C)-(I), (D)-(IV)
- (c) (A)-(II), (B)-(III), (C)-(I), (D)-(IV)
- (d) (A)-(IV), (B)-(I), (C)-(II), (D)-(III)

38. What was the realization of communist member Somnath Lahiri about the Constituent Assembly ?
- (a) He felt that the minority communities were over represented in the constitution.
- (b) He realized that the dark hand of British imperialism was still hanging over the deliberations of the Assembly.
- (c) He complained that environmental issue was not addressed enough by the Assembly.
- (d) He demanded more legal amenities to propagate class hierarchies in society.

39. "The Constituent Assembly was British-made and was working the British plans as the British should like it to be worked out". This statement was given in the constituent Assembly by :
- (a) Jawaharlal Nehru
- (b) Dr. B.R. Ambedkar
- (c) Somnath Lahiri
- (d) Sardar Patel

40. Arrange the following events in chronological order.
- (A) British Prime Minister Attlee meets Indian leaders.
- (B) Constitution was signed.
- (C) Cabinet Mission announces its constitutional scheme.
- (D) Last meeting of the Interim Government.
- (E) Muslim League announces Direct Action Day.

Choose the **correct** answer from the options given below :
- (a) (E), (C), (D), (A), (B)
- (b) (C), (E), (A), (D), (B)
- (c) (A), (C), (D), (E), (B)
- (d) (D), (A), (C), (E), (B)

Directions for Questions 41 to 45:

Read the passage given below to answer the following questions.

On that day in Supa

On 16 May 1875, the District Magistrate of Poona wrote to the Police Commissioner :

On arrival at Supa on Saturday 15 May I learnt of the disturbance.

One house of a moneylender was burnt down; about a dozen were forcibly broken into and completely gutted of their content. Account papers, bonds, grains, country cloth were burnt in the street where heaps of ashes are still to be seen.

The chief constable apprehended 50 persons. Stolen property worth Rs. 2,000 was recovered. The estimated loss is over Rs. 25,000. Moneylenders claim it is over 1 lakh. Deccan riots commission

41. Identify the common pattern of peasant revolts in western India :
    (a) Sahukars were attacked, account books burnt and debt bonds destroyed.
    (b) Moneylenders were attacked and separate Parganas were created.
    (c) Plains were raided, tribute from zamindars was demanded and wars were fought with taluqdars.
    (d) Negotiations were made with the sahukars and in case of failed negotiations sahukars houses were set on fire.

42. Identify one of the measures used by the British to control the peasant revolts :
    (a) Tributes were given to the peasants.
    (b) Police arrested few people and stolen property recovered.
    (c) Taxes on the produce were mitigated.
    (d) New farm policies were introduced.

43. In the nineteenth century, peasants in various parts of India rose in revolt against ___________ and ___________.
    (a) British, sahukars
    (b) Kotwals, traders
    (c) Moneylenders, grain dealers
    (d) British, taluqdars

44. Supa is a large village in ___________ district.
    (a) Birbhum
    (b) Bhagalpur
    (c) Rajmahal
    (d) Pune

45. How much was the gap between the loss of property claimed by the moneylenders and that estimated by the British ?
    (a) Rs. 25,000 and more
    (b) Rs. 50,000 and more
    (c) Rs. 75,000 and more
    (d) Rs. 1 lakh and more

Directions for Questions 46 to 50:

Read the passage given below to answer the following questions.

What taluqdars thought

The attitude of the taluqdars was best expressed by Hanwant Singh, the Raja of Kalakankar, near Rae Bareli. During the mutiny, Hanwant Singh had given shelter to a British officer and conveyed him to safety. While taking leave of the officer, Hanwant Singh told him. Sahib, your countrymen came into this country and drove out our King. You sent your officers round the districts to examine the titles to the estates. At one blow you took from me lands which from time immemorial had been in my family. I submitted. Suddenly misfortune fell upon you. The people of the land rose against you. You came to me whom you had despoiled. I have saved you. But now-now I march at the head of my retainers to Lucknow to try and drive you from the country.

46. Hanwant Singh was the Raja of a place which was located near :
    (a) Bareilly   (b) Rae Bareli
    (c) Garhmukteshwar   (d) Meerut

47. How did Hanwant Singh treat the British officer ?
    (a) He gave him shelter
    (b) He was violent on him
    (c) He requested him for a government job
    (d) He secretly told the sepoys about his whereabouts

48. Hanwant Singh complained that :
    (a) The British officer beat him up
    (b) The officer barged into his house
    (c) The British drove out his King
    (d) The police burnt his house

49. What was there in Hanwant Singh's family from time immemorial ?
    (a) His caste
    (b) Precious stone image of Ganesh
    (c) Their horoscope
    (d) His land

50. Where was Hanwant Singh planning to march next?
    (a) Kalakankar   (b) Lucknow
    (c) Rae Bareli   (d) Kanpur

Answer Keys

1. (b)	**2.** (a)	**3.** (d)	**4.** (d)	**5.** (a)	**6.** (c)	**7.** (b)	**8.** (b)	**9.** (c)	**10.** (a)
11. (c)	**12.** (a)	**13.** (a)	**14.** (a)	**15.** (b)	**16.** (a)	**17.** (d)	**18.** (d)	**19.** (b)	**20.** (c)
21. (d)	**22.** (c)	**23.** (b)	**24.** (a)	**25.** (a)	**26.** (a)	**27.** (d)	**28.** (b)	**29.** (c)	**30.** (a)
31. (a)	**32.** (b)	**33.** (d)	**34.** (c)	**35.** (c)	**36.** (a)	**37.** (c)	**38.** (b)	**39.** (c)	**40.** (c)
41. (a)	**42.** (b)	**43.** (a)	**44.** (d)	**45.** (c)	**46.** (b)	**47.** (a)	**48.** (c)	**49.** (d)	**50.** (b)

Explanations

1. (b) Alexander Cunningham, the first Director-General of the Archaeological Survey of India (ASI), often called the father of Indian archaeology

2. (a) The script remains undeciphered to date, it was evidently not alphabetical (where each sign stands for a vowel or a consonant) as it has just too many signs - somewhere between 375 and 400. It is apparent that the script was written from right to left as some seals show a wider spacing on the right and cramping on the left, as if the engraver began working from the right and then ran out of space.

3. (d)

Major Period in Early Indian Archaeology	
2 million BP (Before Present)	Lower Palaeolithic
80,000	Middle Palaeolithic
35,000	Upper Palaeolithic
12,000	Mesolithic
10,000	Neolithic (early agriculturists and pastoralists)
6,000	Chalcolithic (first use of copper)
2600 BCE	Harappan civilisation
1000 BCE	Early iron, megalithic burials
6000 BCE-400 CE	Early Historic

4. (d) • Most of the inscriptions mentioned a king referred to as Piyadassi - meaning "pleasant to behold"

• Historians have used a variety of sources to reconstruct the history of the Mauryan Empire. These include contemporary works, such as the account of Megasthenes (a Greek ambassador to the court of Chandragupta Maurya), which survives in fragments.

• There were five major political centres in the empire - the capital Pataliputra and the provincial centres of Taxila, Ujjayini, Tosali and Suvarnagiri, all mentioned in Asokan inscriptions.

5. (a) Spices, especially pepper, were in high demand in the Roman Empire, as were textiles and medicinal plants, and these were all transported across the Arabian Sea to the Mediterranean

6. (c) • *Arthashastra* - composed by Kautilya or Chanakya

• *Prayaga Prashasti* composed in Sanskrit by Harishena

• Banabhatta was the Asthana Kavi in the court of the emperor Harsha

7. (b) • Suvarnakara - Gold Smith

• Maha Sammata - Great elect

• Sutas - Charioteer bards

• Shrenis - Guilds

8. (b) Satavahana dynasty

9. (c) Once Drona, a Brahmana who taught archery to the Kuru princes, was approached by Ekalavya, a forest-dwelling nishada (a hunting community).

10. (a) Elaborate sacrificial traditions performed by chiefs and kings

11. (c) A conversation between king Ajatasattu, the ruler of Magadha, and the Buddha can be found in Sutta Pitaka

12. (a) Zarathustra in Iran, Kong Zi in China, Socrates, Plato and Aristotle in Greece, and Mahavira and Gautama Buddha

13. (a) Ibn Battuta's book of travels, called Rihla, written in Arabic, provides extremely rich and interesting details about the social and cultural life in the subcontinent in the fourteenth century.

14. (a) Lingayats believe that on death the devotee will be united with Shiva and will not return to this world

15. (b) Many of these ideas influenced Shaivism as well as Buddhism, especially in the eastern, northern and southern parts of the subcontinent.

16. (a) The message of Baba Guru Nanak is spelt out in his hymns and teachings. These suggest that he advocated a form of nirguna bhakti.

17. (d) By the eleventh century Sufism evolved into a well-developed movement with a body of literature on Quranic studies and sufi practices

18. (d) Administrative centres

19. (b) Our understanding of the Virashaiva tradition is derived from vachanas (literally, sayings) composed in Kannada by women and men who joined the movement.

20. (c) The kingdom of Vijayanagar was founded by Harihara and Bukka

21. (d) Maize (makka), was introduced into India via Africa and Spain

22. (c)

Some Major Mughal Chronicles and	
c. 1530	Manuscript of Babur's memoirs in Turkish – saved from a storm – becomes part of the family collection of the Timurids
c. 1587	Gulbadan Begum begins to write the *Humayun Nama*
1589	Babur's memoirs translated into Persian as *Babur Nama*
1589-1602	Abu'l Fazl works on the *Akbar Nama*
1605-22	Jahangir writes his memoirs, the *Jahangir Nama*
1639-47	Lahori composes the first two *daftars* of the *Badshah Nama*
c. 1650	Muhammad Waris begins to chronicle the third decade of Shah Jahan's reign
1668	Alamgir Nama, a history of the first ten years of Aurangzeb's reign compiled by Muhammad Kazim

23. (b)
- In 1555 Humayun defeated the Surs, but died a year later.
- The founder of the empire, Zahiruddin Babur, was driven from his Central Asian homeland, Farghana, by the warring Uzbeks.
- Akbar succeeded in extending the frontiers of the empire to the Hindukush mountains, and checked the expansionist designs of the Uzbeks of Turan (Central Asia) and the Safavids of Iran.
- The last Mughal emperor, Bahadur Shah II, also known as Zafar, died in a British prison in Burma in 1862.

24. (a)

Timeline	
1765	English East India Company acquires Diwani of Bengal
1773	Regulating Act passed by the British Parliament to regulate the activities of the East India Company
1793	Permanent Settlement in Bengal
1800s	Santhals begin to come to the Rajmahal hills and settle there
1818	First revenue settlement in the Bombay Deccan
1820 s	Agricultural prices begin to fall
1840s-50s	A slow process of agrarian expansion in the Bombay Deccan
1855-56	Santhal rebellion
1861	Cotton boom begins
1875	*Ryots* in Deccan villages rebel

25. (a)

Some travellers who left accounts	
Tenth-eleventh centuries 973-1048	Muhammad ibn Ahmad Abu Raihan al-Biruni (from Uzbekistan)
Thirteenth century 1254-1323	Marco Polo (from Italy)
Fourteenth century 1304-77	Ibn Battuta (from Morocco)
Fifteenth century 1413-82	Abd al-Razzaq Kamal al-Din ibn Ishaq al-Samarqandi (from Samarqand)
1466-72 (years spent in India)	Afanasii Nikitich Nikitin (fifteenth century, from Russia)
Sixteenth century 1518 (visit to India)	Duarte Barbosa, d.1521 (from Portugal)
1562 (year of death)	Seydi Ali Reis (from Turkey)
1536-1600	Antonio Monserrate (from Spain)
Seventeenth century 1626-31 (years spent in India)	Muhmud Wali Balkhi (from Balkh)
1600-67	Peter Mundy (from England)
1605-89	Jean-Baptiste Tavernier (from France)
1620-88	Francois Bernier (from France)

26. (a) The European commercial Companies had set up base in different places early during the Mughal era: the Portuguese in Panaji in 1510, the Dutch in Masulipatnam in 1605,

the British in Madras in 1639 and the French in Pondicherry (present-day Puducherry) in 1673.

27. (d) A series of "Praja Mandals" were established to promote the nationalist creed in the princely states.

28. (b) Champaran Movement

29. (c) During the Non-Cooperation Movement thousands of Indians were put in jail. Gandhiji himself was arrested in March 1922 and sentenced six years' imprisonment

30. (a) The Congress convention began in Lahore in December 1929 and Pandit Nehru was the president of the convention.

31. (a) The subsidiary alliance in India was planned by Lord Wellesley

32. (b) Direct Action Day (16 August 1946), also known as the 1946 Calcutta Killings, was a day of nationwide communal riots

33. (d) It was the first nationalist activity in which women participated in large numbers.

34. (c) It was Nehru who moved the crucial "Objectives Resolution",

35. (c) Mughal Emperor Jahangir's court

36. (a) Income tax in India is governed by Entry 82 of the Union List of the Seventh Schedule to the Constitution of India,

37. (c) • N.G. Ranga, a socialist who had been a leader of the peasant movement, urged that the term minorities be interpreted in economic terms.

• Jaipal Singh - Protection of. Adibasi

• J. Nagappa - Problem of the Untouchables

• Hansa Mehta of Bombay demanded justice for women

38. (b) A Communist member, Somnath Lahiri saw the dark hand of British imperialism hanging over the deliberations of the Constituent Assembly

39. (c) Constituent Assembly was British-made and was "working the British plans as the British should like it to be worked out" - Somnath Lahiri

40. (c)

Timeline	
1945	
26 July	Labour Government comes into power in Britain
December-January	General Elections in India
1946	
16 May	Cabinet Mission announces its constitutional scheme
16 June	Muslim League accepts Cabinet Mission's constitutional scheme
16 June	Cabinet Mission presents scheme for the formation of an Interim Government at the Centre
16 August	Muslim League announces Direct Action Day
2 September	Congress forms Interim Government with Nehru as the Vice-President
13 October	Muslim League decides to join the Interim Government
3-6 December	British Prime Minister, Attlee, meets some Indian Leaders; talks fail
9 December	Constituent Assembly begins its sessions
1947	
29 January	Muslim League demands dissolution of Constituent Assembly
16 July	Last meeting of the Intern Government
11 August	Jinnah elected President of the Constituent Assembly of Pakistan
14 August	Pakistan Independence; celebrations in Karachi
14-15 August	At midnight India celebrates Independence
1949	
December	Constitution is signed

41. (a)   **42.** (b)

43. (a)   **44.** (d)

45. (c)   **46.** (b)

47. (a)   **48.** (c)

49. (d)   **50.** (b)

1. Consider the statements regarding identifying the figure of Proto-Shiva as represented on Harrappan seals.

   A. It is shown in the form of Gajapati

   B. It is surrounded by animals

   C. It is seated in a yogic posture

   D. It is shown with the female figure - Parvati

   E. It is suggested by some scholars as a Shaman

   Choose the correct answer from the options given below :

   (a) A, B and C Only   (b) B, C and D Only

   (c) B, C and E Only   (d) C, D and E Only

2. There is an apparent concern for privacy reflected in Harappan domestic architecture. Identify the architectural feature which justifies the same.

   (a) The courtyard was in the centre with rooms on all sides

   (b) There are no windows in the walls along the ground floor

   (c) Every house had its own bathroom paved with bricks

   (d) The drains of the house were connected through the wall to street drain

3. Inscriptions have many limitations. Out of following, choose the options which are limitations

   A. They give information about date and other factual information

   B. Inscriptions may be damaged or letters missing

   C. Many inscriptions have not been deciphered and translated

   D. Many inscriptions may not have survived the ravages of time

   E. Inscriptions give information about political history and achievement of the rulers

   Choose the correct answer from the options given below :

   (a) B, C and D Only   (b) A, B and C Only

   (c) B, D and E Only   (d) C, D and E Only

4. Which among the following was not a political centre of the Mauryan Empire ?

   (a) Tosali   (b) Banawali

   (c) Taxila   (d) Suvamagiri

5. It refers to a form of government where power is exercised by a group of men, often collectively called as rajas

   (a) Monarchy   (b) Dictatorship

   (c) Democracy   (d) Oligarchy

6. Prayag Prashasti was composed by Harishena. It deals with _________ of the ruler ______.

   (a) Legal aspects / Chandragupta I

   (b) Praise / Samudragupta

   (c) Society / Ashoka

   (d) Religious aspect /Ajatasattu

7. Consider the following statements regarding Exogamy. Which is the correct option

   (a) It is found only in Himalayan region

   (b) Marriage takes place outside the Village area

   (c) Marriage is with same kin group

   (d) It is marriage outside the unit

8. Strategies evolved by Brahmans to enforce 'vama' norms

   A. varna order was of divine origin

   B. varna order would ensure better marriage status

   C. They advised the kings to ensure these norms were followed in the kingdoms

   D. Persuade people that status was determined by birth

   E. varna norms would lead to wealth

   Choose the correct answer from the options given below :

   (a) A, B and C Only   (b) A, C and D Only

   (c) D, B and E Only   (d) E, B and C Only

9. What was the objective of team V. S. Sukthankar ?

   (a) To translate Manusmriti in Tamil

   (b) To prepare critical edition of Mahabharata

   (c) To translate Ramayana into English language

   (d) To prepare critical edition of Manusmriti

10. Which of these Buddhist texts deals with philosophical matters ?

    (a) Vinay Pitaka   (b) Sutta Pitaka

    (c) Abhidamma Pitaka   (d) Jatakas

11. Match List I with List II

List I		List II
A. Tree	I.	Represents Mahaparinibbana
B. Empty Seat	II.	The first sermon of the Buddha
C. Wheel	III.	An event in life of Buddha
D. Stupa	IV.	Meditation of the Buddha

Choose the correct answer from the options given below :

(a) A-I, B-III, C- IV, D-II   (b) A-III, B-IV, C-II, D-I

(c) A-II, B-I, C-III, D-IV   (d) A-IV, B-III, C-II, D-I

12. Read the description and name the Veda

The earliest compiled Veda between (1500-1000B.C.) which consists of hymns in praise of deities esp. - Agni, Indra and Soma.

  (a) Sama Veda   (b) YajurVeda

  (c) Rig Veda   (d) Atharva Veda

13. An early globe trotter 'Ibn Battuta' visited India during the reign of

  (a) Ghiyasuddin Tughlaq

  (b) Muhammad Bin Tughlaq

  (c) Iltutmish

  (d) Qutub-Uddin-Aibak

14. Match List I with List II

List I (Religious figure)   **List II (Region)**

A. Basavanna   I. Rajasthan

B. Andal   II. Assam

C. Khwaja Muinuddin Chisti   III. Tamil Nadu

D. Shankaradeva   IV. Karnataka

Choose the correct answer from the options given below :

  (a) A-III, B-II, C-I, D-IV   (b) A-IV, B-III, C-I, D-II

  (c) A-II, B-I, C-III, D-IV   (d) A-IV, B-III, C-II, D-I

15. Who among the following was the disciple of Shaikh Nizamuddin Aulia ?

  (a) Nadir Shah   (b) Amir Khusrau

  (c) Seydi Ali   (d) Mahmud Balkhi

16. Baba Guru Nanak expressed his ideas through __________.

  (a) Bhajans   (b) Dohas

  (c) Suktas   (d) Shabads

17. Which one among the following organisations of United Nations has declared 'Hampi' a world Heritage site ?

  (a) UNICEF   (b) UNDP

  (c) UNESCO   (d) UNHRC

18. Krishnadeva Raya's rule was characterized by expansion and consolidation.

Arrange the following developments in a sequence pertaining to the apogee and decline of the Vijaynagar Empire.

A. By 1542, control at the centre had shifted to another ruling lineage that of Aravidu

B. The rulers of Orissa were subdued and severe defeats were inflicted on the Sultan of Bijapur

C. The Tuluvas replaced the Saluvas

D. The Sangamas were supplanted by the Saluvas

E. Rama Raya, the chief minister of Vijaynagar led the army into battle at Rakshasi-Tangadi (Talikota)

Choose the correct answer from the options given below :

  (a) D, C, B, A, E   (b) A, B, D, E, C

  (c) C, D, E, A, B   (d) B, E, D, A, C

19. Match List I with List II

List I (Building)   **List II (Junction)**

A. Mahanavami Dibba   I. For use of the king and his family

B. Kalvana mandapa   II. Chariot Shrine

C. Hazara Ram Temple III. Divine weddings

D. Vithala Temple   IV. Ritual Structure

Choose the correct answer from the options given below :

  (a) A-I, B-II, C-III, D-IV   (b) A-II, B-III, C-IV, D-I

  (c) A-IV, B-III, C-I, D-II   (d) A-II, B-I, C-IV, D-III

20. Ain-i-Akbari gives accounts of peasants, "a view from top." Which statement justifies it ?

  (a) It was an account of relationship between the state and rural magnates, the Zamindars

  (b) It gives us details about Akbar's ancestors

  (c) Akbar's administration is given in detail

  (d) It talks about Sulh-i-kul

21. The Paharias practiced

  (a) Settled Cultivation

  (b) Shifting Cultivation

  (c) Settled and Shifting Cultivation

  (d) Commercial Cultivation

22. The painting given here was painted by George Chinnery in 1820. This painting depicted :

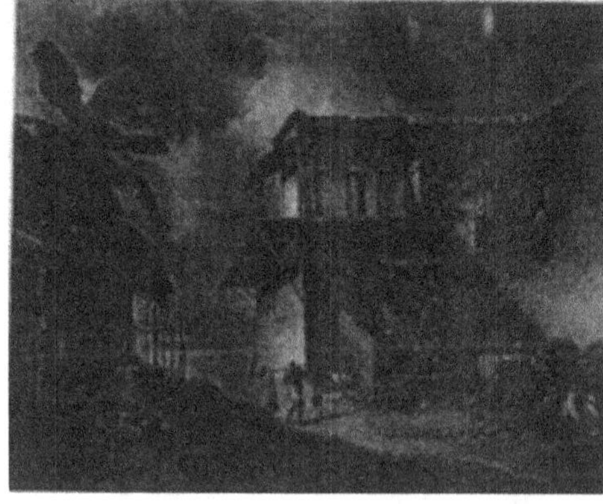

  (a) Bengal village scene (b) A south Indian village

  (c) The plight of ryots   (d) A mahal (estate)

23. When the Permanent Settlement was imposed, __________ was the Raja of Burdwan.

  (a) Tej Chand   (b) Mehtab Chand

  (c) Francis Buchanan   (d) Jagat Seth

24. Following informations are given about Buchanan. Choose the correct options.

   A. Buchanan was a physician

   B. He served in Bengal. Bihar and Orissa

   C. He was the surgeon of Lord William Bentinck

   D. He organized a zoo that became the 'Calcutta Alipore Zoo'

   E. He surveyed the areas under the jurisdiction of East India Company

Choose the correct answer from the options given below :

(a) A, B, C Only   (b) A, D, E Only

(c) B, C, E Only   (d) C, D, E Only

25. The Zamindars defaulted on payment under Permanent Settlement in Bengal. Which is the **incorrect** reason ?

(a) Agricultural prices in 1790s were depressed

(b) Revenue demand fixed was high

(c) Zamindars could pay the British any time of the year

(d) The Settlement limited the power of the Zamindars to collect rent

26. Fart St. George of East India Company was situated at which of the following place ?

(a) Calcutta   (b) Delhi

(c) Bombay   (d) Madras

27. Arrange the following events in correct chronological order

   A. Cabinet Mission   B. Cripps Mission

   C. Khilafat Movement   D. Pakistan Resolution

   E. Jallianwala Bagh Massacre

Choose the correct answer from the options given below :

(a) E, C, D, A, B   (b) E, C, D, B, A

(c) E, C, B, A, D   (d) C, E, D, B, A

28. Read the following and select the correct reasons for the launching of the Civil Disobedience Movement

   A. Salt Law

   B. Rowlatt Satyagraha

   C. Vague offer of Lord Irwin

   D. Dissatisfaction with Simon Commission

   E. Dandi March

Choose the correct answer from the options given below :

(a) A, B and D Only   (b) A, D and E Only

(c) A, C and D Only   (d) A, B and E Only

29. Who among the following leaders belonged to 'Moderate group of Congress' ?

(a) Lala Lajpat Rai

(b) Bal Gangadhar Tilak

(c) Bipin Chandra Pal

(d) Gopal Krishna Gokhale

30. Consider the following events and arrange them in chronological order :

   A. Salt Satyagraha

   B. First public appearance of Gandhi at opening of BHU

   C. Campaign against Rowlatt Act

   D. Champaran Satyagraha

   E. Non-Cooperation Movement

Choose the correct answer from the options given below :

(a) A, B, C, D, E   (b) B, D, C, E, A

(c) B, D, C, A, E   (d) B, E, C, D, A

31. Who among the following leaders advocated radical opposition to colonial rule and broadened the appeal for Swadeshi Movement ?

(a) Gopal Krishna Gokhale

(b) Dada Bhai Naoroji

(c) Surendra Nath Banerjee

(d) Bal Gangadhar Tilak

32. Match List I with List II

List I (Important Leaders)	List II (Their Description)
A. Annie Besant	I. A lawyer of Gujarati Extraction trained in London
B. Gopal Krishna Gokhale	II. A member of the trio "Lal Bal Pal"
C. Bipin Chandra Pal	III. An important leader of the Home Rule Movement
D. Mohammad Ali Jinnah	IV. Gandhiji's political mentor

Choose the correct answer from the options given below :

(a) A-III, B-IV, C-II, D-I   (b) A-I, B- II, C-III, D-IV

(c) A- IV, B-I, C-II, D-III   (d) A-IV, B-II, C-III, D-I

33. Mahatma Gandhi visited __________ Gurudwara to address the Sikh community as part of his effort to restore communal harmony

(a) Nanded Sahib   (b) Harmandar Sahib

(c) Bangla Sahib   (d) Sisganj Sahib

34. Match List I with List II

List I (Member of Constitutional Assembly)	List II (Contribution)
A. S. N. Mukherjee	I. Worked mostly behind the scenes, working to reconcile opposing point of views
B. B. N. Rau	II. Gave critical inputs in the drafting of the constitution
C. Alladi Krishnaswamy Aiyar	III. Prepared a series of background papers on a close study of the political systems obtaining in other countries
D. Sardar Patel	IV. He had the ability to put complex proposals in clear legal language

Choose the correct answer from the options given below :

(a) A-IV, B-II, C-III, D-I

(b) A-I, B-II, C-III, D-IV

(c) A-IV, B-III, C-II, D-I

(d) A-II, B-III, C-IV, D-I

35. Which of these was not part of 'Objectives Resolution' of 1946 ?

(a) India was proclaimed as 'Independent Sovereign Republic'

(b) Citizens were guaranteed justice, equality and freedom

(c) Adequate safeguards for minorities, backward and tribal areas

(d) Separate electorates

36. Place the following events in chronological order :

A. Subhash Chandra Bose wanted freedom with foreign aid

B. Gandhiji launched Quit India movement

C. Uprising of ratings of Royal Indian Navy

D. Constituent Assembly begins its sessions

E. Last meeting of Interim government

Choose the correct answer from the options given below :

(a) A, D, B, C, E

(b) B, A, C, D, E

(c) B, C, A, E, D

(d) C, A, B, D, E

37. What were the arguments against separate electorates by the leaders in the Constituent Assembly ?

A. Separate electorates would guarantee freedom to minorities

B. Feared continued civil war riots and violence

C. It would divide the people

D. It had led to partition and would continue to cause bloodshed

E. It would create harmony amongst communities.

Choose the correct answer from the options given below:

(a) B, C, D Only

(b) E, A, B Only

(c) A, B, D Only

(d) E, A, D Only

38. Dakshayani Velayudhan and Hansa Mehta were members of __________.

(a) Constituent Assembly

(b) NGO Working for physically disabled

(c) NGO Working for women

(d) Language Committee

39. The conquest of Awadh happened in stages. Arrange the different stages of this conquest in a chronological order :

A. Awadh was annexed by Lord Dalhousie on the plea of misgovernment by the nawab

B. The nawab of Awadh could no longer control over the rebellious chiefs and taluqdars

C. The nawab became increasingly dependent on the British to maintain law and order within his kingdom

D. The nawab had to disband his military force and act in accordance with the advice of the British Resident

E. The Subsidiary Alliance had been imposed on Awadh

Choose the correct answer from the options given below :

(a) A, B, C, D, E   (b) E, D, C, B, A

(c) B, A, E, D, C   (d) C, D, E, A, B

40. Identify the person who coined the term Pakistan or Pak-stan

(a) Mohammad Iqbal

(b) Choudhari Rehmat Ali

(c) Mohammad Ali Jinnah

(d) Abdul Latif

Directions for Questions 41 to 45:

Please read the passage and answer the questions that follows.

This is how Chandrabhan Barahman described the Mughal nobility in his book Char Chaman (Four Gardens), written during the reign of Shah Jahan:

People from many races (Arabs. Iranians, Turks. Tajiks. Kurds, Tatars, Russians, Abyssinians and so on) and from many countries (Turkey, Egypt, Syria, Iraq, Arabia, Iran, Khurasan, Turan)- in fact, different groups and classes of people from all societies - have sought refuge in the imperial court, as well as different groups from India, men with knowledge and skills as well as warriors, for example, Bukharis and Bhakkaris, Saiyyads of genuine lineage, Shaikhzadas with noble ancestry, Afghan tribes such as Lodis, Rohillas, Yusufzai, and castes of Rajputs, who were to be addressed as rana, raja, rao, and rayan - i.e. Rathor, Sisodia, Kachhwaha, Hada, Gaur, Chauhan, Panwar, Bhaduriya, Solanki, Bundela, Shekhawat and all the other Indian tribes such as Ghakkar, Khokar, Baluchi, and others who wielded the sword and mansabs from 100 to 7000 zat, likewise landowners from the steppes and mountains, from the regions of Karnataka, Bengal, Assam, Udaipur, Srinagar, Kumaon, Tibet and Kishtwar and so on - whole tribes and groups of them have been privileged to kiss the threshold of the imperial court (i.e. attend the court or find the employment)

41. Identify the same from where the extract has been taken
- (a) Babur Nama
- (b) Ain-i-Akbari
- (c) Alamgir Nama
- (d) Char Chaman

42. Who sought refuge in the Mughal court ?
- (a) Mughals married their daughters with different ethnic groups
- (b) Nobles of Imperial Court liked flowers of different colours
- (c) People from various races, countries and classes
- (d) Officer corps of Mughals were loyal towards Emperors

43. Who worked in the Imperial Court ?
- (a) Nobles who looked after the polaj land for revenue collection
- (b) Nobles who had armies of the paraganas and looked after the welfare of the settlement
- (c) Men with knowledge and skill and who wielded the sword
- (d) Nobles who assessed the Jama

44. Which of the following Communities worked for the Imperial court ?
- A. Bukharis and Bhakkaris
- B. Nobles from North - eastern tribes
- C. Lodis and Rohillas of Afghan tribes
- D. Sisodia, Solanki and Bundelas
- E. Marathas and some tribal groups

Choose the correct answer from the options given below:
- (a) B, C, D Only
- (b) C, D, E Only
- (c) A, C, D Only
- (d) A, C, E Only

45. What kind of mansabs are described in Char Chaman ?
- (a) Only high mansabs
- (b) Mansabs from 100 to 7000 zats
- (c) Mansabs from 100 to 7000 Sawars
- (d) Mansabs of only noblemen

Directions for Questions 46 to 50:

Please read the passage and answer the questions that follows.

In introducing the Permanent Settlement, British officials hoped to resolve the problems they had been facing since the conquest of Bengal. By the 1770s, the rural economy in Bengal was in crisis, with recurrent famines and declining agricultural output. Officials felt that agriculture, trade and the revenue resources of the state could all be developed by encouraging investment in agriculture. This could be done by securing rights of property and permanently fixing the rates of revenue demand. If the revenue demand of the state was permanently fixed, then the company could look forward to a regular flow of revenue, while entrepreneurs could feel sure of earning a profit from their investment, since the state would not siphon it off by increasing its claim. The process, officials hoped, would lead to the emergence of a class of yeomen farmers and rich landowners who would have the capital and enterprise to improve agriculture. Nurtured by the British, this class would also be loyal to the company.

46. Out of the given options, choose the most appropriate one :

The problem that the British officials had been facing since the conquest of Bengal was :
- (a) Rebellion of the Zamindars
- (b) Rebellion of the Jotedars
- (c) The rural economy in Bengal was in crisis, with recurrent famines and declining agricultural output
- (d) Inefficient revenue administration in Bengal

47. Out of the given options, choose the most appropriate one : According to the British officials, the solution to the problems of Bengal was :

(a) Abolition of Zamindari System

(b) Suppression of the Jotedars

(c) Encouraging investment in agriculture

(d) Snatching of the powers of Zamindars

48. Out of the given options, choose the most appropriate one: In the opinion of the British officials, investment in agriculture in Bengal could be encouraged by :

(a) Abolition of Zamindari System

(b) Suppressing the Jotedars

(c) Securing rights of property and permanently fixing the rates of revenue demand

(d) Giving more powers to the Jotedars

49. Out of the given options, choose the most appropriate one: If the revenue demand of the state was permanently fixed, it would have many benefits. Out of the given options, choose the one that would not be a benefit of this policy:

(a) The company could look forward to a regular flow of revenue

(b) entrepreneurs could feel sure of earning of profit from their investment

(c) it would lead to emergence of a class loyal to the company

(d) British exports to India would increase

50. Out of the given options, choose the most appropriate one: A class of yeomen farmers and rich landowners would improve agriculture because

(a) They would have the capital and enterprise

(b) They would have the support of the government

(c) They would have the support of the peasants

(d) They would be actively engaged in foreign trade

Answer Keys

1. (c)	**2.** (b)	**3.** (b)	**4.** (b)	**5.** (d)	**6.** (b)	**7.** (d)	**8.** (b)	**9.** (b)	**10.** (c)
11. (d)	**12.** (c)	**13.** (b)	**14.** (b)	**15.** (b)	**16.** (d)	**17.** (c)	**18.** (a)	**19.** (c)	**20.** (a)
21. (b)	**22.** (a)	**23.** (a)	**24.** (b)	**25.** (c)	**26.** (d)	**27.** (b)	**28.** (b)	**29.** (d)	**30.** (b)
31. (d)	**32.** (a)	**33.** (d)	**34.** (c)	**35.** (d)	**36.** (b)	**37.** (a)	**38.** (a)	**39.** (a)	**40.** (b)
41. (d)	**42.** (c)	**43.** (c)	**44.** (c)	**45.** (b)	**46.** (d)	**47.** (c)	**48.** (c)	**49.** (d)	**50.** (a)

Explanations

1. (c) • In some seals, a figure shown seated cross-legged in a "yogic" posture, sometimes surrounded by animals, has been regarded as a depiction of "proto-Shiva"

• Proto-Shiva seals - The earliest religious text, the Rigveda (compiled c. 1500-1000 BCE) mentions a god named Rudra, which is a name used for Shiva in later Puranic traditions (in the first millennium CE; see also Chapter 4). However, unlike Shiva, Rudra in the Rigveda is neither depicted as Pashupati (lord of animals in general and cattle in particular), nor as a yogi. In other words, this depiction does not match the description of Rudra in the Rigveda. Is this, then, possibly a shaman as some scholars have suggested?

2. (b) What is also interesting is an apparent concern for privacy: there are no windows in the walls along the ground level.

3. (b) Although several thousand inscriptions have been discovered, not all have been deciphered, published and translated. Besides, many more inscriptions must have existed, which have not survived the ravages of time.

4. (b) There were five major political centres in the empire - the capital Pataliputra and the provincial centres of Taxila, Ujjayini, Tosali and Suvarnagiri, all mentioned in Asokan inscriptions.

5. (d) Oligarchy refers to a form of government where power is exercised by a group of men.

6. (b) The Prayaga Prashasti (also known as the Allahabad Pillar Inscription) composed in Sanskrit by Harishena, the court poet of Samudragupta, arguably the most powerful of the Gupta rulers (c. fourth century CE), is a case in point.

7. (d) It is Marriage outside Unit

8. (b) The Brahmanas evolved two or three strategies for enforcing these norms. One, as we have just seen, was to assert that the varna order was of divine origin. Second, they advised kings to ensure that these norms were followed within their kingdoms. And third, they attempted to persuade people that their status was determined by birth.

9. (b) The task of preparing a critical edition of the Mahabharata.

10. (c) The Abhidhamma Pitaka dealt with philosophical matters.

11. (d) The empty seat was meant to indicate the meditation of the Buddha, and the stupa was meant to represent the mahaparinibbana. Another frequently used symbol was the wheel. This stood for the first sermon of the Buddha, delivered at Sarnath.

12. (c) Rig veda

13. (b) Travelling overland through Central Asia, Ibn Battuta reached Sind in 1333. He had heard about Muhammad bin Tughlaq, the Sultan of Delhi, and lured by his reputation as a generous patron of arts and letters, set off for Delhi, passing through Multan and Uch.

14. (b) • In the late fifteenth century, Shankaradeva emerged as one of the leading proponents of Vaishnavism in Assam.
   • The twelfth century witnessed the emergence of a new movement in Karnataka, led by a Brahmana named Basavanna

15. (b) A seventeenth-century painting of Shaikh Nizamuddin Auliya and his disciple Amir

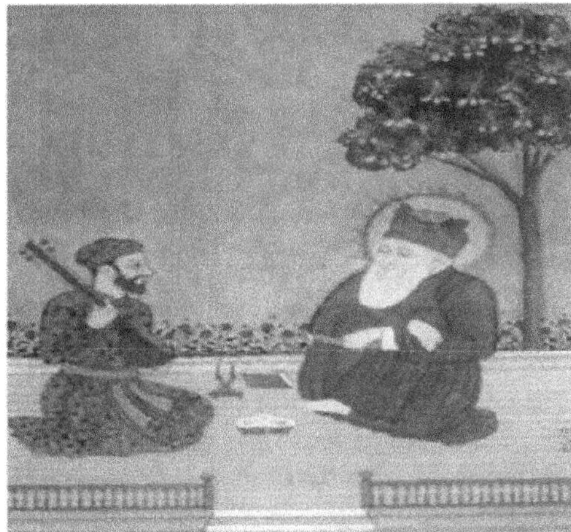

16. (d) He proposed a simple way to connect to the Divine by remembering and repeating the Divine Name, expressing his ideas through hymns called "shabad"

17. (c) In 1986 Hampi declared a World Heritage site by UNESCO

18. (a) • The first dynasty, known as the Sangama dynasty, exercised control till 1485.
   • They were supplanted by the Saluvas, military commanders, who remained in power till 1503 when they were replaced by the Tuluvas. Krishnadeva Raya belonged to the Tuluva dynasty.

19. (c) • A kalyana mandapa, meant to celebrate divine weddings
   • Hazara Rama temple - meant to be used only by the king and his family

20. (a) This text meticulously recorded the arrangements made by the state to ensure cultivation, to enable the collection of revenue by the agencies of the state and to regulate the relationship between the state and rural magnates, the zamindars.

21. (b) They lived around the Rajmahal hills, subsisting on forest produce and practising shifting cultivation.

22. (a) Bengal village scene, painted by George Chinnery, 1820 Chinnery stayed in India for 23 years (1802-25), painting portraits, landscapes and scenes of the everyday life of the common people.

23. (a) When the Permanent Settlement was imposed, Tejchand was the Raja of Burdwan.

24. (b) Who was Buchanan?

   Francis Buchanan was a physician who came to India and served in the Bengal Medical Service (from 1794 to 1815). For a few years he was surgeon to the Governor-General of India, Lord Wellesley. During his stay in Calcutta (present-day Kolkata), he organised a zoo that became the Calcutta Alipore Zoo; he was also in charge of the Botanical Gardens for a short period. On the request of the Government of Bengal, he undertook detailed surveys of the areas under the jurisdiction of the British East India Company. In 1815 he fell ill and returned to England. Upon his mother's death, he inherited her property and assumed her family name Hamilton. So he is often called Buchanan-Hamilton.

25. (c) Zamindars could pay the British any time of the year

26. (d) Fort St. George (or historically, White Town) is a fortress in the coastal city of Chennai, India. Founded in 1639

27. (b) • Jallianwala Bagh Massacre - 1919
   • The Khilafat Movement, (1919-1920) was a movement of Indian Muslims, led by Muhammad Ali and Shaukat Ali
   • Pakistan Resolution - March 24, 1940.
   • Cripps Mission - 1942
   • A Cabinet Mission sent in the summer of 1946

28. (b)

29. (d) Moderates - Gopal Krishna Gokhale

30. (b) • Gandhiji's first major public appearance was at the opening of the Banaras Hindu University (BHU) in February 1916.
- Champaran Satyagraha 1917
- Rowlatt Act - 1919
- Non-cooperation movement 1920
- Salt Satyagraha - 1930

31. (d) Through the Swadeshi movement of 1905-07 it had greatly broadened its appeal among the middle classes. That movement had thrown up some towering leaders - among them Bal Gangadhar Tilak of Maharashtra, Bipin Chandra Pal of Bengal, and Lala Lajpat Rai of Punjab.

32. (a) • Gopal Krishna Gokhale - Gandhiji's political mentor
- Bipin Chandra Pal - The three were known as
- Lal, Bal and Pal",
- Annie Besant - Home Rule
- Mohammad Ali Jinnah, who, like Gandhiji, was a lawyer of Gujarati extraction trained in London.

33. (d) On 28 November 1947, on the occasion of Guru Nanak's birthday, when Gandhiji went to address a meeting of Sikhs at Gurdwara Sisganj

34. (c) • B. N. Rau, Constitutional Advisor to the Government of India, who prepared a series of background papers based on a close study of the political systems obtaining in other countries
- K.M. Munshi from Gujarat and Alladi Krishnaswamy Aiyar from Madras - gave crucial inputs in the drafting of the Constitution.
- Sardar Patel, on the other hand, worked mostly behind the scenes, playing a key role in the drafting of several reports, and working to reconcile opposing points of view

35. (d) Separate electorates was not part of objectives resolution

36. (b) • Quit India struggle of 1942
- Bid by Subhas Chandra Bose to win freedom through armed struggle with foreign aid. - 1942

- Ratings of the Royal Indian Navy in Bombay and other cities in the spring of 1946.
- Constituent Assembly begins its sessions - 1946
- Last meeting of the Interim Government - 1947

37. (a)

38. (a) • Hansa Mehta of Bombay demanded justice for women, not reserved seats, or separate electorates.
- Dakshayani Velayudhan demanded immediate removal of social disabilities

39. (a)

Timeline	
1801	Subsidiary Alliance introduced by Wellesley in Awadh
1856	Nawab Wajid Ali Shah deposed; Awadh annexed
1856-57	Summary revenue settlements introduced in Awadh by the British
1857	
10 May	Mutiny starts in Meerut
11-12 May	Delhi garrisons revolt; Bahadur Shah accepts nominal leadership
20-27 May	Sepoys mutiny in Aligarh, Etawah, Mainpuri, Etah
30 May	Rising in Lucknow
May-June	Mutiny turns into a general revolt of the people
30 June	British suffer defeat in the battle of Chinhat
25 Sept	British forces under have looked and outram enter the Residency in Lucknow
July	Shah Mal killed in battle
1858	
June	Rani Jhansi Killed in battle

40. (b) The name Pakistan was coined in 1933 by Choudhry Rahmat Ali

41. (d)   **42.** (c)

43. (c)   **44.** (c)

45. (b)   **46.** (d)

47. (c)   **48.** (c)

49. (d)   **50.** (a)

1. Some of the Harappan cities were specialised centres for making shell objects - including bangles, ladles and inlay, which were taken to other settlements. Which of the following were such specialised centres?
   A. Kalibangan
   B. Rakhigarhi
   C. Nageshwar
   D. Mohenjodaro
   E. Balakot
   (a) A and B Only
   (b) B and C Only
   (c) C and E Only
   (d) B and D Only

2. Match List I with List

List I (Excavators / Authors)	List II (Their Excavation work / Book)
A. Rakhal Das Banerjii	I. Excavations at Dholavira
B. Dava Ram Sahni	II. Excavations at Mohenjodaro
C. S. N. Roy	III. Excavations at Harappa
D. R. S. Bisht	IV. The story of Indian Archaelogy

   Choose the correct answer from the options given below:
   (a) A-II, B-III, C-IV, D-I
   (b) A-I, B-II, C-III, D-IV
   (c) A-IV, B-III, C-II, D-I
   (d) A-III, B-IV, C-I, D-II,

3. Which of these are correct?
   A. Early Indus Civilisation - Earnest Mackay
   B. Origins of Civilisation - Raymond and Bridget Allchin
   C. Cultured Civilisation - R. E. M. Wheeler
   D. The Indus Civilisation - G. L. Possehl
   E. Understanding Harappa - Shareen Ratnagar
   Choose the correct answer from the options given below:
   (a) A, B, C Only
   (b) A, B, C, D Only
   (c) A, B, D, E Only
   (d) A, B, C, D, E

4. The languages in which the Ashokan inscriptions were written:
   (a) Pali, Sanskrit and Aramaic
   (b) Pali, Sanskrit and Greek
   (c) Pali, Prakrit and Greek
   (d) Prakrit, Aramaic and Greek

5. Means of claiming high status by Kushanas was to identify with variety of deities.
   Which of the following statements does not hold true to prove the statement?
   (a) Colossal statue of Kushana ruler have been found installed in a shrine.
   (b) Many Kushana ruler adopted to the devaputra
   (c) Kushana ruler promoted worship of king alone with the God
   (d) Coins with king Kanishka on obverse and deity on the reverse side have been found

6. First ruler in India to issue coins that can be definitively attributed to particular king were ______.
   (a) The Guptas
   (b) Kushanas
   (c) Indo Greeks
   (d) Shakas

7. __________ is the term used when descent is traced through the mother.
   (a) Exogamy
   (b) Patriliny
   (c) Matriliny
   (d) Endogamy

8. A critical edition of Mahabharata was prepared by:
   (a) V. S. Sukthankar, A noted Indian Sanskritist
   (b) A team comprising dozens of scholars under the leadership of V. S. Sukthankar
   (c) R. E. M. Wheeler
   (d) Alexander Cummingham

9. The Sanskrit play Mrichchhkatika was written in the fourth century by -
   (a) Banabhatta
   (b) Shrudraka
   (c) Kautilya
   (d) Harisena

10. Match List I with List II

List I (Buddhist Philosophy)	List II (Meaning)
A. Dukkha	I. Salvation
B. Nibbara	II. Fellow feeling
C. Metta	III. Soulless
D. anatts	IV. sorrow

   Choose the correct answer from the options given below:
   (a) A-IV, B-I, C-III, D-II
   (b) A-IV, B-II, C-I, D-III
   (c) A-IV, B-I, C-II, D-III
   (d) A-IV, B-III, C-I, D-II

11. According to the ancient Sanskrit religious texts, women had access to which of the following?
    (a) Ancestral properties
    (b) Properties won in gambling
    (c) Stridhan
    (d) Land

12. This Buddhist text included rules and regulations for those who joined the Sangha and monastic order.

(a) Vinaya Pitaka   (b) Dipavamsa

(c) Abhidhama Pitaka   (d) Sutta Pitaka

13. Who found the services of the slaves indespensible for carrying women and men on palanquins or dola?

(a) Abdur Razzak   (b) Al-Biruni

(c) Abdul Fazl   (d) Ibn Batuta

14. Which among the following was a great poet and musician who was the disciple of Hazrat Nizamuddin Auliya?

(a) Shaikh Muinuddin Sijzi

(b) Abu'l Hassan - al -Hujwiri

(c) Quli Khan

(d) Amir Khussrau

15. Match List I with List II

List I (Religious and Cultural Terms)	List II (Their Description)
A. Great Tradition	I. In the form of a stone smeared with ochre
B. Little Tradition	II. The principal deities of the Vedic pantheon
C. Worship of the Goddess	III. Local practices followed by the peasants
D. Agni, Indra, Soma	IV. Rituals and customs observed by peasants that emanated from dominant social categories

Choose the correct answer from the options given below:

(a) A-I, B-II, C-III, D-IV   (b) A-IV, B-III, C-II, D-I

(c) A-IV, B-III, C-I, D-II   (d) A-III, B-II, C-IV, D-I

16. Which of the following statements regarding Baba Guru Nanak Dev are correct?

A. He was born in Nankara Sahib

B. He advocated a form of Saguna Bhakti

C. He expressed his ideas through Shabdas in Punjabi

D. He laid the foundation of Khalsa Panth

E. He appointed Guru Angad Dev as his Successor

Choose the correct answer from the options given below:

(a) A, B, D Only

(b) B, C and E Only

(c) C, D and E Only

(d) A, C and E Only

17. Match List I with List II

List I (Rulles during 14th – 16th Centuty)	List II (Regions)
A. Gajapati	I. Tamil Nadu
B. Sultans	II. Karnataka
C. Cholas	III. Orissa
D. Hoysala	IV. Deccan

Choose the correct answer from the options given below:

(a) A-I, B-III, C-IV, D-II   (b) A-III, B-IV, C-I, D-II

(c) A-IV, B-III, C-II, D-I   (d) A-II, B-I, C-III, D-IV

18. Which of the following are the correct statements about king Krishnadeva Raya?

A. Krishnadeva belonged to Saluva dynasty

B. He defeated Bijapur and Golconda in the battle of Talikota

C. He is credited with building temples and gopurmms

D. He founded Suburban township as Nagalapuram

E. He expanded and consolidated the Vijayanagar empire

Choose the correct answer from the options given below:

(a) A, B and C   (b) B, C and D

(c) C, D and E   (d) A, C and D

19. Where is Brihadeshwara temple located?

(a) Madurai   (b) Chennai

(c) Cochin   (d) Thanjavur

20. Ahom kings belonged to;

(a) Orissa   (b) Assam

(c) Kashmir   (d) Gujrat

21. Who described painting as a 'Magical Art'?

(a) Ibn Batuta   (b) Abu'l Fazl

(c) Abdul Hamid Lahori   (d) Abdus Samad

22. The Ibadat Khana was famous for:-

(a) Receiving Royal guests

(b) Holding interfaith discussions

(c) To entertain the Rajput wives

(d) Holding Royal meetings

23. Which of the following statements regarding mansabdari system of Mughals are true?

A. It was the military-cum-bureaucratic apparatus of the Mughal administration

B. The mansabdars were paid in cash or in jagirs

C. Two numerical designations were given to mansabs - zat and swar

D. The mansabdars of 1,000 Zat were ranked as 'Mir Baksti'.

E. The mansabdars were also called as chaudhari and qazi

Choose the correct answer from the options given below:

(a) B, C and D   (b) C, D and E
(c) A, C and E   (d) A, B and C

24. Who made the Persian language as the official language in the Mughal Court?

(a) Babar   (b) Humayun
(c) Akbar   (d) Jahangir

25. Akbar sent an ambassador to invite Jesuit priests from;

(a) Cochin   (b) Goa
(c) Lisbon   (d) Surat

26. According to the East India Company's Sunset law:

(a) Nobody should venture outside his house after the sunset
(b) If payment did not come in by sunset of the specific date, the Zamindari was liable to be auctioned
(c) After the sunset, hunting of wild animals was prohibited
(d) No trading activity was allowed after the sunset.

27. The battle between the hoe and the plough continued for long. The hoe and the plough were the symbols of:

(a) The British and the Indians
(b) The paharias and the samthals
(c) The Zamindars and the Zotedars
(d) The dikus and the samthals

28. Which of the following was the first province in India where the colonial rule of East India Company was established?

(a) Bengal   (b) Awadh
(c) Bombay   (d) Deccan

29. Who introduced Zamindari system during East India Company rule?

(a) Lord Clive   (b) Lord Wellesley
(c) Lord Cornwallis   (d) Lord William Bentinck

30. Why Amravati did not survive ?

(a) Because it was not known to anyone.
(b) Because it was not preserved.
(c) Because people did not give importance to it.
(d) Because they started making other stupas.

31. "The life was gone out of the body and the body of this town had been left lifeless..." This is related :

(a) The sad demise of Rani Laxmi Bai
(b) Nawab Wajid Ali Shahs's exile from Awadh
(c) Bahadur Shah's exile to Rangoon
(d) The sad demise of Rana Sahib

32. The war, due to which Britishers developed Mount-Abu as a hill station, was the ______

(a) Gurkha war   (b) Anglo-Maratha war
(c) Battle of Buxar   (d) Battle of Plassey

33. Arrange the following important events of the national movement of India in the chronological order:

A. KHILAFAT - Non - Cooperation Movement
B. AHMEDABAD Satyagraha
C. ROWLATT Satyagraha
D. CHAMPARAN Satyagraha
E. KHEDA Satyagraha

Choose the correct answer from the options given below:

(a) A, B, C, D, E   (b) E, D, C, B, A
(c) D, B, E, C, A   (d) B, E, A, D, C

34. The judge who presided over Mahatma Gandhi's trial and remarked. "Even those who differ from you in politics look upon you as a man of high ideals and of even saintly life"?

(a) Justice Louis Fischer
(b) Justice Willington
(c) Justice D. G. Tendulkar
(d) Justice C. N. Broomfield

35. "There is no salvation for India unless you strip yourself of this jewellery and hold it in trust for your countrymen in India."

Who said this and on what occasion?

(a) Jawaharlal Nehru while introducing the objectives resolution
(b) Mahatma Gandhi at the opening of BHU
(c) Dr. B. R. Ambedkar over a discussion of the Hindu Code Bill
(d) Sardar Patel in the Constituent Assembly

36. In 1937 election, the congress won a comprehensive victory. Now, out of 11 provinces, the congress had "Prime Ministers" in:

(a) 7 Provinces   (b) 9 Provinces
(c) 8 Provinces   (d) 11 Provinces

37. The Non Cooperation movement was called off by Mahatma Gandhi after the incident of _______.

(a) Champaran   (b) khera
(c) chouri - Choura   (d) Bardoli

38. Why did Mahatma Gandhi support the Khilafat issue?

(a) To protest against Salt Law
(b) To protest against Jallianwala Bagh incident
(c) To divide Hindu-Muslim against British rule
(d) To unite the people of India for the Caliphate of Turkey

39. Consider the following events and arrange them in correct sequence from earlier to latest:

    A. Wavell Plan

    B. Cabinet Mission

    C. Direct Action Day

    D. Formation of Interim Government

    E. India became Independent

Choose the correct answer from the options given below:

    (a) A, B, C, D, E   (b) B, C, D, A, E

    (c) C, D, A, B, E   (d) D, A, B, C, E

40. Khudai Khidmatgar Organisation was associated with which of the following leaders?

    (a) Maulana Abul kalam

    (b) KHAN Abdul Ghaffar Khan

    (c) Muhammad Ali Jinnah

    (d) Sikander Hay at Khan

Directions for Questions 41 to 45:

Please read the passage and answer the questions that follows.

The national movement in the twentieth century drew its inspiration from the events of 1857. A whole world of nationalist imagination was woven around the revolt. It was celebrated as the first war of independence in which all sections of the India came together to fight against the imperial rule.

Art and literature, as much as the writing of history, have helped in keeping alive the memory of 1857. The leaders of the revolt were presented as heroic figures leading the country into battle, rousing the people to righteous indignation against the oppressive imperial rule. Heroic poems were written about the valour of the queen who, with the sword in one hand and reins of her horse in the other, fought for the freedom of her motherland. Rani of Jhansi was represented as a masculine figure chasing the enemy, slaying British soldiers and valiantly fighting till her last. Children in many parts of India grow up reading the lines of Subhadra Kumari Chauhan: "Khoob lari mardani who to Jhansi wali rani thi" (like a man, she fought, she was the Rani of Jhansi). In popular prints Rani Lakshmi Bai is usually portrayed in battle armour, with a sword in hand and riding a horse, a symbol of the determination to resist injustice and alien rule.

41. The revolt of 1857 is significant in the history of national movement of India because:-

    (a) The Indians fought valiantly against the British in this revolt.

    (b) The Indians defeated the British for the first time, in this revolt.

    (c) The national movement in the twentieth century drew its inspiration from the events of 1857.

    (d) The revolt of 1857 had no parallel in the world history

42. The revolt of 1857 was celebrated by the Indians as:

    (a) The First war of Independence

    (b) The war of Freedom

    (c) The war against the foreign rule

    (d) The revolution for the Liberty, Equality and Fraternity

43. The memory of 1857 are kept alive by way of:

    (a) Remembering it as an unforgettable event.

    (b) Constructing a museum by the British government to conserve the archaeological remains of the revolt of 1857

    (c) Art and literature, as much as the writing of history, have helped in keeping alive the memory of 1857.

    (d) Celebrating the anniversary of the revolt of 1857 every year

44. The leaders of the revolt of 1857 were presented as:

    (a) The most honest persons of the earth

    (b) The kind and philanthropic persons

    (c) The Fanatics

    (d) Heroic figures leading the country into battle, rousing the people to righteous indignation against the oppressive imperial rule

45. In popular prints Rani Lakshmi Bai is usually portrayed as:

    (a) A symbol of Cowardice

    (b) A symbol of the determination to resist injustice and alien rule.

    (c) A symbol of weakening of women

    (d) A symbol of extraordinary charity

Directions for Questions 46 to 50:

Please read the passage and answer the questions that follows.

The members of the Constituent Assembly were not elected on the basis of universal franchise. In the winter of 1945-46 provincial elections were held in India. The Provincial legislatures then chose the representatives of the Constituent Assembly. The Constituent Assembly that came into being was dominated by one party: the Congress. The Congress swept the general seats in the provincial elections, and the Muslim League captured most of the reserved Muslim seats. But the league chose to boycott the Constituent Assembly, pressing its demand for Pakistan with a separate constitution. The socialists too were initially unwilling to join, for they believed the Constituent Assembly was a creation of the British, and therefore incapable of being truly autonomous. In effect, therefore, 82 per cent of the members of the Constituent Assembly were also members of the Congress. The Congress however was not a party with one voice. Its members differed in their opinion on critical issues. Some members were inspired by socialism while others were defenders of landlordism. Some were close to communal parties while others were assertively secular. Through the national movement Congress members had learnt to debate their ideas in public and negotiate their differences, Within the Constituent Assembly too. Congress members did not sit quiet.

46. The elections which were held during winter of 1945-46 were _______

(a) Congress Election

(b) Provincial Election

(c) Panchayat Election

(d) Election for municipality

47. The Constituent Assembly was dominated by which party?

(a) Indian National Congress

(b) Muslim League

(c) Labours Party of India

(d) Jan Sangh

48. Based on the information given about making of the Constituent Assembly.

Choose the most suitable combination from the following options:

A. 82% of the members of the Constituent Assembly were also members of the Congress

B. The socialists were initially unwilling to join, for they believed the Constituent Assembly was a creation of the British, and therefore incapable of being truly autonomous.

C. The Muslim league swept the general seats in the provincial elections

D. The Muslim league chose to boycott the Constituent Assembly, pressing its demand for Pakistan with a separate constitution

Choose the correct answer from the options given below:

(a) C and D Only   (b) B and C Only

(c) A and C Only   (d) A, B and D Only

49. Some members of the congress were defenders of _______

(a) Factionaism   (b) Pluralism

(c) Landlordism   (d) Tourism

50. Through the national movement Congress members had learnt to _______ their ideas in public and their differences.

(a) debate, negotiate   (b) debate, create

(c) negotiate, create   (d) support, spread

Answer Keys

1. (c)	**2.** (a)	**3.** (c)	**4.** (d)	**5.** (c)	**6.** (c)	**7.** (c)	**8.** (a)	**9.** (b)	**10.** (c)
11. (c)	**12.** (a)	**13.** (d)	**14.** (d)	**15.** (c)	**16.** (d)	**17.** (b)	**18.** (c)	**19.** (d)	**20.** (b)
21. (b)	**22.** (b)	**23.** (d)	**24.** (c)	**25.** (b)	**26.** (b)	**27.** (b)	**28.** (a)	**29.** (c)	**30.** (b)
31. (b)	**32.** (b)	**33.** (c)	**34.** (d)	**35.** (b)	**36.** (c)	**37.** (c)	**38.** (d)	**39.** (a)	**40.** (b)
41. (c)	**42.** (a)	**43.** (c)	**44.** (d)	**45.** (b)	**46.** (b)	**47.** (a)	**48.** (d)	**49.** (c)	**50.** (a)

Explanations

1. (c) If you locate Nageshwar and Balakot, you will notice that both settlements are near the coast. These were specialised centres for making shell objects - including bangles, ladles and inlay - which were taken to other settlements.

2. (a) Subsequently, seals were discovered at Harappa by archaeologists such as Daya Ram Sahni in the early decades of the twentieth century, in layers that were definitely much older than Early Historic levels. Another archaeologist, Rakhal Das Banerji found similar seals at Mohenjodaro, leading to the conjecture that these sites were part of a single archaeological culture. Based on these finds, in 1924.

As S.N. Roy noted in The Story of Indian Archaeology, "Marshall left India three thousand years older than he had found her."

In 1990 R.S. Bisht begins excavations at Dholavira.

3. (c) • FROM ERNEST MACKAY: Early Indus Civilisation, 1948

• Raymond and Bridget Allchin. 1997: Origins of a Civilization. Viking, New Delhi.

• Shereen Ratnagar. 2001: Understanding Harappa. Tulika, New Delhi.

• G.L. Possehl. 2003: The Indus Civilization. Vistaar, New Delhi

4. (d) Most Asokan inscriptions were in the Prakrit language while those in the northwest of the subcontinet were in Aramaic and Greek. Most Prakrit inscriptions were written in the Brahmi script; however, some, in the northwest, were written in Kharosthi. The Aramaic and Greek scripts were used for inscriptions in Afghanistan.

5. (c) The notions of kingship Kushans wished to project are perhaps best evidenced in their coins and sculpture. Colossal statues of Kushana rulers have been found installed in a shrine at Mat near Mathura (Uttar Pradesh). Similar statues have been found in a shrine in Afghanistan as well. Some historians feel this indicates that the Kushanas considered themselves godlike. Many Kushana rulers also adopted the title devaputra, or "son of god", possibly inspired by Chinese rulers who called themselves sons of heaven.

6. (c) The first coins to bear the names and images of rulers were issued by the Indo-Greeks, who established control over the north-western part of the subcontinent c. second century BCE.

7. (c) Matriliny is the term used when descent is traced through the mother.

8. (a) One of the most ambitious projects of scholarship began in 1919, under the leadership of a noted Indian Sanskritist, V.S. Sukthankar.

9. (b) Sanskrit texts and inscriptions used the term vanik to designate merchants. While trade was defined as an occupation for Vaishyas in the Shastras, a more complex situation is evident in plays such as the Mrichchhakatika written by Shudraka (c. fourth century CE),

10. (c) According to Buddhist philosophy, the world is transient (anicca) and constantly changing; it is also soulless (anatta) as there is nothing permanent or eternal in it. Within this transient world, sorrow (dukkha) is intrinsic to human existence. The Buddha emphasised individual agency and righteous action as the means to escape from the cycle of rebirth and attain self-realisation and nibbana, literally the extinguishing of the ego and desire - and thus end the cycle of suffering for those who renounced the world. The importance attached to conduct and values rather than claims of superiority based on birth, the emphasis placed on metta (fellow feeling) and karuna (compassion), especially for those who were younger and weaker than oneself, were ideas that drew men and women to Buddhist teachings.

11. (c) The women were allowed to retain the gifts they received on the occasion of their marriage as stridhana (literally, a woman's wealth).

12. (a) The Vinaya Pitaka included rules and regulations for those who joined the sangha or monastic order.

13. (d) Slaves were generally used for domestic labour, and Ibn Battuta found their services particularly indispensable for carrying women and men on palanquins or dola.

14. (d) There is a painting of seventeenth-century depicts Shaikh Nizamuddin Auliya and his disciple Amir Khusrau.

15. (c) The terms great and little traditions were coined by a sociologist named Robert Redfield in the twentieth century to describe the cultural practices of peasant societies. He found that peasants observed rituals and customs that emanated from dominant social categories, including priests and rulers. At the same time, peasants also followed local practices that did not necessarily correspond with those of the great tradition. These he included within the category of little tradition.

Such instances of integration are evident amongst goddess cults as well. Worship of the goddess, often simply in the form of a stone smeared with ochre, was evidently widespread.

The principal deities of the Vedic pantheon, Agni, Indra and Soma, become marginal figures, rarely visible in textual or visual representations.

16. (d) Baba Guru Nanak (1469-1539) was born in a Hindu merchant family in a village called Nankana Sahib near the river Ravi in the predominantly Muslim Punjab. The message of Baba Guru Nanak is spelt out in his hymns and teachings. These suggest that he advocated a form of nirguna bhakti. He proposed a simple way to connect to the Divine by remembering and repeating the Divine Name, expressing his ideas through hymns called "shabad " in Punjabi, the language of the region. He appointed one of his disciples, Angad, to succeed him as the preceptor (gur u), and this practice was followed for nearly 200 years.

17. (b) Establishment of the Gajapati kingdom of Orissa (1435); On their northern frontier, the Vijayanagara kings competed with contemporary rulers - including the Sultans of the Deccan and the Gajapati rulers of Orissa - for control of the fertile river valleys and the resources generated by lucrative overseas trade. Some of the areas that were incorporated within the empire had witnessed the development of powerful states such as those of the Cholas in Tamil Nadu and the Hoysalas in Karnataka.

18. (c) Krishnadeva Raya belonged to the Tuluva dynasty. Krishnadeva Raya's rule was characterised by expansion and consolidation. This was the time when the land between the Tungabhadra and Krishna rivers (the Raichur doab) was acquired (1512), the rulers of Orissa were subdued (1514) and severe defeats were inflicted on the Sultan of Bijapur (1520). Krishnadeva Raya is credited with building some fine temples and adding impressive gopurams to many important south Indian temples. He also founded a suburban township near Vijayanagara called Nagalapuram after his mother. Some of the most detailed descriptions of Vijayanagara come from his time or just after.

19. (d) Ruling elites in these areas had extended patronage to elaborate temples such as the Brihadishvara temple at Thanjavur and the Chennakeshava temple at Belur.

20. (b) In Assam, the Ahom kings had their paiks, people who were obliged to render military service in exchange for land. The capture of wild elephants was declared a royal monopoly by the Ahom kings.

21. (b) The historian Abu'l Fazl described painting as a "magical art": in his view it had the power to make inanimate objects look as if they possessed life.

22. (b) Akbar's quest for religious knowledge led to interfaith debates in the ibadat khana at Fatehpur Sikri between learned Muslims, Hindus, Jainas, Parsis and Christians. Akbar's religious views matured as he queried scholars of different religions and sects and gathered knowledge about their doctrines.

23. (d) All holders of government offices held ranks (mansabs) comprising two numerical designations: zat which was an indicator of position in the imperial hierarchy and the salary of the official (mansabdar), and sawar which indicated the number of horsemen he was required to maintain in service. In the seventeenth century, mansabdars of 1,000 zat or above ranked as nobles (umara, which is the plural of amir).

24. (c) It was Akbar who consciously set out to make Persian the leading language of the Mughal court.

25. (b) Akbar was curious about Christianity and dispatched an embassy to Goa to invite Jesuit priests.

26. (b) According to the Sunset Law, if payment did not come in by sunset of the specified date, the zamindari was liable to be auctioned.

27. (b) By this time in fact there were newer intimations of danger. Santhals were pouring into the area, clearing forests, cutting down timber, ploughing land and growing rice and cotton. As the lower hills were taken over by Santhal settlers, the Paharias receded deeper into the Rajmahal hills. If Paharia life was symbolised by the hoe, which they used for shifting cultivation, the settlers came to represent the power of the plough. The battle between the hoe and the plough was a long one.

28. (a) Bengal was the first province where East India Company established its colonial rule.

29. (c) Lord Cornwallis was the commander of the British forces during the American War of Independence and the Governor General of Bengal when the Permanent Settlement was introduced there in 1793.

30. (b) In 1796, a local raja who wanted to build a temple stumbled upon the ruins of the stupa at Amaravati. He decided to use the stone, and thought there might be some treasure buried in what seemed to be a hill.

31. (b) The widespread sense of grief and loss at the Nawab's exile was recorded by many contemporary observers. One of them wrote: "The life was gone out of the body, and the body of this town had been left lifeless ... there was no street or market and house which did not wail out the cry of agony in separation of Jan-i-Alam." One folk song bemoaned that "the honourable English came and took the country" (Angrez Bahadur ain, mulk lai linho).

32. (b) Simla (present-day Shimla) was founded during the course of the Gurkha War (1815-16); the Anglo-Maratha War of 1818 led to British interest in Mount Abu; and Darjeeling was wrested from the rulers of Sikkim in 1835.

33. (c) Mahatma Gandhi was to spend much of 1917 in Champaran, seeking to obtain for the peasants security of tenure as well as the freedom to cultivate the crops of their choice. The following year, 1918, Gandhiji was involved in two campaigns in his home state of Gujarat. First, he intervened in a labour dispute in Ahmedabad, demanding better working conditions for the textile mill workers. These initiatives in Champaran, Ahmedabad and Kheda marked Gandhiji out as a nationalist with a deep sympathy for the poor. Gandhiji called for a countrywide campaign against the "Rowlatt Act" in 1919. The Khilafat Movement, (1919-1920) was a movement of Indian Muslims, led by Muhammad Ali and Shaukat Ali.

34. (d) During the Non-Cooperation Movement thousands of Indians were put in jail. Gandhiji himself was arrested in March 1922, and charged with sedition. The judge who presided over his trial, Justice C.N. Broomfield, made a remarkable speech while pronouncing his sentence. "It would be impossible to ignore the fact," remarked the judge, "that you are in a different category from any person I have ever tried or am likely to try. It would be impossible to ignore the fact that, in the eyes of millions of your countrymen, you are a great patriot and a leader. Even those who differ from you in politics look upon you as a man of high ideals and of even saintly life."

35. (b) The opening of the BHU, he said, was "certainly a most gorgeous show". But he worried about the contrast between the "richly bedecked noblemen" present and "millions of the poor" Indians who were absent. Gandhiji told the privileged invitees that "there is no salvation for India unless you strip yourself of this jewellery and hold it in trust for your countrymen in India". "There can be no spirit of self-government about us," he went on, "if we take away or allow others to take away from the peasants almost the whole of the results of their labour. Our salvation can only come through the farmer. Neither the lawyers, nor the doctors, nor the rich landlords are going to secure it."

36. (c) In 1935, however, a new Government of India Act promised some form of representative government. Two years later, in an election held on the basis of a restricted franchise, the Congress won a comprehensive victory. Now eight out of 11 provinces had a Congress "Prime Minister", working under the supervision of a British Governor.

37. (c) In February 1922, a group of peasants attacked and torched a police station in the hamlet of Chauri Chaura, in the United Provinces (now, Uttar Pradesh and Uttaranchal). Several constables perished in the conflagration. This act of violence prompted Gandhiji to call off the movement altogether.

38. (d) If non-cooperation was effectively carried out, said Gandhiji, India would win swaraj within a year. To further broaden the struggle he had joined hands with the Khilafat Movement that sought to restore the Caliphate, a symbol of Pan-Islamism which had recently been abolished by the Turkish ruler Kemal Attaturk.

39. (a) I. In 1945, a Labour government came to power in Britain and committed itself to granting independence to India. Meanwhile, back in India, the Viceroy, Lord Wavell, brought the Congress and the League together for a series of talks.

II. A Cabinet Mission sent in the summer of 1946 failed to get the Congress and the League to agree on a federal system that would keep India together while allowing the provinces a degree of autonomy.

III. After the talks broke down, Jinnah called for a "Direct Action Day" to press the League's demand for Pakistan.

IV. Early in 1946 fresh elections were held to the provincial legislatures. The Congress swept the "General" category, but in the seats specifically reserved for Muslims the League won an overwhelming majority.

V. The formal transfer of power was fixed for 15 August. When that day came, it was celebrated with gusto in different parts of India.

40. (b) Khan Abdul Gaffar Khan is associated with Khudai Khidmatgar Organization.

41. (c) The national movement in the twentieth century drew its inspiration from the events of 1857. A

42. (a) 1857 was celebrated as the First War of Independence in which all sections of the people of India came together to fight against imperial rule.

43. (c) Art and literature, as much as the writing of history, have helped in keeping alive the memory of 1857.

44. (d) The leaders of the revolt were presented as heroic figures leading the country into battle, rousing the people to righteous indignation against oppressive imperial rule.

45. (b) Rani of Jhansi was represented as a masculine figure chasing the enemy, slaying British soldiers and valiantly fighting till her last.

46. (b) The members of the Constituent Assembly were not elected on the basis of universal franchise. In the winter of 1945-46 provincial elections were held in India.

47. (a) The Constituent Assembly that came into being was dominated by one party: the Congress.

48. (d) The Socialists too were initially unwilling to join, for they believed the Constituent Assembly was a creation of the British, and therefore incapable of being truly autonomous. In effect, therefore, 82 per cent of the members of the Constituent Assembly were also members of the Congress.

49. (c) Some members were inspired by socialism while others were defenders of landlordism.

50. (a) Through the national movement Congress members had learnt to debate their ideas in public and negotiate their differences. Within the Constituent Assembly too, Congress members did not sit quiet.

1. In 1857 the sepoys of Meerut appealed to the old Mughal emperor to accept the leadership of the revolt because:
   (a) They loved and respected Bahadur Shah
   (b) They were afraid of the British retaliation
   (c) To fight the British. leadership and organisation were required
   (d) The sepoys were fans of the superior generalship quality of Bahadur Shah

2. The court poet of Samudragupta who composed Prayaga Prashasti (also known as the Allahabad Pillar Inscription) in Sanskrit was:
   (a) Harisena
   (b) Banabhatta
   (c) Kautilya
   (d) Kalhana

3. The marriage practice within a unit-a kin group, caste or a group living in the same locality, is known as:-
   (a) Polygamy
   (b) Polyandry
   (c) Exogamy
   (d) Endogamy

4. Tamil Sangam literature refers to slaves as ______.
   (a) Pannai
   (b) Adimai
   (c) Uzhavar
   (d) Vellalar

5. Arrange the following mature harappan sites from east to west.
   A. Harappa
   B. Suktagendor
   C. Amri
   D. Kalibangan
   E. Chahudaro
   Choose the correct answer from the option given below:
   (a) A, C, D, B, E
   (b) A, B, C, D, E
   (c) D, A, E, C, B
   (d) E, D, A, C, B

6. Match the placed List II from the excavated objects given in List I

List I	List II
A. Terracotta model of plough	I. Dholavira
B. Traces of canals	II. Nageshwar
C. Water reservoirs	III. Banawali
D. Shell objects	IV. Shortugai, Afghanistan

Choose the correct answer from the options given below:
(a) A-III, B-I, C-II, D-IV
(b) A-III, B-IV, C-I, D-II
(c) A-III, B-II, C-IV, D-I
(d) A-II, B-III, C-I, D-IV

7. The Rajasuya and Ashwamedha of the later Vedic Period were:
   (a) The rulers of the Mahajanapadas
   (b) Elaborate sacrifices
   (c) Imperial festivals
   (d) The branches of medical science

8. The Upanishads showed the curiosity of people about:
   A. The meaning of life
   B. The possibility of life after death
   C. The rebirth due to past actions
   D. The nature of the ultimate reality
   E. The significance of the Sacrificial tradition
   Choose the correct answer from the options given below"
   (a) A, B, D, E only
   (b) A, B, C, D only
   (c) B, C, D, E only
   (d) A, C D, E only

9. Who was the traveler whose account described Delhi as a vast city, with a great population, the largest in India: -
   (a) Ibn Battuta
   (b) Al-Biruni
   (c) Manucci
   (d) Francois Bernier

10. The Vijaynagara kings claimed that they ruled on behalf of the Hindu God:-
    (a) Lord Shiva
    (b) Vithala
    (c) Lord Balaji
    (d) Shri Virupaksha

11. Match the List I with List IE and choose the correct answer.

List I	List II
A. Kanyadana	I. The most important Dharamasutra and Dharamashastra
B. Stridhana	II. It was named after a vedic seer
C. Gotra	III. The gift of a daughter in marriage
D. Manusmriti	IV. A Woman's wealth

Choose the correct answer from the options given below:
(a) A-III, B-IV, C-II, D-I
(b) A-I, B-II, C-III, D-IV
(c) A-IV, B-III, C-II, D-I
(d) A-II, B-I, C-IV, D-III

12. Who among the following leaders gave emphasis on 'Hindustani' for the national language?

(a) T.A Ramalingam Chellur

(b) R.V Dhulekar

(c) Mahatma Gandhi

(d) Jawaharlal Nehru

13. Arrange the following events in chronological order:

A. The cabinet mission announces its constitutional scheme.

B. The labour Government comes into power in Britain.

C. The Constitution is signed

D. The Constituent Assembly begins its sessions

E. Partition of India

Choose the correct answer from the options given below:

(a) B, A, D, E, C

(b) E, D, C, B, A

(c) A, B, C, D, E

(d) B, A, E, D, C

14. Match List I with List II

List I Prominent Personalities in the history of Nationalist movement	List II Their Description
A. Annie Desant	I. A prominent follower of Gandhiji
B. C.N. Broomfield	II. An important leader of Congress
C. Kamaladevi Chattaopadhyay	III. The judge who presided over Gandhiji's trial
D. Sarojini Naidu	IV. The socialist activist who persuaded Gandhiji not to restrict the salt March protests to men alone

Choose the correct answer from the options given below:

(a) A-I, B-II, C-III, D-IV

(b) A-II, B-III, C-IV, D-I

(c) A-IV, B-III, C-II, D-I

(d) A-III, B-I, C-II, D-IV

15. Select the correct arrangement of the following as per the ascending sequence of occurrence-

A. Quit India Movement

B. Royal Indian Navy Rising

C. The great Calcutta Killings of August 1946

D. Independence day of India

Choose the correct answer from the options given below:

(a) B, C, A, D   (b) C, D, B, A

(c) A, B, C, D   (d) D, C, B, A

16. Whose constitutional status remained ambiguous at the time of Independence?

(a) Tribals   (b) Minorities

(c) Depressed Classes (d) Princely States

17. In Bengal, A Rich Asami meant ________.

(a) A Farmer having one acre of land

(b) A Farmer having a pair of bullock

(c) A Farmer having a plough

(d) A Farmer having ten acre of land

18. In which year Babur defeated Ibrahim Lodhi, the Delhi Sultan, at Panipat in ________ and became the first Mughal emperor:

(a) 1555   (b) 1526

(c) 1540   (d) 1605

19. Select the correct arrangement of the following dynasties in the sequence of their occurrence-

A. Tuluva dynasty

B. Aravidu

C. Sangama dynasty

D. Saluvas

Choose the correct answer from the options given below:

(a) A, B, C, D   (b) C, D, A, B

(c) D, C, B, A   (d) A, C, B, D

20. Identify the given figure and tick the correct one:

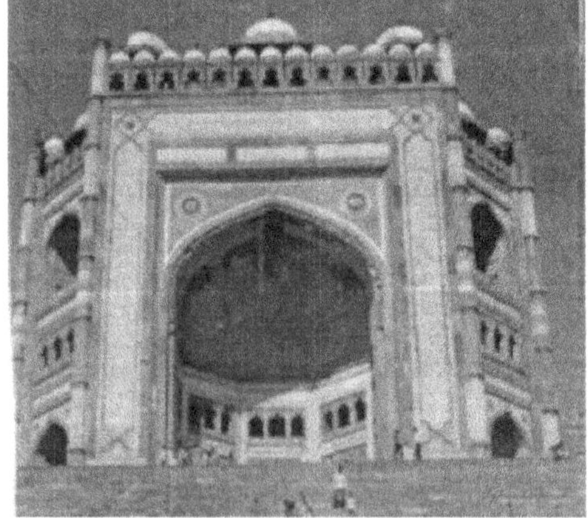

(a) The Red Fort at Agra

(b) The Red Fort at Shahjahanabad

(c) The Buland Darwaza at Fatehpur Sikri

(d) The Dargah of Moinuddin Chishti at Ajmer

21. The combined armies of which States routed the army of Rama Rai in 1565?

    A. Golkonda, Ahmednagar, Bidar

    B. Ahmednagar, Berar, Bijapur

    C. Bijapur, Ahmedanagar, Bidar

    D. Bijapur, Ahmednagar, Golkonda

    Choose the correct answer from the options given below:

    (a) A and B only   (b) A and C only

    (c) D and B only   (d) D only

22. The Mughal empire was among the large territorial empires in Asia that had managed to consolidate power and resources during the sixteenth and seventeenth centuries. Which of the following empires was not enjoying the same power but positioned similar to the Mughals?

    (a) Mings (China)   (b) Safavid (Iran)

    (c) Ottoman (Turkey)   (d) Mongol (Mongolia)

23. Select the correct match of the term with their meanings.

List - I : The Terms	List - II : Their meanings
A. Nazr	I. The lotus blossom set with jewels
B. Padma Murassa	II. A small sum of money
C. Khwajasara	III. The concubines
D. Aghacha	IV. Slave eunuchs

Choose the correct answer from the options given below:

(a) A-II, B-I, C-IV, D-III

(b) A-I, B-II, C-III, D-IV

(c) A-IV, B-III, C-II, D-I

(d) A-III, B-IV, C-I, D-II

24. Which of the following was built by Akbar to commemorate his conquest of Khandesh in Gujrat?

    (a) Bada Imambara

    (b) Jama Masjid

    (c) Siddi Bashir

    (d) Buland Darwaza

25. Select the correct match of List I and List II

List I - Leaders of the Revolt of 1857	List II - Region they belonged to
A. Nawab WajidAli Shah	I. Delhi
B. Rani Lakshmi Bai	II. Kanpur
C. Nana Sahib	III. Jhansi
D. Bahadur Shah Zafar	IV. Awadh

Choose the correct answer from the options given below:

(a) A-III, B-II, C-IV, D-I

(b) A-II, B-IV, C-III, D-I

(c) A-IV, B-III, C-II, D-I

(d) A-III, B-IV, C-II, D-I

Directions for Questions 26 and 27: Answer the questions on the basis of given map.

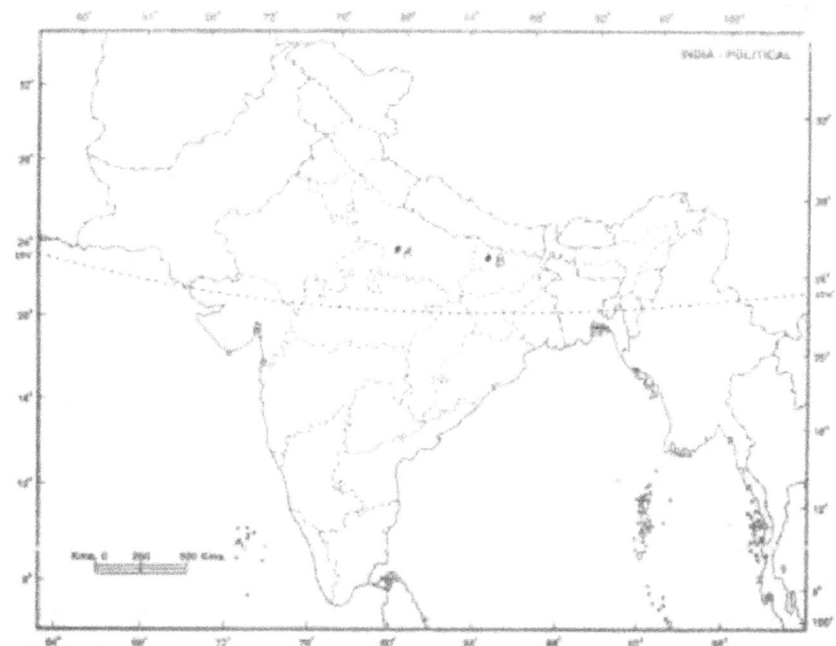

26. Identify the place marked as 'A' in the given political map of India- One of the of the Principal centre of Revolt of 1857 led by Nana Sahib
    (a) Lucknow
    (b) Kanpur
    (c) Awadh
    (d) Jhansi

27. Identify the place marked as 'B' from the given options and clue-

    Mahatma Gandhi's campaign for the peasants security of tenure as well as freedom to cultivate the crops of their choice
    (a) Kheda, Gujarat
    (b) Ahmedabad, Gujarat
    (c) Champaram, Bihar
    (d) Chauri Chaura, UP

28. The people were annoyed by the British because:
    A. British land revenue settlements had dispossessed land holders both big and small
    B. Foreign commerce had driven artisans and weavers to ruin.
    C. The firangi were accused of destroying a way of life that was familiar and cherished.
    D. The British rule had developed India economically as well as educationally.
    E. The British were biased against the Hindus
    Choose the correct answer from the options given below:
    (a) A, B, D only
    (b) A, B, C only
    (c) C, D, E only
    (d) A, C, E only

29. After loosing the battle of Kannauj in 1540 where did Humayun take refuge in the court of:
    (a) Uzbeks of Uzbekistan
    (b) Chaghtai of Turkey
    (c) Mings of China
    (d) Safavid's of Iran

30. Under Sulh-i-kul, all religion had freedom of expression but on certain condition. Identify the condition.
    (a) Close connection with state
    (b) Not to undermine the authority of state
    (c) Freedom of expression only to certain community
    (d) Freedom of expression was only given to a particular gender of religion

31. Select the correct arrangement of the following items starting from the one which occurred first to the one that took place in the last:
    A. Beginning of the sepoy Revolt in Meerut
    B. Abolition of Sati
    C. Passing of the Widow Remarriage Act
    D. Queen's Proclamation
    Choose the correct answer from the options given below:
    (a) B, C, A, D
    (b) C, B, C, D
    (c) D, A, B, C
    (d) A, B, C, D

32. Mahatma Gandhi used to publish the letters written to him in his journal _______.
    (a) New Delhi
    (b) Harijan
    (c) Young India
    (d) Indian Opinion

33. Mahatma Gandhi's American biographer Louis Fisher described the three elements of the 'Non - Cooperation'
    Select the correct one
    A. Denial
    B. Renunciation
    C. Self-discipline
    D. Courage
    E. Compassion
    Choose the correct answer from the options given below:
    (a) C, D, E only
    (b) B, C, D only
    (c) A, B and C only
    (d) A, C, E only

34. Identify the name of the Urdu Poet who composed 'Sare Jahan Se Accha Hindustan Hamara'.
    (a) Ruqsana Begum
    (b) Mohammad Iqbal
    (c) Faiz Ahmed Faiz
    (d) Sahir Ludhianvi

35. Who played the role of the chief draftsman for the constituent assembly?
    (a) N. C. Ranga
    (b) Buddha Bhagat
    (c) Sardar Tara Singh
    (d) S.N. Mukherjee

36. Choose the most appropriate option

    Gandhiji hoped that in future the Indians and Pakistani shall always be like:

    (a) The bitter enemies

    (b) Good neighbours

    (c) Friends and brothers helping and respecting one another

    (d) Not having any relation with each other

37. Identify the central feature of the constitution on which substantial agreement was done:

    (a) Hindi- the language of the nation

    (b) A strong center

    (c) The granting of the Vote to every adult Indian

    (d) The rights of the minorities

38. Identification of the upper and middle class Indians during the reign of Britishers in India:

    (a) Maharajas

    (b) Lawyers

    (c) Merchants

    (d) Craftsmen

39. Which of the following statements regarding Constituent Assembly is NOT correct?

    (a) The members of the Assembly were elected by the members of Provincial Legislatures

    (b) The members of the Assembly were elected on the basis of Universal franchise

    (c) The Muslim League chose to boycott the Constituent Assembly

    (d) Civil servant B.N. Rau was constitutional advisor to the Government of India

40. Who of the following was moderate leader of the Congress?

    (a) Gopal Krishna Gokhale

    (b) Bal Gangadhar Tilak

    (c) Lala Lajpat Rai

    (d) Bipin Chandra Pal

Directions for Quesitons 41 to 45:

Please read the passage and answer the questions that follows.

Some of the earliest bhakti movements (c. sixth century) were led by the Alvars (literally, those who are "immersed" in devotion to Vishnu) and Nayanars (literally, leaders who were devotees of Shiva). They travelled from place to place singing hymns in Tamil in praise of their gods. Dining their travels, the Alvars and Nayanars identified certain shrines as abodes of their chosen deities. Very often large temples were later built at these sacred places. These developed as centers of pilgrimage. Singing compositions of these poet-saints became part of temple rituals in these shrines, as did worship of the saints' images. Some historians suggest that the Alvars and Nayanars initiated a movement of protest against the caste system and the dominance of Brahmanas or at least attempted to reform the system. To some extent, this is corroborated by the fact that bhaktas hailed from diverse social backgrounds ranging from Brahmanas to artisans and cultivators and even from castes considered "untouchable".

41. Some of the earliest movement were started in ________.

    (a) Eighth century

    (b) Seventh centurv

    (c) Sixth century

    (d) Fourth century

42. Which of the following was not a part of Alvars?

    (a) Fakir

    (b) Brahman

    (c) Women

    (d) Farmers

43. Find the common link in each group and fill in the blank accordingly ________ : Nalayira Divya prabandham:

    (a) Brahmanas. Vedas

    (b) Nayanars, Rig veda

    (c) Alvars, Tamil Veda

    (d) Alvars, Nayanars

44. Singing compositions of ________ became part of temple rituals in all shrines.

    (a) Poet- Saints

    (b) Poet - politicians

    (c) Poet - Businessman

    (d) Poet - Artisans

45. Alvars were the devotee of lord Vishnu while the Naynars were the devotee of:

    (a) Lord Shiva

    (b) Lord Surya

    (c) Lord Varun

    (d) Lord Brahma

Directions for Quesitons 46 to 50:

Please read the passage and answer the questions that follows.

Referring to the condition of zamindars and the auction of lands, the fifth Report stated:

The revenue was not realised with punctuality and lands to a considerable extent were periodically exposed to sale by auction. In the native year 1203 corresponding with 1796-97, the land advertised for sale comprehended a jumma or assessment of sicca rupees 28,70,061, the extent of land actually sold bore a jumma or assessment of 14,18,756, and the amount of purchase money sicca rupees 17,90,416. In 1204, corresponding with 1797-98 the land advertised was for sicca rupees 26,66,191, the quantity sold was for sicca rupees 22,74,076, and the purchase money sicca rupees 21,47,580. Among the defaulters were some of the oldest families of the country. Such were the rajahs of Nuddea, Rajeshaye, Bishenpore (all districts of Bengal), ... and others, the dismemberment of whose estates at the end of each succeeding year, threatened them with poverty and ruin, and in some instances presented difficulties to revenue officers, in their efforts to preserve undiminished the amount of public assessment.

46. The main concept or theme on which 'The fifth report is based is given below.

Find the incorrect information that is related to fifth report.

(a) The causes of collapse of traditional Zamindari power

(b) The estimation of the scale on which Zamindars were losing their land (auction of zamindars)

(c) The ingenious methods they used to retain their Zamindaris

(d) It talks about pathetic condition of business class.

47. The Fifth report talks about the defaulters who were from the oldest families of the country. In given below which was the family not mentioned as defaulter family.

(a) The raj ahs of Nuddea

(b) The rajahs of Raje Shave

(c) The rajahs of Bishenpore

(d) Rajahs of Kathiawad

48. The Fifth report based on company's misrule and maladministration mentions where difficulties of the revenue officers:

(a) Revenue officers were responsible for the law and order of the region.

(b) Revenue officers were also working as Zamindars.

(c) The revenue officers were facing problem in maintaining the collection of the revenue assessment.

(d) The revenue officers faced hardship in fighting the forces

49. Fifth report on the administration and activities of the east India company in India reproduced different issues. Find the off one out issue which is not related to the fifth report.

(a) It reproduced petitions of Zamindars and ryots

(b) It reproduced reports of collectors from different districts.

(c) It also reproduced statistical tables on revenue returns of Bengal and Madras written by officials

(d) It reproduced the record of stories and rocks and the different state and layers of soil.

50. Which report produced by a select committee became the basis of intense parliamentary debates on the nature of the East India Company's rule in India?

(a) The Buchanan report

(b) Maharaja Mehtab Chand's proclamation

(c) The Fifth Report

(d) East India Company Archives report

Answer Keys

1. (c)	**2.** (a)	**3.** (d)	**4.** (b)	**5.** (c)	**6.** (b)	**7.** (b)	**8.** (b)	**9.** (a)	**10.** (d)
11. (a)	**12.** (c)	**13.** (a)	**14.** (b)	**15.** (c)	**16.** (d)	**17.** (d)	**18.** (b)	**19.** (b)	**20.** (c)
21. (d)	**22.** (b)	**23.** (b)	**24.** (d)	**25.** (c)	**26.** (b)	**27.** (c)	**28.** (b)	**29.** (d)	**30.** (b)
31. (a)	**32.** (b)	**33.** (c)	**34.** (b)	**35.** (d)	**36.** (c)	**37.** (c)	**38.** (b)	**39.** (b)	**40.** (a)
41. (c)	**42.** (a)	**43.** (c)	**44.** (a)	**45.** (a)	**46.** (d)	**47.** (d)	**48.** (c)	**49.** (d)	**50.** (c)

Explanations

1. (c) To fight the British, leadership and organization were required

2. (a) • Harisena, also called Harishena or Hirisena, was a 4th-century Sanskrit poet, panegyrist, and government minister.
   • He was an important figure in the court of Gupta emperor, Samudragupta. His most famous poem, written c. 345 C.E., describes the bravery of Samudragupta and is inscribed on the Allahabad Pillar.

3. (d) Endogamy is the practice of marrying within a specific social group, religious denomination, caste, or ethnic group

4. (b) Adimai slaves are mentioned in early Tamil Sangam literature. Even today, the word 'adimai' implies slave, and the plural for slaves is 'adimaigal'.

5. (c)

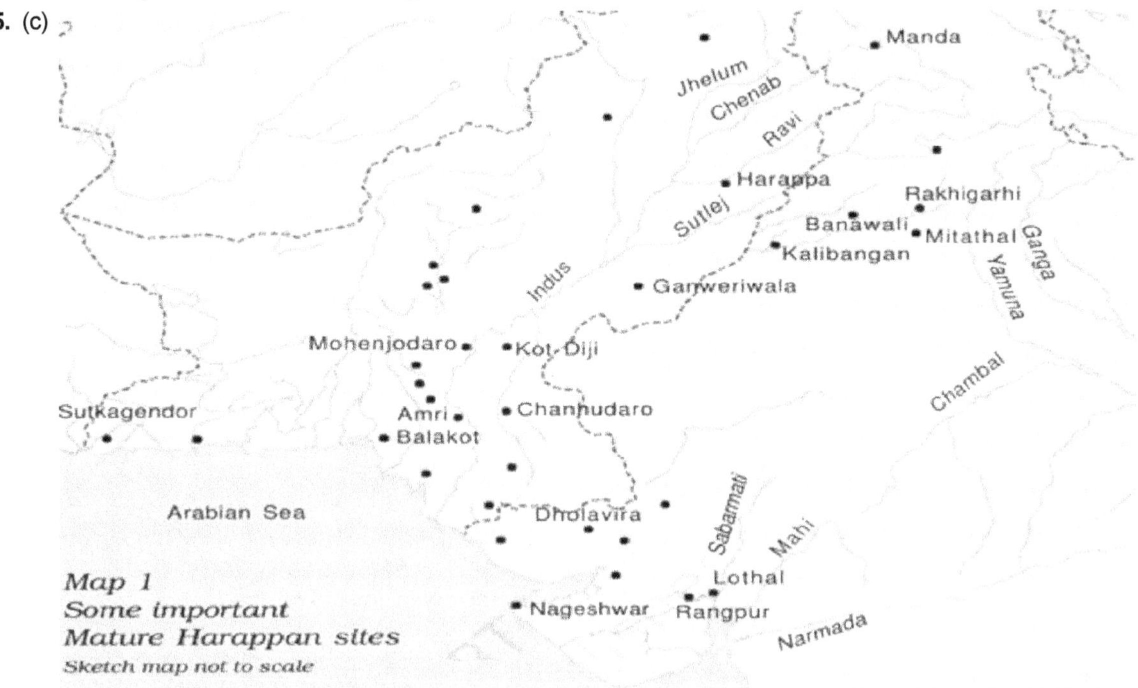

6. (b) • Water reservoirs found in Dholavira (Gujarat)
   • Traces of canals have been found at the Harappan site of Shortughai in Afghanistan

7. (b) Elaborate sacrifices

8. (b) Many ideas found in the Upanishads (c. sixth century BCE onwards) show that people were curious about the meaning of life, the possibility of life after death and rebirth.

9. (a) Ibn Battuta described Delhi as a vast city, with a great population, the largest in India. Daulatabad (in Maharashtra) was no less, and easily rivalled Delhi in size.

10. (d) Virupaksha was their family God. The kings claimed to rule on behalf of the God Virupaksha.

11. (a) • Kanyadana - gift of a daughter in marriage
    • Stridhana - Woman's wealth
    • Gotra - named after a vedic seer
    • Manusmriti - Dharamasutra and Dharamashastra

12. (c) According to Mahatma Gandhi Hindustani would be the ideal language of communication between dieverse communities.

13. (a)

1945	
26 July	Labour Government comes into power in Britain
December-January	General Elections in India
1946	
16 May	Cabinet Mission announces its constitutional scheme
16 June	Muslim League accepts Cabinet Mission's constitutional scheme
16 June	Cabinet Mission presents scheme for the formation of an Interim Government at the Centre
16 August	Muslim League announces Direct Action Day
2 September	Congress forms Interim Government with Nehru as the Vice-President
13 October	Muslim League decides to join the Interim Government
3-6 December	British Prime Minister, Attlee, meets some Indian leaders; talks fail
9 December	Constituent Assembly begins its sessions

14. (b) • Justice C.N. Broomfield presided over the trial of Gandhiji
- The socialist activist Kamaladevi Chattopadhyay had persuaded Gandhiji not to restrict the protests to men alone.

15. (c) Quit India Movement
Royal Indian Navy Rising
The great Calcutta Killings of August 1946
Independence day of India

16. (d) When the British left India, the constitutional status of these princes remained ambiguous.

17. (d) In Bengal, on the other hand, five acres was the upper limit of an average peasant farm ; 10 acres would make one a rich *asami*.

18. (b) In 1526, the Mughal forces of Babur, the Timurid ruler of Kabulistan, defeated the much larger ruling army of Ibrahim Lodi, Sultan of Delhi.

19. (b) The first dynasty, known as the Sangama dynasty, exercised control till 1485. They were supplanted by the Saluvas, military commanders, who remained in power till 1503 when they were replaced by the Tuluvas. Krishnadeva Raya belonged to the Tuluva dynasty.

20. (c) The enormous arched gateway (Buland Darwaza) was meant to remind visitors of the Mughal victory in Gujarat.

21. (d) In 1565 Rama Raya, the chief minister of Vijayanagara, led the army into battle at Rakshasi-Tangadi (also known as Talikota), where his forces were routed by the combined armies of Bijapur, Ahmadnagar and Golconda.

22. (b) The Safavid kings of Iran

23. (b) • Slave eunuchs (khwajasara) moved between the external and internal life of the household as guards, servants, and also as agents for women dabbling in commerce.
- The concubines (*aghacha* or *the lesser agha*) occupied the lowest position in the hierarchy of females intimately related to royalty.
- A courtier never approached the emperor empty handed: he offered either a small sum of money (*nazr*) or a large amount (*peshkash*).
- Jewelled ornaments were often given as gifts by the emperor. The lotus blossom set with jewels (*padma murassa*) was given only in exceptional circumstances.

24. (d) Buland Darwaza

25. (c) • Nana Sahib - Kanpur
- Bahadur Shah Zafar - Delhi
- Rani Lakshmi Bai - Jhansi
- Nawab wajid Ali Shah - Awadh

26. (b) Kanpur

27. (c) Champaran

28. (b)

29. (d) 1540-55 - Humayun defeated by Sher Shah, in exile at the Safavid court

30. (b) Not to undermine the authority of state

31. (a) • The British established laws to abolish customs like sati (1829) and to permit the remarriage of Hindu widows.
- 1857 - Mutiny starts in Meerut

32. (b) Mahatma Gandhi used to publish the letters written to him in his journal Harijan.

33. (c) It entailed denial, renunciation, and self-discipline.

34. (b) Allama Muhammad Iqbal

35. (d) S. N Mukherjee was the chief draftsman of the Constitution in the Constituent Assembly.

36. (c)

37. (c) Granting of the vote to every adult citizen

38. (b)

39. (b) The members of the Constituent Assembly were not elected on the basis of universal franchise.

40. (a) Gopal Krishna Gokhale

41. (c)   **42.** (a)

43. (c)   **44.** (a)

45. (a)   **46.** (d)

47. (d)   **48.** (c)

49. (d)   **50.** (c)

POLITICAL SCIENCE

1. Match **List - I** with **List - II**.

List - I (Leaders)		List - II (Country)
A.	Josip Broz Tito	I. India
B.	Gamal Abdel Nasser	II. Ghana
C.	Jawahar Lal Nehru	III. Yugoslavia
D.	Kwame Nkrumah	IV. Egypt

   Choose the **correct answer** from the options given below:
   (a) A-II, B-III, C-I, D-IV
   (b) A-III, B-IV, C-I, D-II
   (c) A-IV, B-III, C-I, D-II
   (d) A-III, B-II, C-I, D-IV

2. During Cold War Era, the Western alliance formed an organization :
   (a) North Atlantic Treaty Organization (NATO)
   (b) Warsaw Pact
   (c) New International Economic Oder (NIEO)
   (d) Non Alignment Movement (NAM)

3. Which of the following are correct about Arms Control treaties ?
   A. Limited Test Ban Treaty (LTBT) signed by the U.S., U.K. and USSR
   B. Strategic Arms Limitation Tasks (SALT-1) came into force in 1972
   C. Nuclear non-Proliferation Treaty (NPT) came into force on 5th March 1972
   D. Strategic Arms Reduction Treaty I (START-1) was signed by USSR President Mikhail Gorbachev and the US President Jimmy Carter.
   E. Treaty on the Limitation of Anti-Ballitle Missile system (ABM Treaty) was signed in 1972

   Choose **the most appropriate** answer from the options given below:
   (a) A, B, C, D, E only
   (b) B, C, D, E only
   (c) A, B, E only
   (d) B, C, D only

4. Which of the following is **not** a consequence of the disintegration of the USSR?
   (a) End of Bipolarity
   (b) Emergence of Unipolar World
   (c) Emergence of Commonwealth of Independent States
   (d) Emergence of the United Nations

5. The model of transition by 'Shock Therapy' was influenced by :
   (a) UNESCO & UNICEF
   (b) World Bank & WTO
   (c) IMF & World Bank
   (d) UNDP & UNEP

6. The First Gulf War was also known by the name:
   (a) Operation Desert Storm
   (b) Global War on Terror
   (c) Computer War
   (d) Hot War

7. The Global War Against Terror was declared by which US President?
   (a) George H.W. Bush
   (b) Bill Clinton
   (c) Boris Yeltsin
   (d) George W. Bush

8. Choose from the following the causes of the rise of the Chinese Economy:
   A. Four Modernisations
   B. Open Door Policy
   C. Special Economic Zones
   D. Adoption of the policy of political and economic isolation
   E. Privatisation of agriculture

   Choose the **most appropriate** answer from die options given below :
   (a) A, B, C, E only
   (b) A, B, C, D only
   (c) B, C, D, E only
   (d) A, C, D, E only

9. Which incident favoured fast track establishment of the European Union?
   (a) Emergence of NATO
   (b) Establishment of Warsaw Pact
   (c) Disintegration of Soviet Union
   (d) Emergence of NAM

10. Which country adopted "Open Door Policy" for its economic development?
    (a) India
    (b) Sri Lanka
    (c) Japan
    (d) China

11. The Principle of 'Common but differentiated responsibilities' is associated with:

(a) Kyoto Protocol, 1997

(b) India's Energy Conservation Act, 2001

(c) Montreal Protocol, 1987

(d) Rio Declaration at the Earth Summit 1992

12. The Indigenous populations is defined as comprising the descendants of peoples who inhabited the present territory of a country at the time when persons of a different culture or ethnic origin arrived there from other parts of the world and overcame them. This definition is given by:

(a) The Indian Constitution

(b) The WHO

(c) The IMF

(d) The UN

13. Match **List - I** with **List - II**.

List - I	**List - II**
(The Political Parties)	**(The country to which they belong)**
A. The MDP	I. Nepal
B. The PPP	II. Bangladesh
C. The Awami League	III. Pakistan
D. The SPA	IV. The Maldives

Choose the **correct answer** from the options given below:

(a) A-IV, B-III, C-II, D-I   (b) A-I, B-II, C-III, D-IV

(c) A-II, B-I, C-IV, D-III   (d) A-III, B-IV, C-I, D-II

14. Match **List - I** with **List - II**.

List - I (Event)	**List - II (Year)**
A. SAARC Charter	I. 1996
B. Farakka Treaty	II. 1966
C. Shimla Agreement	III. 1985
D. Tashkent Agreement	IV. 1972

Choose the **correct answer** from the options given below

(a) A-IV, B-II, C-III, D-I

(b) A-II, B-III, C-I, D-IV

(c) A-III, B-I, C-IV, D-II

(d) A-I, B-IV, C-II, D-III

15. How many judges are there in the International Court of Justice (ICJ) and what is their tenure?

(a) 15 Judges with 5 years tenure

(b) 15 Judges with 9 years tenure

(c) 15 Judges with 6 years tenure

(d) 9 Judges with 15 years tenure

16. Name the UN Secretary General who initiated an enquiry into UN reforms in 1997?

(a) Ban ki Moon

(b) Kofi Annan

(c) Antonio Guetteres

(d) Dag Hammerskjold

17. Identify the non-governmental organisations out of the following:

(a) The UN

(b) The Red Cross

(c) The World Health Organisation

(d) The World Bank

18. Match **List - I** with **List - II**.

List - I (Concept)	**List - II (Definition)**
A. Security	I. Political Violence which deliberately targets civilians
B. Terrorism	II. Protection of People
C. Migration	III. Freedom from threats
D. Human Security	IV. Voluntarily leaving one's own country for better opportunities

Choose the **correct answer** from the options given below:

(a) A-III, B-II, C-IV, D-I

(b) A-III, B-I, C-IV, D-II

(c) A-III, B-IV, C-II, D-I

(d) A-II, B-III, C-I, D-IV

19. Arrange the following agreements on Environment in chronological order.

A. Antarctic Environmental Protocol

B. Antarctic Treaty

C. Earth Summit

D. Montreal Protocol

E. Kyoto Protocol

Choose the **most appropriate** answer from the options given below:

(a) B, D, A, C, E

(b) B, A, C, D, E

(c) B, D, A, E, C

(d) D, A, E, C, B

20. Identify the statement **not** correct about globalisation.

(a) It is a multi-dimensional phenomenon

(b) It has both negative and positive consequences

(c) It leads to cultural homogenization

(d) It is purely an economic phenomenon

21. Globalisation need not always be positive, it can have negative consequences for the people. Identify the statements true about Globalisation :

A. Globalisation fundamentally deals with flows of ideas, capital, commodities and people

B. It has emerged merely because of the availability of improved communications

C. Globalisation results in worldwide interconnectedness

D. It is a multidimensional concept

E. Globalisation does not reduce state capacity

Choose the **most appropriate** answer from the options given below :

(a) A and E only

(b) A, C, D only

(c) C and D only

(d) B and E only

22. Which Soviet leader is held responsible for the Great Terror of the 1930s and elimination of rivals within the party ?

(a) Mikhail Bakunin

(b) Mikhail Gorbachev

(c) Leonid Brezhnev

(d) Joseph Stalin

23. Tha National Coordination Committee for Railwayman's struggle in 1974 has led by :

(a) George Fernandas

(b) Jai Prakash Narayan

(c) Morarji Desai

(d) Jagjivan Ram

24. Identify the Minister and the his/her Portfolio under Jawaharlal Nehru's first Cabinet of Free India.

Match List -1 with List - II.

List - I (Minister)		List - II (Portfolio)
A. Rajkumari Amrit Kaur	I.	Minister of Communication
B. Maulana Azad	II.	Deputy Prime Minister
C. Sardar Vallabhbhai Patel	III.	Health Minister
D. Rafi Ahmed Kidwai	IV.	Education Minister

Choose the **correct answer** from the options given below :

(a) A-II, B-I, C-IV, D-III

(b) A-III, B-IV, C-II, D-I

(c) A-IV, B-III, C-I, D-II

(d) A-I, B-III, C-II, D-IV

25. Match List - I with List - II.

List – I		List - II
(State)		(Carved out from)
A. Haryana	I.	Bombay State
B. Gujarat	II.	Andhra Pradesh
C. Meghalaya	III.	Punjab
D. Telengana	IV.	Assam

Choose the **correct answer** from the options given below :

(a) A-II, B-I, C-IV, D-III   (b) A-I, B-II, C-III, D-IV

(c) A-IV, B-III, C-I, D-II   (d) A-III, B-I, C-IV, D-II

26. Identify the Leader :

A. He was the first Deputy Prime Minister of India

B. He was the first Home Minister of India

C. He played an important role in National Integration

D. He was the member of committee on fundamental rights in constitutional assembly

Choose the **most appropriate** answer from the options given below :

(a) Jai Prakash Narayan

(b) Morarji Desai

(c) Sardar Vallabhbhai patel

(d) K. Kamaraj

27. NITI Aayog was constituted in place of :

(a) Central Vigilance Commission

(b) Regulatory Authority

(c) Development Commission

(d) Planning Commission

28. The First Summit of the NAM was held in September 1961 in :

(a) Bandung (Indonesia)

(b) Cairo (Egypt)

(c) Accra (Ghana)

(d) Belgrade (Yugoslavia)

29. Match List - I with List - II.

List - I		List - II
(Leaders)		(Their Description)
A. Zulfikar Ali Bhutto	I.	He made secret visit to china via Pakistan
B. General Ayub Khan	II.	Leader of the Awami League
C. Sheikh Mujibur Rahman	III.	He signed the Tashkent Agreement
D. Henry Kissinger	IV.	He signed Shimla Agreement

Choose the **correct answer** from the options given below :

(a) A-IV, B-III, C-II, D-I

(b) A-I, B-II, C-III, D-IV

(c) A-II, B-I, C-IV, D-III

(d) A-III, B-II, C-I, D-IV

30. Which Article of the Indian Constitution directs the state to promote international peace and security ?

(a) Article 32

(b) Article 51

(c) Article 352

(d) Article 21

31. Jai Prakash Narayan was the moving force behind the formation of Janata Party. Following are the points related to Jai Prakash Narayan. Which of the following statements is **not** correct about Jai Prakash Narayan :

(a) Surrender of dacoits in Chambal

(b) Leader of Bihar Movement

(c) Negotiations with Mizo Rebels

(d) Bhoodan Movement

32. Which one of the following is incorrect about Raj Kumari Amrit Kaur ?

(a) She was a Gandhian and freedom fighter

(b) She belonged to a royal family of Kapurthala

(c) She was die member of Constituent Assembly

(d) Minister for Education in independent India's first ministry

33. Match List - I with List - II.

List - I (Leader)	List - II (Associated with)
A. Indira Gandhi	I. OBC reservations
B. Narendra Dev	II. Congress Socialist Party
C. B.R. Ambedkar	III. Drafting of Constitution
D. B.P. Mandal	IV. Garibi Hatao

Choose the **correct** answer from the options given below :

(a) A-IV, B-II, C-III, D-I

(b) A-I, B-III, C-II, D-I

(c) A-I, B-II, C-III, D-IV

(d) A-II, B-IV, C-I, D-III

34. Morarji Desai was a prominent leader of which party.

(a) Congress (O)

(b) Communist Party of India (Marxist)

(c) Communist Party of India (Marxist - Leninist)

(d) Congress

35. In 1947, Jammu and Kashmir was ruled by a Hindu ruler named :

(a) Sawai Jai Singh

(b) Raja Pratap Singh

(c) Raja Ajit Singh

(d) Hari Singh

36. These amendments introduced women reservations in local level political offices :

(a) 42nd and 44th Amendments

(b) 72nd and 76th Amendments

(c) 73th and 74th Amendments

(d) 78th and 79th Amendments

37. The Bahujan Samaj Party emerged in 1984 under the leadership of :

(a) H.D. Deve Gowda

(b) Chandra Shekhar

(c) Kanshi Ram

(d) B.P. Mandal

38. After the fall of the Janta Party, the supporters of Jana Sangh formed the Bhartiya Janata Party (BJP) in:

(a) 1979   (b) 1980

(c) 1982   (d) 1981

39. The Recommendations of Mandal Commission were implemented by which of the following :

(a) United Front Government

(b) National Front Government

(c) National Democratic Alliance Government

(d) United Progressive Alliance Government

40. Which Lok Sabha elections in India were held in 2004 ?

(a) 10th Lok Sabha

(b) 14th Lok Sabha

(c) 15th Lok Sabha

(d) 16th Lok Sabha

Directions for Quesitons 41 to 45:

Please read the passage and answer the questions that follows.

Shastri was the country's Prime Minister from 1964 to 1966. During Shastri's brief Prime Minister ship, the country faced two major challenges. India was still recovering from the economic implications of the war with China, failed monsoons, drought and serious food crisis presented grave challenges. Besides the country also faced a war with Pakistan in 1965. Shastri's famous slogan 'Jai Jawan Jai Kisan symbolised the country's resolve to face both these challenges.

41. The country's Prime Minister from the period of 1964 to 1966 was :

- (a) Morarji Desai
- (b) Lal Bahadur Shastri
- (c) Jawaharlal Nehru
- (d) Indira Gandhi

42. The country faced grave challenges like :

- (a) War, Drought
- (b) Unemployment, Population
- (c) Poverty, Violence
- (d) Health Epidemic

43. Tire famous slogan 'Jai Jawan Jai Kisan' was given by :

- (a) Jag Jivan Ram
- (b) Ram Manohar Lohia
- (c) Jawaharlal Nehru
- (d) Lal Bahadur Shastri

44. India and Pakistan had a conflict which resulted in war in which year ?

- (a) 1966
- (b) 1965
- (c) 1970
- (d) 1975

45. An agreement was signed between Lal Bahadur Shastri and Mohd. Ayub Khan named as :

- (a) Instrument of Accession
- (b) Shimla Agreement
- (c) Tashkent Agreement
- (d) Merger Agreement

Directions for Quesitons 46 to 50:

Please read the passage and answer the questions that follows.

The cultural effect of globalisation leads to the fear that this process poses a threat to cultures in the world. It does so, because globalisation leads to the rise of a uniform culture or what is called cultural homogenisation. The rise of a uniform culture is not tire emergence of a global culture. What we have in the name of a global culture is the imposition of western culture on the rest of the world. The culture of the politically and economically dominant society leaves its imprint on a less powerful society, and the world begins to look more like the dominant power wishes it to be. Those who make this argument often draw attention to the 'Mc Donaldisation' of the world, with cultures seeking to buy into the dominant American dream. This is dangerous for the whole of humanity, for it leads to the shrinking of the rich cultural heritage of the entire globe.

While cultural homogenisation is an aspect of globalisation, the same process also generates precisely the opposite effect. It leads to each culture becoming more different and distinctive. This phenomenon is called cultural heterogenisation.

46. Imposition of Western Culture on the rest of the world happens in the name of :

- (a) Cultural heterogenisation
- (b) Uniform culture
- (c) Global culture
- (d) Common culture

47. Cultural heterogenisation is about :

- A. a uniform culture in tire world
- B. 'Mc Donaldisation' of the world
- C. Each culture becoming more distinctive
- D. Importance of culture of economically dominant society
- E. Each culture becoming more different

Choose the **correct** answer from the options given below :

- (a) C and E only
- (b) A, C, E only
- (c) A, D and E only
- (d) B, C and E only

48. Globalisation poses a threat to culture in the world because :

- (a) It leads to rise of a Uniform culture
- (b) It leads to cultural heterogenisation
- (c) It leads to multipolar world
- (d) It concentrates decision making power in global South countries

49. 'Mc Donaldisation' of the world refers to :

- (a) Politically dominant society
- (b) Rich cultural heritage of the entire globe
- (c) Cultural heterogenisation
- (d) Influence of dominant American Dream

50. The culture of the politically and economically dominant society leaves its imprint on a less powerful society in the form of :

- A. Cultural dominance
- B. Shrinking of the rich cultural heritage of the entire globe
- C. International exposure to the cultures of the developing nations
- D. Cultural homogenisation
- E. More political space for die global South

Choose the **correct** answer from the options given below :

- (a) A, B, C and D only
- (b) A, B and C only
- (c) B, C and D only
- (d) A, B, D and E only

Answer Keys

1. (b)	**2.** (a)	**3.** (c)	**4.** (d)	**5.** (c)	**6.** (a)	**7.** (d)	**8.** (a)	**9.** (c)	**10.** (d)
11. (a)	**12.** (d)	**13.** (a)	**14.** (c)	**15.** (b)	**16.** (b)	**17.** (b)	**18.** (b)	**19.** (c)	**20.** (d)
21. (b)	**22.** (d)	**23.** (a)	**24.** (b)	**25.** (d)	**26.** (c)	**27.** (d)	**28.** (d)	**29.** (a)	**30.** (b)
31. (c)	**32.** (d)	**33.** (a)	**34.** (a)	**35.** (d)	**36.** (c)	**37.** (c)	**38.** (b)	**39.** (b)	**40.** (b)
41. (b)	**42.** (a)	**43.** (d)	**44.** (b)	**45.** (c)	**46.** (b)	**47.** (a)	**48.** (a)	**49.** (d)	**50.** (c)

Explanations

1. (b) The founders of the Non-Aligned Movement (NAM) were Jawaharlal Nehru of India, Kwame Nkrumah of Ghana, Nasser of Egypt, Sukarno of Indonesia and Tito of Yugoslavia.

2. (a) The western alliance was formalised into an organisation, the North Atlantic Treaty Organisation (NATO), which came into existence in April 1949.

3. (c) NUCLEAR NON-PROLIFERATION TREATY (NPT) Allows only the nuclear weapon states to have nuclear weapons and stops others from aquiring them. For the purposes of the NPT, a nuclear weapon state is one which has manufactured and exploded a nuclear weapon or other nuclear explosive device prior to 1 January 1967. So there are five nuclear weapon states: US, USSR (later Russia), Britain, France and China. Signed in Washington, London, and Moscow on 1 July 1968. Entered into force on 5 March 1970. Extended indefinitely in 1995.

4. (d) First of all, it meant the end of Cold War confrontations. The ideological dispute over whether the socialist system would beat the capitalist system was not an issue any more.

5. (c) Shock therapy influenced by World bank and IMF

6. (a) The first gulf war are also known as Operation desert storm

7. (d) US presidency by George W. Bush of the Republican Party, son of the earlier President George H. W. Bush. Unlike Clinton, Bush had a much harder view of US interests and of the means by which to advance them. As a part of its 'Global War on Terror', the US launched 'Operation Enduring Freedom'

8. (a) China followed its own path in introducing a market economy. The Chinese did not go for 'shock therapy' but opened their economy step by step. The privatisation of agriculture in 1982 was followed by the privatisation of industry in 1998. Trade barriers were eliminated only in Special Economic Zones (SEZs) where foreign investors could set up enterprises

9. (c) The collapse of the Soviet bloc put Europe on a fast track and resulted in the establishment of the European Union in 1992.

10. (d) China started 'open door policy'.

11. (a) CBDR are associated with Kyoto protocol, 1997.

12. (d) The UN defines indigenous populations as comprising the descendants of peoples who inhabited the present territory of a country at the time when persons of a different culture or ethnic origin arrived there from other parts of the world and overcame them.

13. (a) In June 2005, the parliament of the Maldives voted unanimously to introduce a multiparty system. The Maldivian Democratic Party (MDP) dominates the political affairs of the island. The MDP won the 2018 Elections

14. (c) 1996 December: India and Bangladesh sign the Farakka Treaty for sharing of the Ganga Waters.

15. (b) International Court of Justice:

Fifteen judges elected for nine years by absolute majority in both the General Assembly and the Security Council. Based in The Hague.

16. (b) On 1 January 1997, the UN Secretary-General Kofi Annan initiated an inquiry into how theUN should be reformed.

17. (b) Red cross is an Non – governmental organization

18. (b) Terrorism refers to political violence that targets civilians deliberately and indiscriminately .

19. (c) There have been many path-breaking agreements such as the 1959 Antarctic Treaty, the 1987 Montreal Protocol, and the 1991 Antarctic Environmental Protocol.

20. (d) It is wrong to assume that globalisation has purely economic dimensions, just as it would also be mistaken to assume that it is a purely cultural phenomenon.

21. (b) At the most simple level, globalisation results in an erosion of state capacity, that is, the ability of government to do what they do.

22. (d) Joseph Stalin (1879-1953) Successor to Lenin and led the Soviet Union during its consolidation (1924-53); began rapid industrialisation and forcible collectivisation of agriculture; credited with Soviet victory in the Second World War; held responsible for the Great Terror of the 1930s, authoritarian functioning and elimination of rivals within the party.

23. (a) The National Coordination committee of railwayman was led by George Fernades

24. (b) Rajkumariamritkaur was first health minister of India under Nehru cabinet

25. (d) The social composition of the State changed first with Partition and later on after the carving out of Haryana and Himachal Pradesh.

26. (c) SardarVallabhbhai Patel (1875-1950): Leader of the freedom movement; Congress leader; follower of Mahatma Gandhi; Deputy Prime Minister and first Home Minister of independent India; played an important role in the integration of Princely States with India; member of important committees of the Constituent Assembly on Fundamental Rights, Minorities, Provincial Constitution, etc

27. (d) NITI Aayog was created in the place of Planning commission

28. (d) The First summit of NAM was held in Belgrade in September 1961.

29. (a) The correct answer is Indira Gandhi and Zulfikar Ali Bhutto. On the day of 02 July 1972, Shimla Agreement was signed between Indira Gandhi and Zulfiqar Ali Bhutto at Shimla of Himachal Pradesh

30. (b) Article 51 of the constitution talks about International peace and security

31. (c) LoknayakJayaprakash Narayan negotiations with the naga rebels

32. (d) She was Health minister

33. (a) Indira Gandhi given the slogan garibihatao

34. (a) Morarjidesai was the prominent leader of Congress(o)

35. (d) Harisingh was ruled Jammu and Kashmir in 1947

36. (c) 73rd and 74th Constitutional amendment introduce women reservation in local bordies

37. (c) According to Kanshi Ram, when he founded the party in 1984, the Bahujans comprised 85 percent of India's population, but were divided into 6,000 different castes.

38. (b) BhartiyaJanata Party Formed in 1980.

39. (b) National front government decided to implement Mandal commission reservation of obc

40. (b) It was 14th Loksabha election

41. (b) LalBahadurshastri was PM of India from 1964 to 1966

42. (a) War and Drought was the two grave challenge in front of India

43. (d) Jai Jawan Jai Kisan slogan was given by Lalbahadurshastri

44. (b) 1965 was the year when India and Pakistan fought a war

45. (c) Tashkent Agreement was signed

46. (b) Uniform culture

47. (a) Cultural Heterogenisation is culture become more distinctive and different

48. (a) It leads to rise of uniform culture

49. (d) Influence of dominanat American dream

50. (c)

1. Who were the founder members of the NAM?
   (a) Gamal Abdel Nasser, Nikita Khrushchev, Liyakat Ali
   (b) Sukarno, Jawahar Lal Nehru, Fidel Castro
   (c) Kwame Nkrumah, Jawahar Lal Nehru, Sukarno
   (d) Marshal Tito, Indira Gandhi, Kwame Nkrumah

2. Which statement is not correct about the Security Council of UN?
   (a) There are fifteen members
   (b) The decision of the Security Council is binding on all UN members
   (c) The ten member's (non-permanent) are elected by a process of voting in the Security Council
   (d) There are five permanent members

3. United States of America dropped two atomic bombs on the Japanese cities of Hiroshima and Nagasaki in:
   (a) August 1942
   (b) August 1945
   (c) September 1942
   (d) September 1945

4. The Non-Aligned Movement is best described as the policy of:
   (a) Staying away from alliances
   (b) Neutrality
   (c) Isolationism
   (d) Fleeing away from world affair's

5. Which among the following is not an outcome of the disintegration of the USSR?
   (a) End of the ideological war between the US and the USSR
   (b) Birth of CIS
   (c) Change in the balance of power in the world order
   (d) Formation of SAARC

6. Who was the founder of the Bolshevik Communist Party?
   (a) Joseph Stalin
   (b) Nikita Khrushchev
   (c) Vladimir Lenin
   (d) Leonid Brezhnev

7. Soviet Union invaded Afghanistan under whose leadership ?
   (a) Nikita Khrushchev   (b) Leonid Brezhnev
   (c) Mikhail Gorbachev   (d) Joseph Stalin

8. Which President of the U.S.A, hailed the emergence of a 'new world order?'
   (a) Bill Clinton   (b) George H. W. Bush
   (c) George W. Bush   (d) Barak Obama

9. In the year 2003, U.S.A launched its invasion of Iraq under which of the following code name ?
   (a) Operation Enduring freedom
   (b) Operation Desert Storm
   (c) Operation Iraqi Revolution
   (d) Operation Iraqi freedom

10. The Nobel Peace Prize award for the year 2012 was given to which of the following ?
    (a) ASEAN   (b) EU
    (c) NATO   (d) WTO

11. Which of the following is not an objective of ASEAN?
    (a) Accelerate economic growth
    (b) Social progress
    (c) Cultural development
    (d) Accelerate political integration

12. In 1972, China ended its political isolation with the establishment of relations with
    (a) India   (b) United States
    (c) France   (d) Italy

13. In 1988, the visit of which Prime Minister to China proved to be an impetus for an improvement in India - China relations ?
    (a) Atal Bihari Vajpayee
    (b) Manmohan Singh
    (c) Rajiv Gandhi
    (d) P. V. Narasimha Rao

14. Arrange the following aspects of Europe's integration in the correct order of their appearance.
    A. Marshall Plan
    B. Lisbon Treaty coming into force
    C. Croatia becomes the 28th member of EU
    D. Schengen Agreement abolishing border controls amongst the EU members
    E. Referendum in Britain that initiated the process of Britain's exit from the EU

    Choose the correct answer from the options given below :
    (a) B, C, A, D and E   (b) A, D, B, C and E
    (c) C, D, A, B and E   (d) A, B, D, C and E

15. The first country in South Asian region to liberalise its economy.

(a) Nepal   (b) Sri Lanka

(c) Bhutan   (d) India

16. Identify the country of South Asia where Monarchy is still in existence.

(a) Sri Lanka   (b) Nepal

(c) Bhutan   (d) Maldives

17. The popular struggle against West Pakistani domination in 1971 was led by :

(a) Ziaur Rahman

(b) Lt. Gen. H. M. Ershad

(c) Sheikh Mujibur Rahman

(d) Sheikh Imtiyaz

18. A major regional initiative by the South Asian states to evolve cooperation began in 1985 by

(a) SAFTA   (b) SAARC

(c) NAM   (d) ASEAN

19. The Shimla Agreement between India and Pakistan was signed in which of the following year ?

(a) 1970   (b) 1971

(c) 1972   (d) 1976

20. WTO is serving as the successor to which of the following organization?

(a) World Health Organisation (WHO)

(b) General Agreement on Trade Tariffs (GATT)

(c) General Arrangement on Free and Fair Trade (GAFFT)

(d) U.N. Development Programme (UNDP)

21. Among the Permanent members of UN Security Council, which country used the maximum number of veto power from 1945-2018?

(a) USA

(b) USSR/Russia

(c) UK

(d) China

22. Arrange the following in chronological order:

A. Membership of the UN Security Council expanded from 11 to 15

B. Creation of the World Bank

C. Establishment of a Human Rights Council

D. UN Secretary General Kofi Anann initiated an inquiry into how the UN should be reformed

Choose the correct answer from the options given below:

(a) A, C, B, D   (b) D, B, A, C

(c) A, B, D, C   (d) B, A, D, C

23. As a part of Aims Control, the Anti-Ballistic Missile (ABM) Treaty was signed in 1972 between which countries ?

(a) China and United States

(b) India and China

(c) China and Soviet Union

(d) United States and Soviet Union

24. India ratified the Paris Climate Agreement in which of the following years ?

(a) 2012   (b) 2015

(c) 2016   (d) 2018

25. The term Mc Donaldisation draws attention towards the cultural dominance of which country?

(a) France   (b) Italy

(c) Russia   (d) USA

26. Choose the correct statements about Chipko movement

A. It began in Uttarakhand

B. Women actively participated in the movement

C. Forest department allotted land to liquor making industry

D. The movement achieved a victory

E. The straggle soon spread across tire world

Choose the correct answer horn the options given below:

(a) A, B, C only

(b) B, D, E only

(c) A, D, E only

(d) A, B, D only

27. From the following statements, which one is false in relation to World Social Forum.

(a) It is a global platform

(b) It opposes neo-liberal globalization

(c) It is a wide coalition including labour, youth, women activists

(d) It supports neo-liberal globalization

28. Who was India's first Health Minister?

(a) B. R. Ambedkar

(b) Rafi Ahmed Kidwai

(c) Rajkumari Amrit Kaur

(d) A. K. Gopalan

29. The Constitution of India came into effect on

(a) 26 November 1949

(b) 26 January 1950

(c) 15 August 1950

(d) 15 August 1947

30. 'Frontier Gandhi' was a title given to which of the following ?
   (a) Nathu Ram Godse
   (b) Mohd. Iqbal
   (c) Khan Abdul Gaffar Khan
   (d) Shyama Prasad Mukherjee

31. The States reorganisation Commission was appointed by the Central Government in the year
   (a) 1952　　　　(b) 1953
   (c) 1955　　　　(d) 1956

32. Meghalaya was carved out of Assam in the year
   (a) 1970　　　　(b) 1972
   (c) 1969　　　　(d) 1975

33. Name the person who is nicknamed as "Milkman of India."
   (a) Sundarlal Bahuguna
   (b) Choudhary Charan Singh
   (c) Verghese Kurien
   (d) J. C. Cornelius

34. India conducted its first nuclear test in the year
   (a) 1950　　　　(b) 1964
   (c) 1974　　　　(d) 1998

35. Indus Water Treaty of 1960 was signed between which of the following ?
   (a) India and Bangladesh
   (b) India and Afghanistan
   (c) India and Nepal
   (d) India and Pakistan

36. The Tashkent Agreement of 1966 between India and Pakistan was mediated by which country ?
   (a) United States
   (b) Soviet Union
   (c) China
   (d) France

37. The Panchsheel Agreement was signed between which countries ?
   (a) India and Pakistan
   (b) India and China
   (c) India and Nepal
   (d) India and Sri Lanka

38. Wliat was the 'Kamraj Plan' ?
   (a) Social Control of Banks
   (b) Senior congressman to resign from office to make way for younger party worker's
   (c) Nationalization of General Insurance
   (d) Ceiling on urban property and income

39. In order to enquire into the allegations of abuse of power during emergency period, the Janata Party Government appointed a commission under which of the following ?
   (a) Justice Jagmohan Lal Sinha
   (b) Justice A. N. Ray
   (c) Justice J. C. Shah
   (d) Justice H. J. Kania

40. From the following list of events, which of the following is not related to J. P. Narayan?
   (a) Delhi March, 1975
   (b) Tota1 Revolution
   (c) Bihar Movement
   (d) Cliipko Movement

Directions for Quesitons 41 to 45:

Please read the passage and answer the questions that follows.

The Soviet system, however, became very bureaucratic and authoritarian, making life very difficult for its citizens. Lack of democracy and absence of freedom of speech stifled people who often expressed their dissent in jokes and cartoons. Most of the institutions of the Soviet state needed reform: the one-party system represented by the Communist Party of Soviet Union had tight control over all institutions and was unaccountable to the people. The party refused to recognize the urge of people in the fifteen different republics that formed the Soviet Union to manage their own affairs including their cultural affairs. Although, on paper, Russia was only one of the fifteen republics that altogether constituted the USSR, in reality Russia dominated everything and people from other regions felt neglected and often suppressed.

41. How did the people of the Soviet Union express their dissent?
   (a) By organizing big rallies
   (b) By writing articles against government
   (c) By organizing stage shows
   (d) By making jokes and cartoons

42. How many republics were there in USSR?
   (a) 15
   (b) 12
   (c) 3
   (d) 10

43. Which of the following is not a reason for the disintegration of Soviet Union?
   (a) Bureaucratic and authoritarian system
   (b) Lack of democracy and freedom
   (c) Russian dominance river Soviet Union
   (d) Capitalist policies followed by the state

44. Which statement is not correct about the Communist Party of the Soviet Union?

(a) It had tight control over all institutions

(b) It was accountable to people

(c) It refused to recognize the urge of the people in the fifteen republics

(d) It was a representation of the one party system

45. Which statement is not correct about the republics of USSR?

(a) There were fifteen republics

(b) Russian people felt neglected by other republics

(c) The Union of all the republics was called the USSR

(d) Russia was the most dominant republic

Directions for Quesitons 46 to 50:

Please read the passage and answer the questions that follows.

The China war dented India's image at home and abroad. India had to approach the Americans and the British for military assistance to tide over the crisis. The Soviet Union remained neutral during the conflict. It induced a sense of national humiliation and at the same time strengthened a spirit of nationalism. Some of the top army commanders either resigned or were retired. Nehru's close associate and the then Defence Minister V. Krishna Menon had to leave the cabinet. Nehru's own stature suffered as he was severely criticized for his naive assessment of the Chinese intentions and the lack of military preparedness. For the first time, a no-confidence motion against his government was moved and debated in the Lok Sabha. Soon thereafter, the Congress lost some key by-elections to Lok Sabha. The political mood for the country had begun to change.

The Sino-Indian conflict affected the opposition as well. This and the growing rift between China and the Soviet Union created irreconcilable difference within the Communist Party of India (CPI). The pro-USSR faction remained within the CPI and moved towards closer ties with the Congress. The other faction was for sometime closer to China and was against any ties with the Congress. The party split in 1964 and the leaders of the latter faction formed the Communist Party of India (Marxist) (CPI-M). In the wake of the China war many leaders from those that became CPI (M) were arrested for being pro-China.

46. What was the context of the passage?

(a) Soviet-Indian Conflict

(b) Sino-Indian Conflict

(c) Sino-Soviet Conflict

(d) American-British Conflict

47. During the Sino-China conflict, what was the response of Soviet Union towards India ?

(a) Supported

(b) Neutral

(c) Opposed

(d) Openly participated in the conflict against India

48. During the conflict who was the Defence Minister of India?

(a) A. K. Gopalan

(b) Jawaharlal Nehru

(c) V. Krishna Menon

(d) Sardar Vallabh Bhai Patel

49. During the conflict which of the following countries did India approach for military assistance ?

(a) USA and Soviet Union

(b) USA and Britain

(c) Soviet Union and China

(d) China and USA

50. The Communist Party of India (CPI) had split in the year 1964 in the wake of which of the following ?

(a) Pakistan war

(b) China war

(c) Bangladesh war

(d) Kargil war

Answer Keys

1. (c)	**2.** (c)	**3.** (b)	**4.** (a)	**5.** (d)	**6.** (c)	**7.** (b)	**8.** (b)	**9.** (d)	**10.** (b)
11. (d)	**12.** (b)	**13.** (c)	**14.** (b)	**15.** (b)	**16.** (c)	**17.** (c)	**18.** (b)	**19.** (c)	**20.** (b)
21. (b)	**22.** (d)	**23.** (d)	**24.** (c)	**25.** (d)	**26.** (d)	**27.** (d)	**28.** (c)	**29.** (b)	**30.** (c)
31. (b)	**32.** (b)	**33.** (c)	**34.** (c)	**35.** (d)	**36.** (b)	**37.** (b)	**38.** (b)	**39.** (c)	**40.** (d)
41. (d)	**42.** (a)	**43.** (d)	**44.** (b)	**45.** (b)	**46.** (b)	**47.** (b)	**48.** (c)	**49.** (b)	**50.** (b)

Explanations

1. (c) The group was started in Belgrade in 1961. It was created by Yugoslavia's President, Josip Broz Tito, India's first Prime Minister, Jawaharlal Nehru, Egypt's second President, Gamal Abdel Nasser, Ghana's first president Kwame Nkrumah, and Indonesia's first President, Sukarno.

2. (c) The non-permanent members are elected in a manner so that they represent all continents of the world.

3. (b) The world war ended when the United States dropped two atomic bombs on the Japanese cities of Hiroshima and Nagasaki in August 1945, causing Japan to surrender

4. (a) NAM is a policy for staying away from Alliances

5. (d) Formation of SAARC was not an outcome of disintegration of soviet union.

6. (c) Vladimir Lenin (1870-1924) Founder of the Bolshevik Communist party; leader of the Russian Revolution of 1917 and the founder-head of the USSR during the most difficult period following the revolution (1917-1924);

7. (b) Leonid Brezhnev (1906-82) Leader of the Soviet Union (1964- 82); proposed Asian Collective Security system; associated with the détente phase in relations with the US; involved in suppressing a popular rebellion in Czechoslovakia and in invading Afghanistan

8. (b) The US President George H.W. Bush hailed the emergence of a 'new world order'.

9. (d) Operation Iraqi freedom

10. (b) 2012 : The EU is awarded the Nobel Peace Prize.

11. (d) The objectives of ASEAN were primarily to accelerate economic growth and through that 'social progress and cultural development'.

12. (b) The Chinese leadership took major policy decisions in the 1970s. China ended its political and economic isolation with the establishment of relations with the United States in 1972.

13. (c) Rajiv Gandhi's visit to China in December 1988 provided the impetus for an improvement in India–China relations.

14. (b) 2009 December: The Lisbon Treaty came into force.

15. (b) Sri Lanka was one of the first developing countries to successfully control the rate of growth of population, the first country in the region to liberalise the economy, and it has had the highest per capita gross domestic product (GDP) for many years right through the civil war

16. (c) Bhutan became a constitutional monarchy in 2008.

17. (c) Sheikh Mujiburrehman

18. (b) SAARC was formed in 1985

19. (c) Shimla agreement was signed in 1972

20. (b) WTO is successor of General Agreement on Trade and Tarrifs

21. (b) USSR/Russia used the maximum number of veto power from 1945-2018

22. (d) The Human Rights Council in 2005; awarded the 2001 Nobel Peace Prize

23. (d) United states and soviet union signed Anti-Ballistic missile treaty.

24. (c) India ratified the Paris Climate Agreement on 2 October 2016.

25. (d) Cultural dominance of US

26. (d) Chipko movement was started in Uttrakhand and only spread in the state.

27. (d) The World Social Forum (WSF) is another global platform, which brings together a wide coalition composed of human rights activists, environmentalists, labour, youth and women activists opposed to neo-liberal globalisation. The first WSF meeting was organised in Porto Alegre, Brazil in 2001. The fourth WSF meeting was held in Mumbai in 2004. The latest WSF meeting was held in Brazil in March 2018.

28. (c) Rajkumari Amrit kaur was first Health minister

29. (b) 26th January 1950 Constitution of India came into force

30. (c) Khan Abdul gaffar khan was also known as frontier Gandhi

31. (b) These struggles forced the Central Government into appointing a States Reorganisation Commission in 1953 to look into the question of redrawing of the boundaries of states.

32. (b) Meghalaya was carved out of Assam in 1972.

33. (c) Verghese Kurien was known as Milk man of India

34. (c) India conducted first nuclear test in 1974

35. (d) Indus water treaty was signed between India and Pakistan

36. (b) Tashkent agreement 1966 mediated by Soviet Union

37. (b) India and China signed Panchsheel agreement
38. (b) He proposed that all senior Congress leaders should resign from their posts and devote all their energy to the re-vitalization of the Congress. In 1963 he suggested to Nehru that senior Congress leaders should leave ministerial posts to take up organisational work.
39. (c) Justice J.C shah commission was appointed
40. (d) Chipko movement was not related to J.P Narayan
41. (d) By joke and cartoons
42. (a) 15 Republics were in USSR
43. (d) Capitalist policy was not followed by Soviet Union
44. (b) Communist party of Soviet Union was not accountable to the people
45. (b) Russian people were more dominant as compared to other countries
46. (b) Sino-India conflict
47. (b) Soviet union response was neutral
48. (c) Defence minister V. Krishnamenon was resigned
49. (b) USA and Britain
50. (b) China war cause the split in communist party of India

1. Mikhail Gorbachev became the General Secretary of the communist party of Soviet Union in the year :
   - (a) 1982
   - (b) 1985
   - (c) 1986
   - (d) 1991

2. Which of the following statements are true about Antarctic continental region ?
   - A. It has a limited terrestrial life and a highly productive Marine ecosystem
   - B. The region extends over 1000 million square kilometers
   - C. The region is subjected to special regional rules of environmental protection
   - D. Some parts of it are degraded by waste as a result of oil spills
   - E. It is disturbing the climate equilibrium

   Choose the **correct** answer from the options given below :
   - (a) A, B, C and D only
   - (b) A, C, D and E only
   - (c) C, D and E only
   - (d) A, C and D only

3. Match **List - I** with **List - II**.

List - I (Country)	List - II (Status/Position During the cold war period)
A. Spain	I. Neutral country
B. Romania	II. Non-aligned state
C. Sweden	III. Warsaw Pact Member
D. Yugoslavia	IV. NATO member

   Choose the **correct** answer from the options given below :
   - (a) A-II, B-III, C-IV, D-I
   - (b) A-II, B-IV, C-I, D-III
   - (c) A-IV, B-III, C-I, D-II
   - (d) A-III, B-I, C-II, D-IV

4. With reference to the Soviet Union, arrange the following events in a chronological order.
   - A. Mikhail Gorbachev elected as the General Secretary of Communist Party.
   - B. Secessionist movements in Chechnya and Dagestan.
   - C. Revival of the Russian Economy.
   - D. Introduction of Multiparty polities in the Soviet Parliament (Duma)
   - E. Disintegration of Soviet Union

   Choose the **correct** answer from the options given below :
   - (a) A, B, D, C, E
   - (b) E, C, D, A, B
   - (c) A, D, E, C, B
   - (d) C, B, A, E, B

5. When did the Soviet System came into being ?
   - (a) After the Russian Revolution
   - (b) After the Second World War
   - (c) After the 1990's
   - (d) After the 1970's

6. Which among the following combination given below are features of Soviet System ?
   - A. It aimed to abolish institutions of private property in the country.
   - B. The economy was developed and was at par with the US economy.
   - C. The system was centered around the communist party and allowed political opposition.
   - D. The state ownership was the dominant mode of ownership in this system.
   - E. The institution of state was of paramount importance in the soviet system.

   Choose the **correct** answer from the options given below :
   - (a) A, B, D only
   - (b) A, C, E only
   - (c) A, D, E only
   - (d) B, D, E only

7. Match **List - I** with **List - II**.

List - I (UN Secretary General)	List - II Term (Period of Office)
A. Trygve Lie	I. 1972-1981
B. Dag Hammarskjold	II. 1961-1971
C. U Thant	III. 1953-1961
D. Kurt Waldheim	IV. 1946-1952

   Choose the **correct** answer from the options given below :
   - (a) A-I, B-II, C-III, D-IV
   - (b) A-II, B-III, C-IV, D-I
   - (c) A-IV, B-III, C-II, D-I
   - (d) A-IV, B-I, C-III, D-II

8. Which of the following statement is **not** true about India's Nuclear Policy/Programme ?

(a) It is a policy of NO FIRST USE

(b) It reiterates India's Commitment to global, verifiable nuclear disarmament

(c) It prohibits India to be a member of Nuclear Suppliers Group (NSG)

(d) It opposes partisan treaties like CTBT & NPT

9. What is Schengen Visa ?

(a) One Visa from just one of the EU countries allows a person entry in most other European Union Countries

(b) Two Visas from two EU countries allows a person entry in the USA

(c) A Special type of Visa given to refugees coming to EU countries

(d) A type of Visa given to the family member of Green Card holders.

10. Which of the following steps taken by China to develop the market economy is wrong ?

(a) Introduction of SEZs

(b) Privatisation of agriculture

(c) Use of Shock Therapy

(d) Removal of Trade barriers

11. The 'ASEAN way' reflects :

(a) the life style of ASEAN members

(b) Is a form of interaction among ASEAN members that is informal non confrontationist & Cooperative

(c) Is the defense policy followed by the ASEAN members

(d) Is the road that connects all the ASEAN countries

12. Western Europe's economy was revived after the second World War by :

(a) NATO

(b) Maastricht Treaty

(c) Marshall Plan

(d) IMF

13. Sharing of river waters has been a source of conflict between these neighbors despite the World Bank's interventionist approach in 1960s to resolve the problem. Identify the correct pair of countries in the above context.

(a) India and Bangladesh

(b) India and Nepal

(c) India and Pakistan

(d) Bhutan and Bangladesh

14. Choose the correct statements about 'Hindutva'.

A. Hindutva literally means 'Hinduness'.

B. It was defined by V.D. Savarkar as the basis of Indian Nationhood.

C. Hindutva is a religion.

D. Hindutva is opposed to all other religions.

E. 'Hindutva' believes that a strong nation can be built on a strong and united national culture

Choose the **correct** answer from the options given below :

(a) C, D, E only

(b) A, B, E only

(c) A, C, D only

(d) B, C, D only

15. What does the expression South Asia convey ?

(a) Cultural ethos

(b) One Geo-political space

(c) Coexistence of rivalries and goodwill

(d) Deeper Integration

16. Match **List - I** with **List - II**.

List - I (Description of Country)	List - II (Country)
A. The first country to liberalize its economy in the South Asian Region	I. India
B. Centrally located and shares borders with most of the South Asian Countries	II. The Maldives
C. Earlier the island had the Sultan as the head of this state, now its a republic	III. Bhutan
D. A landlocked country with a monarchy	IV. Sri Lanka

Choose the **correct** answer from the options given below :

(a) A-I, B-II, C-IV, D-III

(b) A-IV, B-I, C-II, D-III

(c) A-III, B-IV, C-I, D-II

(d) A-II, B-III, C-I, D-IV

17. Which one of the following is **not** an element of traditional notion of security ?

(a) Military threat from another country

(b) Policies of Deterrence and defense

(c) Forming schemes for fostering human security

(d) Alliance building through written treaties

18. Environmental issues were brought to the center stage of Global politics by :

(a) Montreal protocol

(b) Antarctica Treaty

(c) The Earth Summit

(d) Kyoto protocol

19. Which of the following statements are true about globalization ?

A. It led to an interconnected world despite of national political boundaries.

B. Globalisation led to cultural homogenisation (Global culture)

C. It has far reaching impacts in Social, Economic and Political spheres.

D. It is primarily seen as an economic phenomenon.

E. Globalisation has led to the growth of non state actors.

Choose the **correct** answer from the options given below :

(a) A, C, D, E only   (b) A, B, C, D only

(c) A, B, C, E only   (d) A, B, D, E only

20. The First World Social Forum (WSF) meeting was held in.

(a) Spain   (b) India

(c) Brazil   (d) France

21. Non Congressism was a strategy that advocated :

(a) Keep Congress out of power

(b) Keep non-Communist parties out of power

(c) Build one party

(d) Keep Socialist parties out of power

22. Match List - I with List - II.

List – I (Leaders)	List – II (Constituencies of 1967 Election)
A. K Kamraj	I. Maharashtra
B. S.K. Patil	II. Tamil Nadu
C. Atulya Ghosh	III. Bihar
D. K.B. Sahav	IV. West Bengal

Choose the **correct** answer from the options given below :

(a) A-II, B-I, C-IV, D-III

(b) A-IV, B-II, C-III, D-I

(c) A-III, B-I, C-IV, D-II

(d) A-II, B-III, C-IV, D-I

23. Arrange the following in chronological order :

A. Tashkent Agreement

B. Planning Commission set up

C. Formation of Bangladesh

D. First General Elections of India

E. Partition of India

Choose the **correct** answer from the options given below :

(a) E, B, D, C, A

(b) A, E, B, D, C

(c) D, E, C, B, A

(d) E, B, D, A, C

24. Vishalandhra movement was related to :

(a) Independence from princely rule in Andhra Region

(b) Demand for huge allocation for irrigation projects

(c) Partition of India

(d) Demand for formation of separate Andhra province based on language

25. What was, Sardar Patel's first cabinet rank in Independent India.

(a) Deputy Prime Minister and Home Minister

(b) Home Minister and Finance Minister

(c) Prime Minister

(d) Prime Minister and Home Minister

26. First Five Year Plan emphasized on :

A. Construction of Mega Dams to improve irrigation facilities.

B. Rapid Import substitution and self reliance.

C. Land Reforms.

D. Setting up of heavy industries

E. Quick structural reforms

Choose the **correct** answer from tire options given below :

(a) A and D only   (b) A and C only

(c) A and E only   (d) A and B only

27. Arrange the following events between India - Pakistan in chronological manner.

A. Bangladesh war

B. Sharing of Indus River Water

C. Proxy war between India & Pakistan armies in Kashmir after Partition

D. Pakistan's armed attack in the Rann of Kutch

Choose the **correct** answer from the options given below :

(a) A, C, D, B   (b) B, A, D, C

(c) C, B, D, A   (d) D, C, A, B

28. According to Indian Constitution, which Article deals with 'Promotion of International Peace and Security'?

(a) Article 50 (b) Article 51

(c) Article 52 (d) Article 53

29. Match **List - I** with **List - II**.

List - I		List - II
(Conference)		**(Description)**
A. Bandung Conference	I.	Between Lal Bahadur Shastri and Ayub Khan
B. Yalta Conference	II.	Between Indira Gandhi and Zulfikar Ali Bhutto
C. Shimla Agreement	III.	'Big Three' decides to organise a United Nations Conference
D. Tashkent Agreement	IV.	Afro-Asian Conference in Indonesia

Choose the correct answer from the options given below :

(a) A-I, B-II, C-III, D-IV

(b) A-I, B-III, C-IV, D-II

(c) A-II, B-IV, C-I, D-III

(d) A-IV, B-III, C-II, D-I

30. What cabinet minister rank was Atal Bihari Vajpayee holding during his visit to China in 1979.

(a) Prime Minister

(b) External Affairs Minister

(c) Finance Minister

(d) Defence Minister

31. On 25 June 1975, government declared that there was a threat of internal disturbances and therefore invoked which of the following article in the constitution :

(a) Article 354

(b) Article 370

(c) Article 352

(d) Article 19

32. Who amongst the following returned the 'Padma Shri' award in protest against the 'Suspension of democracy'?

(a) Fanishwarnath Renu

(b) J.C. Shah

(c) Jaya Prakash Narayan

(d) Charu Majumdar

33. The commission set up enquiry into the excesses committed during emergency was headed by:

(a) Justice Jagmohan Lal Sinha

(b) Justice J.C. Shah

(c) Justice A.N. Ray

(d) Justice M.N. Venkatachaliah

34. Who among the following was the first non Congress Prime Minister ?

(a) Morarji Desai

(b) V.P. Singh

(c) Chandra Shekhar

(d) I.K. Gujral

35. Match **List - I** with **List - II**.

List - I	List - II
(Names of Leaders)	**(Movements/ Association with)**
A. Laldenga	I. President of Akali Dal
B. Harchand Singh Longowal	II. Leader of National Conference
C. Sheikh Mohammad Abdullah	III. Self-respect movement
D. EV Ramaswamy Naicker	IV. Leader of Mizo National Front

Choose the **correct** answer from the options given below :

(a) A-II, B-I, C-III, D-IV

(b) A-II, B-III, C-IV, D-I

(c) A-IV, B-I, C-II, D-III

(d) A-IV, B-I, C-III, D-II

36. Right to Information Bill received Presidential assent in :

(a) June 2004

(b) June 2005

(c) June 2006

(d) June 2007

37. The Bahujan Samaj Party (BSP) was founded in the year.

(a) 1980

(b) 1984

(c) 1985

(d) 1990

38. Mandal Commission recommended what percentage of reservation in jobs for OBC's in the Central Government.

(a) 15% (b) 10%

(c) 30% (d) 27%

39. Prime Minister Deve Gowda led which of the following Alliance/ Front ?

(a) National Front

(b) United Front

(c) Left Front

(d) United Progressive Alliance

40. In 1989 the National Front Government was led by :

(a) Chandrashekhar

(b) Jyoti Basu

(c) V.P. Singh

(d) L.K. Advani

Directions for Quesitons 41 to 45:

Please read the passage and answer the questions that follows.

Reform and improvement are key to the functioning of any organization. The UN is no exception. There have been various demands for structural reform in the Security Council, a key organ of UN responsible for maintaining international peace and security. Security Council consists of 15 members and there has been on going debate to increase the strength of its non - permanent members. Currently 10 non - permanent members are selected for two- year term. This is suggested keeping in mind the changing regional dynamics and economic development of several nations.

Apart from change in UNSC, member states have also been demanding expulsion of veto power held by the 5 permanent members. Although UNSC was expanded from 11 to 15 in 1965, there was no significant change for the permanent members, They continued to hold more power.

Another structural reform that has been discussed over the years is about the range of issues to be brought within its jurisdiction should UN play a more effective part in security missions or expand its horizon to include issues relating to health, education human rights, gender, social justice, equality to name a few. Established on 24th October 1945 immediately after the second World War, UN needs were to be reformed. It needs to represent contemporary political realities; reflect the decisions of all member states and showcase an equitable representation. That truly will create a robust UN system or it will meet the same fate as its predecessor, the League of Nations.

41. UN was established in the year.

(a) 1945

(b) 1948

(c) 1946

(d) 1951

42. Identify the incorrect statement about the UN system:

(a) UN was established immediately after World War II.

(b) The UN day is celebrated on the 24th of October every year.

(c) UN was founded as a succession to the League of Nations.

(d) It came into existence in 1948

43. Identify the most appropriate reason for demanding reform of the UN Security Council:

(a) To expand the jurisdiction of UN over international issues.

(b) To make it more representative and equitable geographically.

(c) To resolve conflicts quickly around the globe.

(d) To increase financial contribution to UN General Assembly.

44. The non-permanent members of the UN Security Council are elected for a period of :

(a) two years

(b) three years

(c) four years

(d) five years

45. Why were the permanent members of the UN Security Council given the VETO power ?

(a) They initiated the idea of an international organization for the first time.

(b) They were more advanced economically.

(c) They were the victors of World War II.

(d) They contributed more to the UN funds.

Directions for Quesitons 46 to 50:

Please read the passage and answer the questions that follows.

The stage was now set for a big political confrontation. The opposition political parties led by Jayaprakash Narayan pressed for Indira Gandhi's resignation and organised a massive demonstration in Delhi's Ramlila grounds on 25 June 1975. Jayaprakash announced a nationwide satyagraha for ther resignation and asked the army, the police and government employees not to obey "illegal and immoral orders". This too threatened to bring the activities of the government to a standstill. The political mood of the country had turned against the Congress, more than ever before. The response of the government was to declare a state of emergency. On 25 June 1975, the government declared that there was a threat of internal disturbances and therefore, it invoked Article 352 of the Constitution. Under the provision of this article the government could declare a state of emergency on grounds of external threat or a threat of internal disturbances. From the wording of the provisions of the Constitution, it is clear that an Emergency is seen as an extra ordinary condition in which normal democratic politics cannot function. Therefore, special powers are granted to the government. On the night of 25 June 1975, the Prime Minister recommended the imposition of Emergency to President Fakhruddin Ali Ahmed. He issued the proclamation immediately.

46. Who was Jayaprakash Narayan ?

   (a) A symbol of opposition to emergency

   (b) The Prime Minister of India during the 1975 emergency

   (c) The President of India during the 1975 emergency

   (d) Indian Gandhi's son and the administrator of her regime

47. Which kind of emergency is imposed in the case of war, external aggression and armed rebellion ?

   (a) National emergency using Article 352

   (b) State emergency using Article 356

   (c) National emergency using Article 324

   (d) Financial emergency using Article 360

48. Who can declare National emergency in India ?

   (a) The Prime Minister

   (b) The President

   (c) The Chief Justice of India

   (d) The Chief Election Commission

49. The massive demonstration was held in Delhi's.

   (a) Lal Qila Maidan

   (b) Jantar Mantar

   (c) Ramlila Grounds

   (d) Mandi House

50. What was the context of the given passage ?

   (a) Assassination of Indira Gandhi

   (b) State of Emergency

   (c) War with Pakistan

   (d) 1977 Elections

Answer Keys

1. (b)	**2.** (d)	**3.** (c)	**4.** (c)	**5.** (a)	**6.** (c)	**7.** (c)	**8.** (c)	**9.** (a)	**10.** (c)
11. (b)	**12.** (c)	**13.** (c)	**14.** (b)	**15.** (b)	**16.** (b)	**17.** (c)	**18.** (c)	**19.** (c)	**20.** (c)
21. (a)	**22.** (a)	**23.** (d)	**24.** (d)	**25.** (a)	**26.** (b)	**27.** (c)	**28.** (b)	**29.** (d)	**30.** (b)
31. (c)	**32.** (a)	**33.** (c)	**34.** (a)	**35.** (c)	**36.** (c)	**37.** (b)	**38.** (d)	**39.** (b)	**40.** (c)
41. (a)	**42.** (d)	**43.** (b)	**44.** (b)	**45.** (c)	**46.** (a)	**47.** (a)	**48.** (b)	**49.** (c)	**50.** (b)

Explanations

1. (b) Mikhail Gorbachev, who had become General Secretary of the Communist Party of the Soviet Union in 1985

2. (d) The Antarctic continental region extends over 14 million square kilometres and comprises 26 per cent of the world's wilderness area,

3. (c) Spain was NATO member during cold war era.

4. (c) 1990 February: Gorbachev strips the Soviet Communist Party of its 72-year-long monopoly on power by calling on the Soviet parliament (Duma) to permit multiparty politics

5. (a) After Russian revolution soviet system came into existence.

6. (c) State ownership was more dominant in Soviet system

7. (c) Trygve Lie (1946-1952) Norway; lawyer and foreign minister; worked for ceasefire between India and Pakistan on Kashmir; criticised for his failure to quickly end the Korean war; Soviet Union opposed second term for him; resigned from the post.

8. (c) India wants to be a member of nuclear supplier group

9. (a) Oh, now I know what a Schengen visa means! Under the Schengen agreement, you have to get a visa from just one of the EU countries and that allows you entry in most of the other European Union countries.

10. (c) Shock therapy was not in china economy model.

11. (b) 'ASEAN Way', a form of interaction that is informal, non-confrontationist and cooperative.

12. (c) Marshal plan revive the economy of western Europe

13. (c) Indus water treaty was signed in 1960 between India and Pakistan to solve the river disputes.

14. (b) Hindutva means Hinduness and defined by V.D savarkar

15. (b) South Asia stands for diversity in every sense and yet constitutes one geo-political space.

16. (b) Sri Lanka was one of the first developing countries to successfully control the rate of growth of population, the first country in the region to liberalise the economy

17. (c) In the traditional conception of security, the greatest danger to a country is from military threats.

18. (c) The 1992 Earth Summit has brought environmental issues to the centre-stage of global politics.

19. (c) Globalisation is a multidimensional concept. It has political, economic and cultural manifestations, and these must be adequately distinguished. It is wrong to assume that globalisation has purely economic dimensions, just as it would also be mistaken to assume that it is a purely cultural phenomenon

20. (c) The first WSF meeting was organised in Porto Alegre, Brazil in 2001.

21. (a) Keep congress out of power

22. (a) K.Kamraj from Tamil nadu and S.K Patil from Maharashtra, Atulya Ghosh from Bihar

23. (d) Partition of India 1947,Planning commission was set up in 1952

24. (d) Vishalandhra movement for creation of Andhra Pradesh

25. (a) Deputy Prime minister and Home minister

26. (b) Construction of mega dams and land reforms

27. (c) Proxy war between India and Pakistan in 1947, Indus water treaty was signed in 1960.

28. (b) Article 51 promotes International peace and security

29. (d) Shimla agreement was signed between India and Pakistan Indira Gandhi and Zulfikar Ali Bhutoo

30. (b) The external affairs minister, Atal Bihari Vajpayee, said his talks with Chinese leaders had "unfrozen" the border issue which has bedevilled relations between India and China for 19 years.

31. (c) Article 352 of the Indian Constitution was invoked during the threats from internal disturbance

32. (a) Fanishwar Nath Renu returned the 'Padamashri' award in protest of suspension of democracy

33. (c) Justice J.C shah commission was appointed by Janta party government

34. (a) Morarji Desai was the First non-congress PM of India

35. (c) The popular movement in the State, led by Sheikh Abdullah of the National Conference, wanted to get rid of the Maharaja, but was against joining Pakistan. The National Conference was a secular organisation and had a long association with the Congress.

36. (c) June 2005 Right to information bill received president assent

37. (b) BSP was formed on 14 April 1984 by high profile charismatic populist leader Kanshi Ram. The political symbol (election symbol) of this party is an elephant.

38. (d) 27% reservation recommended by Mandal commission

39. (b) United front with congress support

40. (c) V.P Singh led National Front government

41. (a) UN was established in 1945

42. (d) UN was established in 1945

43. (b) Should the issue of equitable representation be decided by geography

44. (b) Two years is tenure for non-permanent member

45. (c)

46. (a) A symbol of opposition of congress

47. (a) National emergency under Article 352

48. (b) The President have power to declare National emergency

49. (c) Ramlila ground

50. (b) State of emergency

1. Arrange the following in chronological order:

A. Fall of the Berlin Wall

B. Birth of CIS

C. Coup by the Communist Party hardliners in USSR

D. Gorbachev became the General Secretary of the Communist Party of Soviet Union

Choose the correct answer from the options given below:

(a) A, B, C, D

(b) D, A, C, B

(c) C, A, B, D

(d) D, C, B, A

2. The states formed after the disintegration of USSR are called:

(a) Commonwealth Nations

(b) Commonwealth of Free and Cooperating States

(c) Commonwealth of Sovereign States

(d) Commonwealth of Independent States

3. Who was the Soviet leader during the Cuban Missile crisis?

(a) Mikhail Gorbachev

(b) Boris Yeltsin

(c) Joseph Stalin

(d) Nikita Khrushchev

4. George H.W. Bush was the leader of which party in the United States of America?

(a) Republican Party

(b) Democratic Party

(c) Labour Party

(d) Conservative Party

5. Identify the country which does NOT belong to South Asia.

(a) Srilanka

(b) Maldives

(c) China

(d) Bangladesh

6. The 'Indus River Waters' dispute between India and Pakistan was mediated by which of the following?

(a) IMF

(b) World Bank

(c) United Nations

(d) USSR

7. Match **List - I** with **List - II**.

List - I (Country)		List - II (Political Developments)
A. Pakistan	I.	Emerged as democratic republic in 2008
B. Nepal	II.	Became constitutional monarchy in 2008
C. Bhutan	III.	Multi-party system introduced in 2005
D. Maldives	IV.	Suffered a military coup in 1999

Choose the correct answer from the options given below:

(a) A-IV, B-I, C-II, D-III

(b) A-I, B-III, C-II, D-IV

(c) A-IV, B-I, C-III, D-II

(d) A-I, B-IV, C-II, D-III

8. Match **List - I** with **List - II**.

List - I (Agreement/Treaty)		List - II (Year)
A. Tashkent Agreement	I.	1972
B. Shimla Agreement	II.	1987
C. Indo-Sri Lanka Accord	III.	1996
D. Farakka Treaty	IV.	1966

Choose the correct answer from the options given below:

(a) A-III, B-I, C-II, D-IV

(b) A-IV, B-I, C-II, D-III

(c) A-I, B-IV, C-III, D-II

(d) A-IV, B-II, C-I, D-III

9. Select South Asia country which was a Sultanate till 1968 when it was transformed into a republic with a presidential form of government.

(a) Sri Lanka

(b) Bhutan

(c) Nepal

(d) Maldives

10. The United Nations Organisation was set up through the signing of the United Nations Charter by how many states?

(a) 51 states

(b) 49 states

(c) 45 states

(d) 50 states

11. The examples of res communis humanitatis (global commons) are:

 A. Antarctica

 B. The ocean Floor

 C. The outer space

 D. The forests

 E. The earths atmosphere

 Choose the correct answer from the options given below:

 (a) A, B, C, E only   (b) B, C, D, E only

 (c) A, C, D, E only   (d) A, B, D, E only

12. Choose the term which refers to institutional safeguards to minimize the negative effects of globalization on economically weaker section.

 (a) Economic safety nets

 (b) Social safety nets

 (c) Social security nets

 (d) Economic security nets

13. The full form of NATO is:

 (a) North African Treaty Organisation

 (b) North Atlantic Treaty Organisation

 (c) North American Treaty Organisation

 (d) North Asian Treaty Organisation

14. Which of the following is not associated with Potti Sriramulu?

 (a) Went on a fast in 1946 demanding that temples in the Madras province be closed to dalits.

 (b) A Gandhian worker who left Government job to participate in Salt Satyagraha.

 (c) Undertook a fast unto death from 19th October 1952 demanding separate state of Andhra Pradesh.

 (d) Died during the fast on 15th December 1952.

15. Arrange the following important events of post-independence history of India in a chronological order:

 A. States Reorganisation Act was passed.

 B. States Reorganisation Commission was appointed.

 C. The Prime Minister announced the formation of a separate Andhra Pradesh.

 D. Potti Sriramulu went on indefinite fast that led to his death after 56 days.

 Choose the correct answer from the options given below:

 (a) A, B, C, D   (b) D, C, B, A

 (c) D, C, A, B   (d) C, A, D, B

16. Which is not a correct statement about the concept of 'Hindutva'?

 (a) Hindutva literally means 'Hinduness'

 (b) B.J.P. accepts the idea of 'Hindutva'

 (c) Communist Parties also champion the idea of 'Hindutva'

 (d) V. D. Savarkar defines 'Hindutva' as the basis of Indian Nationhood

17. The first summit of NAM was held in which of the following place and year?

 (a) Belgrade, September 1961

 (b) Ghana, September 1961

 (c) Egypt, September 1962

 (d) Yugoslavia, September 1962

18. Identify the election which is referred to as a 'Political Earthquake'.

 (a) 1971 election

 (b) 1967 election

 (c) 1984 election

 (d) 1977 election

19. Identify the President of the Congress Party at the time of death of Jawaharlal Nehru

 (a) S. K. Patil

 (b) K. Kamraj

 (c) S. Nijalingappa

 (d) N. Sanjeeva Reddy

20. Which amendment was passed during the Emergency?

 (a) 42nd

 (b) 32nd

 (c) 45th

 (d) 35th

21. Who issued the proclamation for Emergency on the night of 25 June 1975?

 (a) Prime Minister Indira Gandhi

 (b) Prime Minister's son Sanjay Gandhi

 (c) President V. V. Giri

 (d) President Fakhruddin Ali Ahmed

22. Basic features of the constitution cannot be amended by the Parliament. This decision was given by the Supreme Court of India in:

 (a) A. K. Gopalan case

 (b) Kesavananda Bharati case

 (c) Maneka Gandhi case

 (d) Raj Narain case

23. Match **List - I** with **List - II**.

List - I (Regional leaders)	List - II (Their states)
A. E. V. Ramasami Naicker	I. Sikkim
B. Laldenga	II. Nagaland
C. Angami Zapu Phizo	III. Mizoram
D. Kazi Lhendup Dorji Khangsarpa	IV. Tamil Nadu

Choose the correct answer from the options given below:

(a) A-I, B-II, C-III, D-IV

(b) A-IV, B-III, C-II, D-I

(c) A-II, B-I, C-IV, D-III

(d) A-III, B-IV, C-I, D-II

24. Who is known as the 'Milkman of India'?

(a) Sardar Patel

(b) Verghese Kurien

(c) E. V. Ramasami Naicker

(d) Kamaraj

25. Choose the wrong statement about Jagjivan Ram from the following options:

(a) Freedom fighter and Congress leader from Bihar

(b) Deputy Prime Minister of India (1977-79)

(c) Finance Minister in the first ministry of free India

(d) Member of Parliament since 1952 till his death

26. Bahujan Samaj Party (BSP) emerged under the leadership of:

(a) B. P. Mandal

(b) Charu Majumdar

(c) Kanshi Ram

(d) K. B. Sahay

27. Match **List - I** with **List - II**.

List - I (Phenomenon/ Concept)	List - II (Description)
A. World Social Forum	I. Ideas moving from one part of the world to another
B. Social Safety Nets	II. Brings together a wide coalition of activists opposed to globalization
C. Mc. Donaldisation	III. Minimise the negative effects of globalization on economically weak
D. Globalisation	IV. Cultures seeking to buy into dominant American dream

Choose the correct answer from the options given below:

(a) A-I, B-II, C-III, D-IV

(b) A-II, B-I, C-IV, D-III

(c) A-II, B-III, C-IV, D-I

(d) A-III, B-II, C-I, D-IV

28. UNHCR stands for:-

(a) the United Nations Health Committee for Refugees

(b) the United Nations High Commission for Reforms

(c) the United Nations High Commission for Refugees

(d) the Union National High Committee for Refugees

29. What is the currency of European Union?

(a) Pound   (b) Dollar

(c) Euro   (d) Ruble

30. Find out the incorrectly matched pair.

(a) Dalit Panthers - Maharashtra

(b) National Fish Workers Forum - Madhya Pradesh

(c) Anti-Arrack Movement - Andhra Pradesh

(d) Right to Information - Rajasthan

31. The Nuclear Non-Proliferation Treaty (NPT) was an arms control treaty, it regulated the acquisition of nuclear weapons. For the purpose of NPT, a nuclear weapon state is one which has manufactured and exploded a nuclear weapon or other nuclear explosive device prior to:

(a) 1 January 1969

(b) 1 January 1967

(c) 1 January 1968

(d) 1 January 1970

32. Match **List - I** with **List - II**.

List - I (Prime Minister)	List - II (Period)
A. A. B. Vajpayee	I. May 2014 onwards
B. Narendra Modi	II. April 1997 to March 1998
C. I. K. Gujral	III. June 1996 to April 1997
D. H. D. Deve Gowda	IV. October 1999 to May 2004

Choose the correct answer from the options given below:

(a) A-I, B-IV, C-III, D-II

(b) A-IV, B-I, C-II, D-III

(c) A-II, B-III, C-IV, D-I

(d) A-III, B-I, C-IV, D-II

33. The idea of one country, one culture and one nation was emphasized by which political party?

- (a) Bharatiya Jana Sangh
- (b) Congress Party
- (c) Swatantra Party
- (d) Communist Party of India

34. Which of the following provides a roadmap for reducing the emission of greenhouse gases to check global warming?

- (a) Rio Summit
- (b) Kyoto Protocol
- (c) Earth Summit
- (d) Agenda 21

35. Match **List - I** with **List - II**.

List - I : Party	List - II : Leader
A. Swatantra Party	I. E M S Namboodiripad
B. Communist Party of India (CPI)	II. C. Rajagopalachari
C. Socialist Party	III. Deen Dayal Upadhyaya
D. Bharatiya Jana Sangh	IV. Acharya Narendra Dev

Choose the correct answer from the options given below:

- (a) A-I, B-II, C-III, D-IV
- (b) A-II, B-I, C-IV, D-III
- (c) A-II, B-IV, C-III, D-I
- (d) A-I, B-II, C-IV, D-III

36. ASEAN was established in the year:-

- (a) 1967
- (b) 1969
- (c) 1972
- (d) 1980

37. The 'Kamaraj Plan' was:

- (a) All senior Congressman should resign from office to make way for younger parry workers
- (b) Mid-day meal scheme for school children should be introduced in India
- (c) Teaching of Hindi should be promoted in Tamil Nadu
- (d) Seats should be reserved for backward castes in government jobs and educational institutions

38. Arrange in the chronological order of their formation.

- A. European Economic Community
- B. European Parliament
- C. Organisation for European Economic Cooperation
- D. European Union
- E. The Council of Europe

Choose the correct answer from the options given below:

- (a) E, A, C, B, D
- (b) A, B, E, C, D
- (c) C, E, A, B, D
- (d) B, D, E, A, C

39. Match **List - I** with **List - II**.

List - I (Leader)	List - II (Party/Organisation)
A. Sheikh Abdullah	I. Sikkim Praja Mandal
B. Kazi Lhendup Dorji Khangsarpa	II. Naga National Council
C. Angami Zapu Phizo	III. National Conference
D. Laldenga	IV. Mizo National Front

Choose the correct answer from the options given below:

- (a) A-I, B-III, C-IV, D-II
- (b) A-II, B-IV, C-I, D-III
- (c) A-III, B-I, C-II, D-IV
- (d) A-IV, B-I, C-II, D-III

40. The Bharatiya Janata Party was formed in:

- (a) 1980
- (b) 1977
- (c) 1975
- (d) 1989

Directions for Quesitons 41 to 45:

Please read the passage and answer the questions that follows.

Students' protests in Gujarat and Bihar, both of which were Congress ruled states, had far reaching impact on the politics of the two States and national politics. In January 1974 students in Gujarat started an agitation against rising prices of food grains, cooking oil and other essential commodities and against corruption in high places. The students protest was joined by major opposition parties and became widespread leading to the imposition of President's rule in the state. The opposition parties demanded fresh elections to the state legislature. Morarji Desai, a prominent leader of Congress (O), who was the main rival of Indira Gandhi when he was in the Congress, announced that he would go on an indefinite fast if fresh elections were not held in the state. Under intense pressure from students, supported by the opposition political parties, assembly elections were held in Gujarat in June 1975. The Congress was defeated in this election.

In March 1974 students came together in Bihar to protest against rising prices, food scarcity, unemployment and corruption. After a point they invited Jayaprakash Narayan (JP), who had given up active politics and was involved in social work to lead the student movement. He accepted it on the condition that the movement will remain non-violent and will not limit itself to Bihar. Thus the students' movement assumed a political character and had national appeal.

People from all walks of life now entered the movement. Javaprakash Narayan demanded the dismissal of the Congress government in Bihar and gave a call for total revolution in the social, economic and political sphere in order to establish what he considered to be true democracy. A series of Bandhs, Gheraos and strikes were organized in protest against the Bihar government. The government, however refused to resign.

41. Assembly elections were held in Gujarat in the year:

(a) July 1976 (b) June 1976

(c) June 1975 (d) June 1974

42. Why Jayaprakash Narayan gave a call for total revolution?

(a) To bring a political change and establish a communist society

(b) To establish true democracy

(c) To totally revolutionise the social and economic structure to establish liberal order

(d) To make himself the Prime Minister of India

43. The correct statements about Gujarat and Bihar movements are:-

A. Gujarat and Bihar were Congress ruled states

B. Students in Gujarat started an agitation in January 1974

C. The student protest was condemned by the opposition parties

D. Jayaprakash Narayan was invited to lead the student movement in Gujarat

E. JP demanded the dismissal of Congress government in Bihar

Choose the correct answer from the options given below:

(a) A, C, D only

(b) B, C, D only

(c) A, B, E only

(d) B, D, E only

44. Why Morarji Desai announced to go on an indefinite fast?

(a) He was the main supporter of Indira Gandhi

(b) If fresh elections were not held in Gujarat

(c) He was a prominent leader of Janata Party

(d) He wanted to take the position of the President of Congress Party

45. Arrange the following in a chronological order.

A. Morarji Desai's announcement to go on indefinite fast

B. Students agitation in Gujarat

C. Congress's defeat in Assembly elections

D. Assembly elections in Gujarat

Choose the correct answer from the option given below:

(a) A, B, C, D (b) A, C, D, B

(c) B, D, C, A (d) B, A, D, C

Directions for Quesitons 46 to 50:

Please read the passage and answer the questions that follows.

The Cold War was not simply a matter of power rivalries of military alliances, and of the balance of power. These were accompanied by a real ideological conflict as well, a difference over the best and the most appropriate wav of organising political, economic and social life all over the world. The western alliance, headed by the US, represented the ideology of liberal democracy and capitalism while the eastern alliance, headed by the Soviet Union, was committed to the ideology of socialism and communism. In 1945, the Allied Forces, led by the US, Soviet Union, Britain and France defeated the Axis Powers led by Germany, Italy and Japan, ending the Second World War (1939-1945). The war had involved almost all the major powers of the world and spread out to regions outside Europe including Southeast Asia, China, Burma (now Myanmar) and parts of India's northeast.

The war devastated the world in terms of loss of human lives and civilian property. In April 1961, the leaders of the Union of Soviet Socialist Republic (USSR) were worried that the United States of America (USA) would invade Communist-ruled Cuba and overthrow Fidel Castro, the president of the small island nation off the coast of the United States. Cuba was an ally of the Soviet Union and received both diplomatic and financial aid from it. Nikita Khrushchev, the leader of the Soviet Union, decided to convert Cuba into a Russian base. In 1962, he placed nuclear missiles in Cuba. The installation of these weapons put the US, for the first time, under fire from close range and nearly doubled the number of bases orcities in the American mainland which could be threatened by the USSR.

46. Axis Powers consists of-

(a) Germany, America and France

(b) America, France and Italy

(c) Germany, Italy and Japan

(d) England, Italy and France

47. What was the anxiety of the Soviet Union in 1961-62?

    (a) Capitalist Revolution in USA

    (b) The USA may invade Cuba and overthrow Castro

    (c) Second World War.

    (d) The Communist revolution in China

48. Allied forces consists of:

    (a) US, USSR, Britain and France

    (b) Germany, Italy and Japan

    (c) US, Germany and Japan

    (d) US, Britain and Germany

49. What is the backdrop of the above passage?

    (a) Socialist Revolution o f USSR

    (b) Capitalist Revolution o f USA

    (c) First World War

    (d) Cold War

50. Fidel Castro was the leader of which country?

    (a) USSR

    (b) USA

    (c) Cuba

    (d) Cambodia

Answer Keys

1. (b)	**2.** (d)	**3.** (d)	**4.** (a)	**5.** (c)	**6.** (b)	**7.** (a)	**8.** (b)	**9.** (d)	**10.** (d)
11. (a)	**12.** (b)	**13.** (b)	**14.** (a)	**15.** (b)	**16.** (b)	**17.** (a)	**18.** (b)	**19.** (b)	**20.** (a)
21. (d)	**22.** (b)	**23.** (b)	**24.** (b)	**25.** (c)	**26.** (c)	**27.** (c)	**28.** (c)	**29.** (c)	**30.** (b)
31. (b)	**32.** (b)	**33.** (a)	**34.** (b)	**35.** (c)	**36.** (a)	**37.** (b)	**38.** (c)	**39.** (c)	**40.** (a)
41. (c)	**42.** (b)	**43.** (c)	**44.** (b)	**45.** (d)	**46.** (c)	**47.** (b)	**48.** (a)	**49.** (d)	**50.** (c)

Explanations

1. (b) The Berlin Wall symbolised the division between the capitalist and the communist world. Built in 1961 to separate East Berlin from West Berlin, this more than 150 kilometre long wall stood for 28 years and was finally broken by the people on 9 November 1989.

2. (d) The declaration on the disintegration of the USSR and the formation of the Commonwealth of Independent States (CIS) came as a surprise to the other republics, especially to the Central Asian ones.

3. (d)

4. (a) Clinton had been succeeded in the US presidency by George W. Bush of the Republican Party, son of the earlier President George H. W. Bush.

5. (c) The expression 'South Asia' usually includes the following countries: Bangladesh, Bhutan, India, the Maldives, Nepal, Pakistan and Sri Lanka.

6. (b) Indus water treaty was mediated by world bank

7. (a) Nepal was a constitutional monarchy with the danger of the king taking over executive powers. In 2008, the monarchy was abolished and Nepal emerged as a democratic republic. Bhutan became a constitutional monarchy in 2008.

8. (b) 1996 December: India and Bangladesh sign the Farakka Treaty for sharing of the Ganga Waters

9. (d) The Maldives, the other island nation, was a Sultanate till 1968 when it was transformed into a republic with a presidential form of government.

10. (d) 1945 June 26: Signing of the UN Charter by 50 nations (Poland signed on October 15; so the UN has 51 original founding members)

11. (a) These are known as res communis humanitatis or global commons. They include the earth's atmosphere, Antarctica (see Box), the ocean floor, and outer space

12. (b) They have emphasised the need to ensure institutional safeguards or creating 'social safety nets' to minimise the negative effects of globalisation on those who are economically weak.

13. (b) NATO - North Atlantic Treaty organization

14. (a) Potti Sriramulu (1901-1952): Gandhian worker; left government job to participate in Salt

Satyagraha; also participated in individual Satyagraha; went on a fast in 1946 demanding that templesp in Madras province be opened to dalits; undertook a fast unto death from 19 October 1952 demanding separate state of Andhra; died during the fast on 15 December 1952.

15. (b) These struggles forced the Central Government into appointing a States Reorganisation Commission in 1953 to look into the question of redrawing of the boundaries of states. The Commission in its report accepted that the boundaries of the state should reflect the boundaries of different languages. On the basis of its report the States Reorganisation Act was passed in 1956.

16. (b) BJP accepts the idea of Hindutva

17. (a) Belgrade 1961 – The first summit of NAM

18. (b) 1967 election was considered as Political earthquake

19. (b) K.Kmaraj was the congress president

20. (a) 42nd Amendment Act 1976 was passed

21. (d) President Fakhruddin Ahmed issued the proclamation of emergency

22. (b) Kesavananda Bharti Case

23. (b) Laldenga is from Mizoram and he was the first chief minister

24. (b) Verghese Kurien is known as Milk man of India.

25. (c) Jagjivan ram was first labour minister in the first ministry of free India

26. (c) Kanshi Ram was the founder of Bahujan Samaj Party

27. (c) They have emphasised the need to ensure institutional safeguards or creating 'social safety nets' to minimise the negative effects of globalisation on those who are economically weak.

28. (c) United Nations High Commission for Refugees (UNHCR)

29. (c) Euro is the currency of European Union

30. (b) National Fish workers forum is from Kerala

31. (b) For the purposes of the NPT, a nuclear weapon state is one which has manufactured and exploded a nuclear weapon or other nuclear explosive device prior to 1 January 1967.

32. (b)

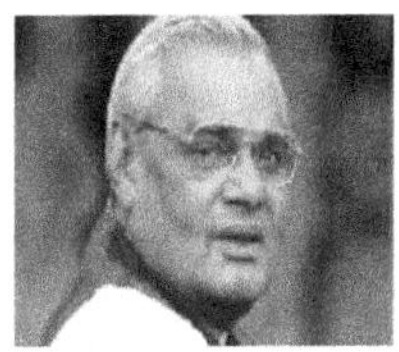

| March **1998** October **1999** | National Democratic |
| October **1999** May **2004** | Alliance led by BJP |

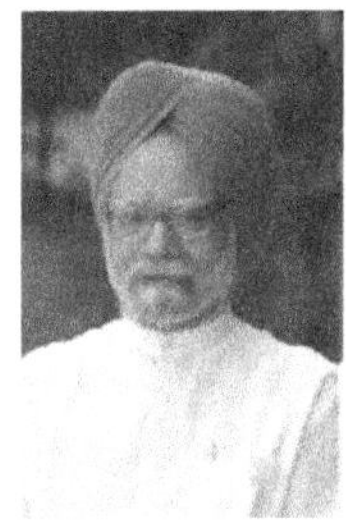

| May **2004** | United Progressive Alliance |
| May **2014** | led by Congress |

33. (a) ***Bharatiya Jana Sangh*** laid emphasis on the idea of one country, one culture and one nation.

34. (b) Kyoto Protocol operationalizes the United Nations Framework Convention on Climate Change by committing industrialized countries and economies in transition to limit and reduce greenhouse gases (GHG) emissions in accordance with agreed individual targets.

35. (c) Acharya Narendra Dev formed socialist party. Deen Dayal Uapdhayaya

36. (a) ASEAN was established in 1967 by five countries of this region — Indonesia, Malaysia, the Philippines, Singapore and Thailand — by signing the Bangkok Declaration.

37. (b) No village remained without a primary school and no panchayat without a high school. Kamaraj strove to eradicate illiteracy by introducing free and compulsory education up to the eleventh standard. He introduced the Midday Meal Scheme to provide at least one meal per day to the lakhs of poor school children.

38. (c) The Council of Europe, established in 1949, was another step forward in political cooperation. Leading to the formation of the European Economic Community in 1957.

39. (c) Sheikh Abdullah was the leader of National conference

40. (a) Bhartiya Janta Party was formed in 1980

41. (c) June 1975

42. (b) To establish true democracy

43. (c) JP Narayan demended the dismall of congress government in Bihar

44. (b) If fresh election were mot held in gujrat

45. (d)

46. (c) Axis Power – Germany, Italy and Japan

47. (b) US may invade Cuba and overthrow President Fidel Castro

48. (a) US, Soviet Union, Britain and France

49. (d) Cold War

50. (c) Cuba President- Fidel Castro

1. If you have to visit the headquarters of SAARC, you would travel to which country?

(a) India   (b) China

(c) Nepal   (d) Maldives

2. At present the functional principal organs of the UN are:

A. The General Assembly

B. The Secretariat

C. The International Court of Justice

D. The Economic and Social Council

E. The Trusteeship Council

Choose the correct answer from the options given below:

(a) A, B, D, E only

(b) B, C, D, E only

(c) A, C, D, E only

(d) A, B, C, D only

3. Match **List - I** with **List - II**.

	List I (UN Secretary		List II (Associated Work)
A.	Ban ki-Moon	I.	Creation of UN Women
B.	Kofi A. Annan	II.	Worked for resolving the Suez Canal dispute
C.	Boutros Boutros Ghali	III.	Established Human Rights Council
D.	Dag Hammarskjold	IV.	Formulated an Agenda for Peace

Choose the correct answer from the options given below:

(a) A-I, B-II, C-IV, D-II

(b) A-III, B-I, C-II, D -IV

(c) A-IV, B-II, C-I, D-III

(d) A-II, B-IV, C-III, D-I

4. The World Council of 'Indigenous people' was formed in the year.

(a) 1972   (b) 1973

(c) 1974   (d) 1975

5. The First World Social Forum (WSF) meeting was organized in:

(a) Mumbai in 2004

(b) Delhi in 2005

(c) Porto Alegre in 2001

(d) Paris in 2001

6. In 1997 in UNFCCC meeting, an international agreement was formulated setting targets for industrialised countries to cut their greenhouse gas emission.

This agreement came to be known as:

(a) Montreal Protocol

(b) Environmental Protocol

(c) Rio Summit

(d) Kyoto Protocol

7. Choose from the fallowing the consequences of the Chinese invasion, 1962.

A. Some of the top Indian army commanders either resigned or were retired and V. Krishna Menon had to leave the cabinet.

B. For the first time, a no-confidence motion against Nehru's government was moved and debated in the Lok Sabha.

C. The Communist Party of India split into CPI and CPI(M).

D. Nagaland was granted statehood; Manipur and Tripura, though UTs were given the right to elect their own legislative assemblies.

E. India signed a 20 year Treaty of Peace and Friendship with the Soviet Union

Choose the correct answer from the options given below:

(a) A, B, D, E only

(b) A, B, C, D only

(c) B, C, D, E only

(d) A, C, D, E only

8. Who signed the instrument of accession with the Government of India on behalf of the Princely state of Jammu and Kashmir?

(a) Liaqat Ali

(b) Hari Singh

(c) Dr. Ambedkar

(d) Sheikh Abdullah

9. The leader who played an important role in the integration of princely states with India.

(a) Acharya Narendra Dev

(b) Sardar Vallabhai Patel

(c) Potti Sriramulu

(d) Lal Bahadur Shastri

10. The form of government adopted by India:

    (a) Representative democracy based on parliamentary form of government

    (b) Representative democracy based on presidential form of government

    (c) Representative democracy with semi presidential form of government

    (d) Representative democracy with least political competition

11. The development planning initiated by India was derailed due to the conflict with neighbours. The war of 1962 embarked India on a military modernization drive resulting in establishment of the Department of Defence Production.

Choose the event responsible for the same.

    (a) Kargil conflict

    (b) Indo-Pak war

    (c) Bangladesh War

    (d) Chinese invasion

12. Find out the wrongly matched pair.

    (a) E. V. Ramasami Naicker - Dravidian Movement

    (b) Sheikh Abdullah - National Conference

    (c) Master Tara Singh - Shiromani Gurudwara Prabhandhak Committee

    (d) Harchand Singh Longowal - Congress

13. An ambitious developmental project was launched in the Narmada Valley of Central India in early 'eighties'. The Narmada and its tributaries flows across three states. Identify those states.

    (a) Andhra Pradesh, Maharashtra and Telangana

    (b) Karnataka, Telangana and Maharashtra

    (c) Madhya Pradesh, Gujarat and Maharashtra

    (d) Madhya Pradesh, Rajasthan and Gujarat

14. Match **List - I** with **List - II**.

List I (Organisations)	List II (Associated leaders)
A. Bharatiya Janata Party	I. Ram Manohar Lohia
B. Bahujan Samaj Party	II. Kanshi Ram
C. Janata party	III. Chaudhary Charan Singh
D. Samyukta Socialist Party	IV. L. K. Advani

Choose the correct answer from the options given below:

    (a) A-IV, B-II, C-III, D-I

    (b) A-I, B-II, C-III, D-IV

    (c) A-IV, B-III, C-II, D-I

    (d) A-II, B-I, C-III, D-IV

15. Match **List - I** with **List - II**.

List I (Governments)	List II (P.M)
A. National Front	I. Narendra Modi
B. United Progressive Alliance	II. I.K. Gujral
C. National Democratic Alliance	III. V.P. Singh
D. United Front	IV. Manmohan Singh

Choose the correct answer from the options given below:

    (a) A-II, B-I, C-IV, D-III

    (b) A-IV, B-III, C-II, D-I

    (c) A-III, B-IV, C-I, D-II

    (d) A-IV, B-II, C-III, D-I

16. Which of the following is not a factor that makes the region of South Asia very turbulent?

    (a) Pending border and water sharing disputes between the states of the region.

    (b) Conflicts arising out of insurgency, ethnic strife, etc.

    (c) India and Pakistan joining the club of nuclear powers.

    (d) Free Trade Agreements between countries of South Asia.

17. The Permanent members of the Security Council are:

    (a) France, Russia, UK, USA, China

    (b) Germany, Japan, USA, Russia, Italy

    (c) Russia, Japan, UK, Canada, US

    (d) France, China, Russia, India, US

18. Arrange the following in order of their occurrence:

    A. Formation of NATO

    B. Fall of Berlin Wall

    C. Cuban Missile Crisis

    D. Formation of Warsaw pact

Choose the correct answer from the option given below:

    (a) A, D, C, B

    (b) A, B, C, D

    (c) A, C, D, B

    (d) D, C, A, B

19. Match **List - I** with **List - II**.

List I (Person)	List II (Associated with)
A. K.N. Raj	I. Rural Industrialisation
B. Verghese Kurien	II. Statistician
C. J. C Kumarappa	III. Milk Cooperatives
D. P. C Mahalanobis	IV. First Five Year Plan

Choose the correct answer from the options given below:

(a) A-IV, B-III, C-I, D-II

(b) A-I, B-IV, C-II, D-III

(c) A-II, B-I, C-IV, D-III

(d) A-III, B-IV, C-II, D-I

20. Identify the political party.

During Emergency, it felt that agitations led by Java Prakash Narayan were mainly by middle classes who opposed the radical policies of the Congress Party.

(a) Bharatiya Jana Sangh

(b) CPI

(c) Bharatiya Lok Dal

(d) Socialist Party

21. Who was the founder member and prominent kisan leader of Bharatiya Lok Dal?

(a) Choudhary Charan Singh

(b) Morarji Desai

(c) Jag Jivan Ram

(d) Ram Manohar Lohia

22. The imposition of Emergency brought out some ambiguities regarding the Emergency provision in the Constitution that have been rectified since. Now 'internal' Emergency can be proclaimed only on the grounds of

(a) Internal disturbances

(b) Protests and movements

(c) Armed rebellion

(d) Mass movements

23. Identify the political party which justifies the imposition of Emergency, on the ground that there was an international conspiracy against the unity of India.

(a) Swatantra Party

(b) Bharatiya Kranti Dal

(c) Communist Party of India

(d) Congress for Democracy

24. In 1951, the Muslim population in India accounted for what proportion of the total population?

(a) 10%   (b) 12%

(c) 15%   (d) 5%

25. Which statement is not correct in the context of the Shah Bano case of 1985?

(a) A 62 year old divorced Muslim woman had filed a case for maintenance.

(b) The BJP criticized the action of Congress government as 'appeasement' of the minority community,

(c) The Supreme Court ruled in Shah Bano's favour.

(d) The orthodox Muslims hailed the decision of Supreme Court.

26. Following are the facts about 'Hindutva'.

A.   It was defined by V.D. Savarkar as the basis of Indian nationhood.

B.   'Hindutva' is the ideology of Communist Party.

C.   Hindutva argues that a strong nation can be built only on the basis of a strong national culture

D.   Hindutva literally means 'Hinduness'

E.   Everyone must not accept India as their 'Fatherland'

Choose the correct answer from the options given below"

(a) A, C, D only

(b) A, B, E only

(c) C, D, E only

(d) B, C, E only

27. Arrange the following statements in a chronological order, as per their occurrence from first to last.

A.   Panchsheel Agreement signed by the Indian PM, Pt. Nehru and the Chinese Premier Zhou Enlai

B.   China occupies the Aksai-Chin area and built a strategic road.

C.   Chinese revolution resulting in establishment of the communist government in China.

D.   China launched a swift and massive invasion and captured some key areas of Arunachal Pradesh.

E.   China took over control of Tibet and established administrative control.

Choose the correct answer from the options given below:

(a) A, D, C, E, B

(b) A, D, B, E, C

(c) C, A, B, D, E

(d) C, E, A, B, D

28. Indira Gandhi and Zulfikar Ali Bhuto signed which of the following agreement on 3rd July 1972?

    (a) Tashkent Agreement

    (b) Shimla Agreement

    (c) Nuclear Non-proliferation Treaty

    (d) Friendship Treaty

29. Match **List - I** with **List - II**.

List I (Leader)		List II (Ministry in first cabinet)
A.	Maidan a Abul Kalam Azad	I. Chief Minister of Madras State
B.	Rajkumari Amrit Kaur	II. Food and Agriculture Minister
C.	Rafi Ahmed Kidwai	III. Education Minister
D.	C. Rajagopalachari	IV. Minister for Health

Choose the correct answer from the options given below:

    (a) A-I, B-III, C-IV, D-II

    (b) A-III, B-IV, C-II, D-I

    (c) A-II, B-III, C-I, D-IV

    (d) A-I, B-IV, C-III, D-II

30. The Bharatiya Janata party traces its roots to:

    (a) Bharatiya Kranti Dal

    (b) Bharatiya Kisan Sangh

    (c) Bharatiya Jana Sangh

    (d) Bharatiya Samaj Party

31. In 1998, India conducted nuclear test in which of the following places?

    (a) Kudankulam

    (b) Tarapur

    (c) Pokhran

    (d) Narora

32. The 1994 UNDP's Human Development Report is associated with which concept of security?

    (a) Nuclear Security

    (b) Human Security

    (c) Collective Security

    (d) Traditional Security

33. India is having a treaty with a country that allows the citizens of the two countries to travel and work in the other country without visas and passports. The country is:

    (a) Bangladesh

    (b) Nepal

    (c) Sri Lanka

    (d) The Maldives

34. Which of the following is not a factor for the European Union to be known as a Supernational Organisation?

    (a) The EU is the world's second biggest economy

    (b) France holds permanent seat at the UN Security Council

    (c) EU is not able to intervene in economic, political and social areas

    (d) Militarily, the EU's combined armed forces are the second largest in the world

35. Which among the following reasons made India an attractive economic partner with US?

    A. Liberalise its economy and integrate it with the global economy.

    B. India's impressive economic growth rates in recent years.

    C. India's increase in its own comprehensive national power.

    D. Role of Indian-American diaspora.

    E. India's lead in establishing a coalition of countries from the developing world.

Choose the correct answer from the options given below:

    (a) A, B, D only

    (b) B, C, E only

    (c) A, D, E only

    (d) C, D, E only

36. Who among the following Chinese leaders is associated with 'Four Modernisation'?

    (a) Deng Xiaoping

    (b) Mao-Tse Tung

    (c) Zhou Enlai

    (d) Ven Ziaobav

37. Which of the following is not a Baltic Republic?

    (a) Estonia

    (b) Georgia

    (c) Latvia

    (d) Lithuania

38. Which one of the following pairs is not correctly matched?

    (a) **Country**   **Founder member of NAM**

        Yugoslavia   Josip Broz Tito

    (b) **Country**   **Founder member of NAM**

        Ghana   Kwane Nkrumah

    (c) **Country**   **Founder member of NAM**

        Vietnam   Sukurno

    (d) **Country**   **Founder member of NAM**

        Egypt   Gamel Abdel Nasser

39. The Cuban Missile Crisis occurred when

   (a) Cuba threatened to invade the US with the help of USSR

   (b) The Soviet Union fired missiles at Cuba

   (c) The US learned that the Soviet Union is converting Cuba into its military base

   (d) The Soviet Union fired missiles at US from Cuba

40. The 'ASEAN way':

   (a) Refers to the life style of the people of ASEAN countries.

   (b) It is a form of interaction that is informal, cooperative and non-confrontationist.

   (c) Refers to the common foreign policy followed by the ASEAN members.

   (d) Refers to the super expressway that connects all the ASEAN members.

Directions for Quesitons 41 to 45:

Please read the passage and answer the questions that follows.

It was in this context of heightened popular discontent and the polarization of political forces that the fourth general election to the Lok Sabha and State Assemblies were held in February 1967. The Congress was facing the electorate for the first time without Nehru.

The results jolted the Congress at both the national and state levels. Many contemporary political observers described the election results as a 'political earthquake'. The Congress did manage to get a majority in the Lok Sabha, but with its lowest tally of seats and share of votes since 1952. Half the ministers in Indira Gandhi cabinet were defeated. The political stalwarts who lost in their constituencies included Kamaraj in Tamil Nadu, S.K. Patil in Maharashtra, Atulya Ghosh in West Bengal and K.B. Sahay in Bihar.

The Congress lost majority in as many as seven states. In Madras state (now called Tamil Nadu) a regional party DMK won power, after having led a massive anti-Hindi agitation by the students against the centre.

41. The 1967 General Elections were the:

   (a) Sixth General Elections

   (b) Fifth General Elections

   (c) Fourth General Elections

   (d) Third General Elections

42. Match **List - I** with **List - II**.

List I (Leader)	List II (State)
A. K. Kamaraj	I. Maharashtra
B. S. K. Patil	II. West Bengal
C. Atulya Ghosh	III. Bihar
D. K. B. Sahay	IV. Tamil Nadu

Choose the correct answer from the options given below:

   (a) A-IV, B-I, C-II, D-III   (b) A-I, B-II, C-III, D-IV

   (c) A-II, B-I, C-III, D-IV   (d) A-IV, B-III, C-I, D-II

43. Contemporary political observers described the election results of 1967 as 'political earthquake'. Identify which one of the following was not a reason for the same.

   (a) Congress did manage to win the Lok Sabha elections but with its lowest tally of seats

   (b) The political stalwarts of Congress lost in their constituencies

   (c) Congress lost the election in 7 states

   (d) Congress was facing the electorate for the first time where some of the leaders like Kamaraj, Patil, Atulva and Sahay won the elections.

44. In 1967, DMK formed the government in Madras because of its policy of:

   (a) Non-Congressism

   (b) Anti-Hindi agitation

   (c) Communist strategies

   (d) Promise of creating a Dravida Nation

45. Which of the following statements are true about 1967 general elections in India?

   A. The Congress did manage to get a majority

   B. The election results were described as 'encouraging' for the Congress

   C. The elections were held in the atmosphere of unision between political forces

   D. DMK won the elections in the state of Madras.

   E. The Congress lost majority in as many as seven states

Choose the correct answer from the options given below:

   (a) A, D and E only   (b) A, B and E only

   (c) A, C and B only   (d) B, D and E only

Directions for Quesitons 46 to 50:

Please read the passage and answer the questions that follows.

Association of South East Asian Nations was established in 1967 with the objective of accelerating economic growth, social progress and cultural development. It was established by five Asian countries by signing the Bangkok Declaration. Over the years, new member states joined and now the strength is 10. Building cooperation through the 'ASEAN way', the member states have broadened its objectives beyond the economic and social spheres.

ASEAN and its associated organisations or bodies have been rapidly growing into an important regional association. Its vision 2020 was to build an outward looking role for ASEAN in the international community. India has also been working closely with ASEAN by building dialogue, interaction and cooperation with member states.

It has also played a very important role in ending conflicts such as Cambodian conflict, East Timor crisis among others. ASEAN just like its logo (representing ten South Asian countries in solidarity through ten stalks of paddy) have proved its strength in acknowledging national sovereignty of each country along with strong commitment to economic development.

46. Which event led to the establishment of ASEAN in 1967?

    (a) The Bandung Conference

    (b) Non-Aligned Movement

    (c) Formation of European Union

    (d) Bangkok Declaration

47. Identify the correct statement about ASEAN.

    (a) It came into existence in 1968

    (b) It was established by 3 Asian countries of the region

    (c) The ASEAN logo represents nine stalks of corn

    (d) It played an important role in resolving the Cambodian conflict

48. What is the total strength of ASEAN?

    (a) Ten

    (b) Twelve

    (c) Fifteen

    (d) Five

49. What was the main objective of its Vision 2020?

    (a) To resolve and mediate regional conflicts

    (b) To build an outward looking role for ASEAN in the international community

    (c) To foster East Asian Cooperation

    (d) To strengthen coordination of security and foreign policy

50. What among the following was NOT the objective of ASEAN?

    (a) Accelerating economic growth

    (b) Social progress

    (c) Military alliance

    (d) Cultural Development

Answer Keys

1. (c)	**2.** (d)	**3.** (a)	**4.** (d)	**5.** (c)	**6.** (d)	**7.** (b)	**8.** (b)	**9.** (b)	**10.** (a)
11. (d)	**12.** (d)	**13.** (c)	**14.** (a)	**15.** (c)	**16.** (c)	**17.** (a)	**18.** (a)	**19.** (a)	**20.** (d)
21. (a)	**22.** (c)	**23.** (c)	**24.** (b)	**25.** (d)	**26.** (a)	**27.** (d)	**28.** (b)	**29.** (b)	**30.** (c)
31. (c)	**32.** (b)	**33.** (b)	**34.** (c)	**35.** (a)	**36.** (c)	**37.** (b)	**38.** (c)	**39.** (c)	**40.** (b)
41. (c)	**42.** (a)	**43.** (d)	**44.** (b)	**45.** (a)	**46.** (d)	**47.** (d)	**48.** (a)	**49.** (b)	**50.** (c)

Explanations

1. (c) SAARC stands for the South Asian Association for Regional Cooperation. It was established when its Charter was formally adopted on 8th December 1985 by the Heads of State or Government of Bangladesh, Bhutan, India, Maldives, Nepal, Pakistan and Sri Lanka. The headquarters of the SAARC Secretariat are in Kathmandu, Nepal.

2. (d) Trusteeship Council

   Suspended on 1 November 1994 with the independence of Palau, the last UN trust territory.

3. (a) Ban Ki-moon (2007-2016) Republic of Korea (South Korea); diplomat and foreign minister; the second Asian to hold the post; highlighted climate change; focused on the Millennium Development Goals and Sustainable Development Goals; worked for the creation of UN Women; emphasised conflict resolution and nuclear disarmament

4. (d) The World Council of Indigenous Peoples was formed in 1975. The Council became subsequently the first of 11 indigenous NGOs to receive consultative status in the UN.

5. (c) The first WSF meeting was organised in Porto Alegre, Brazil in 2001.

6. (d) The Kyoto Protocol is an international agreement setting targets for industrialised countries to cut their greenhouse gas emissions. Certain gases like Carbon dioxide, Methane, Hydro-fluoro carbons etc.

7. (b) Nagaland granted statehood

8. (b) Hari Singh signed the Instrument of Accession with the GOI.

9. (b) Sardar vallabhi Patel played an important role in the integration of princely states

10. (a) Representative democaracy based on parliamentary form of government

11. (d) Chinese invasion on October 1962

12. (d) Harchand singh longowal is from Akali dal.

13. (c) Narmada and its tributaries that flow across three states of Madhya Pradesh, Gujarat and Maharashtra.

14. (a) L.K Advani is from Bhartiya janta party

15. (c) Manmohan singh is from United Progressive alliance

16. (c) The focus was, of course, on the various kinds of conflict in this region: there are pending border and water sharing disputes between the states of the region. Besides, there are conflicts arising out of insurgency, ethnic strife and resource sharing. This makes the region very turbulent.

17. (a) France ,Russia,UK,USA and China are the permanent member of UNSC

18. (a) The Berlin Wall symbolised the division between the capitalist and the communist world. Built in 1961 to separate East Berlin from West Berlin, this more than 150 kilometre long wall stood for 28 years and was finally broken by the people on 9 November 1989

19. (a) Anand, September 09, 2012. Dr. Verghese Kurien, the Father of the White Revolution, passed away in the early hours of today, after a brief illness. He was 91 years old.

20. (d) Jay Prakash Narayan was from Socialist party

21. (a) Chaudhary Charan Singh is the founder of Bhartiya Lok Dal

22. (c) Armed rebellion for internal emergency

23. (c) Communist party of India

24. (b) Muslims to the newly created Pakistan, the Muslim population in India accounted for 12 per cent of the total population in 1951.

25. (d) Shah Bano, a 62-year-old Muslim woman from Indore, Madhya Pradesh, filed a petition in court in April 1978, demanding maintenance from her divorced husband Mohammed Ahmad Khan, a well-known lawyer. Later in November, Khan granted her an irreversible talaq.

26. (a) Hindutva was defined by V.D savarkar

27. (d) Panchsheel agreement was signed in 1954

28. (b) Shimla agreement was signed on 3rd July 1972

29. (b) Maulana Kabul Azad was the first Education minister in first cabinet

30. (c) In 1967 the BJS gained a substantial foothold in the Hindi-speaking regions of northern India. Ten years later the party, led by Atal Bihari Vajpayee, joined three other political parties to form the Janata Party and took over the reins of government. Plagued by factionalism and internal disputes, however, the government collapsed in July 1979. The BJP was formally established in 1980.

31. (c) The Pokhran-II tests were a series of five nuclear bomb test explosions conducted by India at the Indian Army's Pokhran Test Range in May 1998. It was the second instance of nuclear testing conducted by India; the first test, code-named Smiling Buddha, was conducted in May 1974.

32. (b) The concern about human security was reflected in the 1994 UNDP's Human Development Report, which contends.

33. (b) Nepal and India enjoy a very special relationship that has very few parallels in the world. A treaty between the two countries allows the citizens of the two countries to travel to and work in the other country without visas

34. (c) As a supranational organisation, the EU is able to intervene in economic, political and social areas.

35. (a) Role of India- American Diaspora

36. (c) Premier Zhou Enlai proposed the 'four modernisations'(agriculture, industry, science and technology and military) in 1973.

37. (b) Baltic Republics (Estonia, Latvia and Lithuania),

38. (c) The roots of NAM went back to the friendship between three leaders — Yugoslavia's Josip Broz Tito, India's Jawaharlal Nehru, and Egypt's leader Gamal Abdel Nasser — who held a meeting in 1956. Indonesia's Sukarno and Ghana's Kwame Nkrumah strongly supported them. These five leaders came to be known as the five founders of NAM. T

39. (c) In April 1961, the leaders of the Union of Soviet Socialist Republics (USSR) were worried that the United States of America (USA) would invade communist-ruled Cuba and overthrow Fidel Castro, the president of the small island nation off the coast of the United States

40. (b) the 'ASEAN Way', a form of interaction that is informal, non confrontationist and cooperative. The respect for national sovereignty is critical to the functioning of ASEAN

41. (c) Fourth general election

42. (a) K.B Sahay from Bihar

43. (d)

44. (b) Anti-Hindi agitation

45. (a)

46. (d) Bangkok Declaration

47. (d) end of Cambodian conflicts

48. (a) Ten members of ASEAN

49. (b) To build an outward looking role for ASEAN in the international community

50. (c) Millitary alliance is not the objective of ASEAN

PSYCHOLOGY

1. According to Sternberg, persons high on _____ think analytically and critically and succeed in schools.
   - (a) Contextual Intelligence
   - (b) Emotional Intelligence
   - (c) Componential Intelligence
   - (d) Experiential Intelligence

2. Match the List I with List II

List I		List II
A. Performance Tests	I.	can be administrated to Literate people
B. Verbal Tests	II.	do not show a bias To the culture in which they are developed
C. Culture fair tests	III.	require subjects to manipulate objects and other material to perform a task
D. Group tests	IV.	Do not allow an opportunity to be familiar with the subjects feeling

   Choose the correct answer from the options given below:
   - (a) A-II, B-I, C-IV, D-III
   - (b) A-III, B-I, C-II, D-IV
   - (c) A-I, B-II, C-III, D-IV
   - (d) A-IV, B-I, C-II, D-III

3. The evidence for role of environmental influence on intelligence comes mainly from-
   - A. Comparing intelligence of identical twins reared together
   - B. Studying children from disadvantaged homes adopted into families with higher socio emotional and economic status
   - C. Comparing intelligence of fraternal twins reared together
   - D. Comparing identical twins reared together with those reared apart
   - E. Studies that show that environmental deprivation lowers intelligence while good family and school environment increases intelligence

   Choose the correct answer from the options given below:
   - (a) B, D, E only
   - (b) A, D, E only
   - (c) A, B, D only
   - (d) C, D, E only

4. A teacher observes a child showing higher attention span and higher creative abilities than his peers. He is sensitive to environmental changes, has high self esteem and prefers to read biographies of famous people when free. He loves to discover new and unique things. After observing these characteristics, the teacher would identify the student as _______.
   - (a) Intellectually deficient
   - (b) Talented
   - (c) Intellectually average
   - (d) Gifted

5. Which of the following is NOT TRUE about creativity?
   - (a) Manifestations of creativity can be observed in a novel solution to a problem, an invention or in an innovative composition of a poem
   - (b) An ordinary' individual who is engaged in simple occupations like pottery, carpentry, cooking etc cannot be creative
   - (c) Creativity is determined by both heredity and environment
   - (d) Both high and low level of creativity can be found in both highly intelligent and average intelligent people.

6. A student respects social order, is committed to elders, concerned about others and recognizes other's perspectives, the students is high in _______.
   - (a) Social competence
   - (b) Cognitive capacity
   - (c) Emotional competence
   - (d) Entrepreneurial competence

7. Match the List I with List II

List I		List II
A. Seashore's musical	I.	Non-Verbal Test
B. Differential Aptitude test	II.	Performance Test
C. Raven's Progressive Matrices	III.	Generalised Aptitude Test
D. Draw - A- Person Test	IV.	Specialised Aptitude Test

   Choose the correct answer from the options given below:
   - (a) A-IV, B-III, C-I, D-II
   - (b) A-II, B-IV, C-III, D-I
   - (c) A-I, B-II, C-IV, D-III
   - (d) A-III, B-I, C-II, D-IV

8. International classification of Diseases (I CD-10) was proposed by:
   - (a) Word Health Organisation
   - (b) Indian Medical Association
   - (c) American Psychological Association
   - (d) Psychiatric Association

9. Eysenck proposed that ____ refers to the degree to which people are socially outgoing or socially withdrawn.

(a) Neuroticism vs introversion

(b) Extraversion vs introversion

(c) Extraversion vs emotional stability

(d) Extraversion vs Psychoticism

10. Identify the correct sequence of learning for Raghav in accordance with the Behavioural approach

A. He receives appreciation from his parents for eating the disliked vegetables, He is happy that he tried to eat the vegetables.

B. The reinforcement establishing the response can be understood as learning stimulus- response connections and their reinforcement (as noted in above mentioned Raghav's example)

C. Raghav does not like vegetables but eats them because he is hungry.

D. Next time he is hungry he again eats vegetables in anticipation of appreciation (reinforcement)

E. Rahav acquires the taste of those vegetables and finds them good because he is continuously reinforced for eating them

Choose the correct answer from the options given below:

(a) B, E, A, D, C   (b) E, B, A, C, D

(c) C, A, D, H, B   (d) A, C, B, E, D

11. Gordon Allpart considered __________ traits as highly generalised disposition.

They indicate the goal around which a person's entire life seems to revolve.

(a) Cardinal traits   (b) Central traits

(c) Surface traits   (d) Secondary traits

12. Full form of GAS is :

(a) General Adaptation Skills

(b) General Adjustment Skills

(c) General Adaptation Syndrome

(d) General Adjustment Syndrome

13. Identify the correct sequence with respect to bodily response to stress as explained by Selye.

A. Continued exposure to the same stressor or additional stressor drains the body of its resources and leads to the stage of exhaustion

B. Selye observed patients with various injuries and illness in hospital

C. In the alarm reaction stage the individual is ready for fight or flight

D. He noticed a similar pattern of bodily response in all the patients that he observed. He called this pattern General Adaption Syndrome (GAS) which involved three stages

E. In the Resistance stage the parasympathetic nervous system calls for more coutious use of the body's resources

Choose the correct answer from the options given below:

(a) A, E, B, D, C   (b) C, D, B, A, E

(c) B, A, D, C, E   (d) B, D, C, E, A

14. Choose the statement which is not true about Hardiness.

(a) It is a set of beliefs about oneself, the world and how they interact

(b) Studies by kobasa show that people with high levels of stress but low levels of illness share three characteristics

(c) Stress resistant personalities are committed to work, family, hobbies and social life

(d) It consists of 'Three C' i.e., confidence competance and coverage

15. Avoidance oriented strategy involves these steps in order to cope:

A. Minimizing the seriousness of the stress fill situation

B. Coping with logical and analytical thinking

C. Gathering information about one's emotions and feeling

D. Denying the existence of the stress fill situation

E. Replacement of negative thoughts with self-protective thoughts

Choose the correct answer from the options given below:

(a) A, B and E only   (b) B, C and D only

(c) A, C and D only   (d) A, D and E only

16. A person living in a crowded area witnesses quarrelsome neighbors everyday. He faces a lot of problems in reaching work on time. Even while coming back from work, he gets stuck in massive traffic signals. This poses challenges to him.

Identify the source of stress.

(a) Hassles   (b) Traumatic event

(c) Life event   (d) Environmental stress

17. People experiencing delusion of reference feel that-

(a) They hear people talking about them or attach meaning to the actions of others

(b) They are being persecuted by people

(c) They are being loved by people

(d) They have weak memory and do not remember events

18. Which of the following is a key symptom of panic disorder?

(a) Prolonged, vague unemployed fear

(b) Irrational fear of things

(c) Recurrent attacks of intense terror

(d) Inability to stop thinking about a particular idea

19. Match the List I with List II

List I		List II
A.	Diathesis stress model	I.	Abnormal behavior is a symbolic expression of unconscious
B.	Humanistic-existential model	II.	Normal and abnormal behavior ate learnt
C.	Behavior model	III.	Biological predisposition is set off by stressful situation
D.	Psychodynamic model	IV.	Aspects related to human existence

Choose the correct answer from the options given below:

(a) A-I, B-II, C-III, D-IV　　(b) A-III, B-IV, C-II, D-I

(c) A-III, B-II, C-IV, D-I　　(d) A-III, B-IV, C-I, D-II

20. Rita was a victim of the earthquake that occured in her village. She lost her mother and brother in it and was extremely stressed. She is likely to be expressing __________.

(a) Somatic Symptom disorder

(b) Depressive disorder

(c) Post traumatic stress disorder

(d) Bipolar disorder

21. Match the List I with List II

List I		List II
A.	Obsession	I.	Inability to stop thinking of a particular idea
B.	Phobia	II.	need to perform certain behavior repeatedly
C.	Compulsion	III.	Physical symptom in the absence of physical disease
D.	Somatic Symptom	IV.	Irrational fear

Choose the correct answer from the options given below:

(a) A-IV, B-III, C-II, D-I　　(b) A-III, B-II, C-I, D-IV

(c) A-I, B-III, C-II, D-IV　　(d) A-I, B-IV, C-II, D-III

22. The disorder which involves persistent preoccupation about developing a serious disease and constantly working about its possibility is known as __________.

(a) Conversion disorder　　(b) Illness anxiety disorder

(c) Dissociative amnesia (d) Agoraphobia

23. Choose the correct options which explain substance related and addictive disorders.

A. It Includes problems associated with the use and abuse of alcohol cocaine,tabacco and opiods

B. Individual may eat excessive amount of food then purge her-his body of food by using medicines such as laxatives or diuretics

C. An individual body builds up tolerance for the substance

D. It involves excessive intake of high calorie food or subtance such as alcohol or concaine

E. The individual has a distorted body image that leads her him to see himself hers elf as overweight

Choose the correct answer from the options given below:

(a) A, C, E only　　　(b) A, C, D only

(c) C, D, E only　　　(d) B, C, D only

24. A 10 year old was taken to a child psychologist by a social worker as he seemed lost and out of place. When he was found he was hurting a street dog. On being questioned he revealed he ran away from home and had some cash with him that he stole from his mother's purse

Identify the disorder which the child is exhibiting

(a) Autism Spectrum disorder

(b) Intellectual disability

(c) Specific learning disorder

(d) Conduct disorder

25. Arrange the following in the correct order in terms of a person experiencing Bulimia nervosa

A. Bulimia nervosa is a part of a group of disorders called feeding and eating disorders

B. the individual purges his/ her body of food by using medicines such as lakatives and diuretics or by vomiting

C. This eating disorder starts 'with a distorted emotional after purging

D. The individual is relieved of tension and negative emotions after purging

E. The individual eats excessive amounts of food, i.e binges

Choose the correct answer from the options given below:

(a) B, C, A, E, D　　　(b) A, C, E, B, D

(c) C, E, B, D, A　　　(d) E, B, A, C, D

26. The __________ model states that abnormal functioning can result from irrational, inaccurate and illogical thoughts and overgeneralisations.

(a) Psycho dynamic　　(b) Cognitive

(c) Humanistic　　　　(d) Socio cultural

27. Arrange the steps in the modality of treatment in Psycho dynamic therapy.

  A. The therapist overcomes the resistance by repeatedly confronting the patient about it and by uncovering emotions such as anxiety, fear or shame

  B. The process of transference is met with resistance

  C. The outcome of working through is insight

  D. The therapist maintains a permissive attitude that allows the client to continue with his her process of emotional identification. This is the process of transference

  E. The repeated process of using confrontation, clarification an interpretation is known as working through

Choose the correct answer from the options given below:

  (a) D, B, A, E, C

  (b) C, B, D, A, E

  (c) A, C, B, D, E

  (d) B, D, A, E, C

28. Reading brogiaphies of self actualised person, an individual may develop a positive attitude towards hard work and other aspects as the means of achieving success in life. This process of attitude formation as known as learning attitude through __________.

  (a) Association

  (b) Modelling

  (c) Group or cultural norms

  (d) Exposure to information

29. A famous football player changed his attitude towards aerated beverage from positive to negative and developed a positive attitude towards drinking water. A group of youngsters who identified with him and imitated him, also changed their attitude towards aerated beverages from positive to negative. Identify the process of attitude change.

  (a) Balance

  (b) Two-step concept

  (c) Cognitive dissonance

  (d) Cognitive consistency

30. Suppose a person has a little positive attitude towards empowerment of women. After reading about successful women, his attitude becomes more positive towards women empowerment. This direction of attitude changes is to use __________

  (a) Stereotypes   (b) Congruence

  (c) Incongruence   (d) Centrality

31. __________ refers to the cognitive component of attitude, and form the ground on which attitudes stand.

  (a) Belief   (b) Value

  (c) Attitude   (d) Valence

32. A parent praise a teenager for helping out in an after school programme with little kids. As a result, the teen develops a positive attitude towards volunteer work. This is an example of __________.

  (a) Learning attitude through exposure to information

  (b) Learning attitude through observation

  (c) Learning attitude through group as cultural norms

  (d) Learning attitude through rewards and punishment

33. Pro social behavior cannot be explained by:

  (a) Norm of reciprocity

  (b) Norm of equity

  (c) Norm of responsibility

  (d) Norm of intellectual understanding

34. Conformity behavior in a group is likely to be greater if.

  (a) Size of the group is large

  (b) Size of the group is small

  (c) Private expression of opinion exists

  (d) Individuals are independent in their way of thinking

35. Match List I with List II

List I	List II
A. Audience	I. Impulsivity
B. Mobs	II. Complimentary skills
C. Team	III. No cohesiveness
D. Crowd	IV. Passive

Choose the correct answer from the options given below:

  (a) A-I, B-II, C-III, D-IV

  (b) A-IV, B-III, C-II, D-I

  (c) A-IV, B-I, C-II, D-III

  (d) A-II, B-IV, C-III, D-I

36. Arrange the sequence of group formation in correct order as suggested by Tuckman.

  A. Norming   B. Performing

  C. Storming   D. Adjourning

  E. Forming

Choose the correct answer from the options given below

  (a) B, A, D, C, E   (b) D, C, E, A, B

  (c) E, C, A, B, D   (d) A, B, C, D, E

37. In an experiment Latane and his associates, asked a group of male students to clap or cheer as loudly as possible. They varied the group size; individual were either alone, or in groups of two, four and six. The results of the study showed that although the total amount of noise rose up, as size increased, the amount of noise produced by each participant dropped. Each participant put in less effort as the group size increased. Identify the phenomenon.

(a) Social Facilitation

(b) Social Inhibition

(c) Group Polarisation

(d) Social Loafing

38. The attributes associated with an affective psychologist are

A. Positive regard for others

B. Ability to Sympathise

C. Ability to empathise

D. Authenticity

E. Paraphrasing

Choose the correct answer from the options given below

(a) A, B, C, D only   (b) A, C, E, B only

(c) A, C, D, E only   (d) A, B, D, E only

39. __________ refers to the state in which a person feels that she/he has lost something valuable, and is not getting something what she he deserves.

(a) Discrimination   (b) Social disadvantage

(c) Stereotypes   (d) Deprivation

40. Arrange the following in terms of increasing interpersonal physical distance (according to Hall)

A. Public Distance

B. Social Distance

C. Intimate Distance

D. Personal Distance

Choose the correct answer from the options given below:

(a) C, D, B, A   (b) A, B, C, D

(c) B, C, A, D   (d) D, A, C, B

Directions for Quesitons 41 to 45:

Please read the passage and answer the questions that follows.

Projective techniques is a term that eNcompasses any test or procedure designed to increase insight into individuals by allowing them to respond freely to ambiguous stimuli. The underlying assumption is that, when faced with unstructured or ambiguous stimuli, people will reveal aspects of their personality, in their attempt to structure the material.

Projective techniques comprise inkblot methods, story-telling methods, figure drawing methods, and sentence completion methods. In addition to being less structured than objective measures, these four types of projective methods differ from each other in their degree of ambiguity which often resides mainly in their stimuli or in their instruction.

41. Projective techniques are based on __________ theory of personality that tells us, a large part of human behaviour is governed by unconscious motives.

(a) Psychoanalytic   (b) Behavioral

(c) Cultural   (d) Humanistic

42. Select, which one of them is not a projective technique.

(a) Rorschach Inkblot test

(b) Sentence completion test

(c) Eysenck Personality Questionnaie

(d) Draw a person test

43. __________ and __________ are the true stages of Rorschach imkblot test.

(a) Performance proper, enquiry

(b) Social desirability, Acquiescence

(c) Middle category bias, extreme category bias

(d) Structural, unstructured

44. Out of the following which one is not a feature of projective techniques?

(a) Ambiguous/ unstructured stimuli

(b) They suffer from social desirability

(c) No correct or incorrect responses

(d) Each response is considered to reveal a significant aspect of personality

45. Select the projective technique in which the subject is asked to tell a story describing the situation presented in the picture.

(a) Draw -a- person test

(b) Sentence completion test

(c) Rosenzweig's picture- frustration test

(d) The Thematic Apperception test

Directions for Quesitons 46 to 50:

Please read the passage and answer the questions that follows.

Psychotherapy is a treatment for healing of psychological distress. Is not a homogenous treatment method. There are about 400 different types of psychotherapies some of them Focus on acquiring self-understanding while other therapies are more action oriented. Pscho-analysis, behavioral, cognitive and humanistic are the important systems of psycho therapy. All therapeutic approaches are correctives and helping in nature. The effectiveness of a therapeutic approach for a patient depends on a number of factors such as severity[7] of the disorder, degree of distress faced by others, availability of time, therapeutic alliance, effort etc. The therapist requires to see professionally trained before embarking on the journey of psychotheraphy. Try to recollect how you were given rewards, praises and tokens for your good work.

46. When one has the compassion and pity towards the suffering of another but is not able to feel like another person it is called __________.

(a) Unconditional positive regard

(b) Empathy

(c) Sympathy

(d) Non Judgmental Attitude

47. In your growing up years in school at times you get rewarded by being given gold stars and black stars when you did something wrong you could collect these gold and stars could covert into, a this is an example of __________

(a) Positive Reinforcement

(b) Differential Reinforcement

(c) Token economy

(d) Vicarious learning

48. You have recently observed that you have started doing things like your Psychology teacher. You have started dressing up like her. You try to be more systematic and organised like her. This is a perfect example of __________

(a) Modelling

(b) Systematic learning

(c) Principle of Reciprocal Inhibition

(d) Aversive Conducting

49. There are several non specific factors associated with psychotherapy like motivation to change oneself, expectation of improvement after receiving treatment etc. This can be as __________ variable

(a) Therapist

(b) Patient

(c) Audience

(d) Treatment

50. __________ indicates that positive warm of the therapist is not dependent on what the client reveals or does in the therapy Sessions.

(a) Catharsis

(b) Judgmental Attitude

(c) Empathy

(d) Unconditional positive regard

Answer Keys

1. (c)	**2.** (b)	**3.** (a)	**4.** (d)	**5.** (b)	**6.** (a)	**7.** (a)	**8.** (a)	**9.** (b)	**10.** (c)
11. (a)	**12.** (c)	**13.** (d)	**14.** (d)	**15.** (d)	**16.** (a)	**17.** (a)	**18.** (c)	**19.** (b)	**20.** (c)
21. (d)	**22.** (b)	**23.** (b)	**24.** (d)	**25.** (b)	**26.** (b)	**27.** (a)	**28.** (d)	**29.** (b)	**30.** (b)
31. (a)	**32.** (d)	**33.** (d)	**34.** (b)	**35.** (c)	**36.** (c)	**37.** (d)	**38.** (b)	**39.** (d)	**40.** (a)
41. (a)	**42.** (c)	**43.** (a)	**44.** (b)	**45.** (d)	**46.** (c)	**47.** (c)	**48.** (a)	**49.** (b)	**50.** (d)

Explanations

1. (c) Componential Intelligence : Componential or analytical intelligence is the analysis of information to solve problems. Persons high on this ability think analytically and critically and succeed in schools.

2. (b) Group tests, however, do not allow an opportunity to be familiar with the subjects' feelings. Individual tests allow people to answer orally or in a written form or manipulate objects as per the tester's instructions. Group tests generally seek written answers usually in a multiple-choice format.

3. (a) With respect to the role of environment, studies have reported that as children grow in age, their intelligence level tends to move closer to that of their adoptive parents. Children from disadvantaged homes adopted into families with higher socioeconomic status exhibit a large increase in their intelligence scores.

4. (d) Giftedness is exceptional general ability shown in superior performance in a wide variety of areas.

5. (b) An ordinary individual who is engaged in simple occupations like pottery, carpentry, cooking, etc. can also be creative.

6. (a) Social competence (respect for social order, commitment to elders, the young and the needy, concern about others, recognising others' perspectives).

7. (a) Raven's Progressive Matrices (RPM) Test is an example of a non-verbal test.

8. (a) Classification of psychological disorders has been done by the WHO (ICD-10) and the American Psychiatric Association (DSM-5).

9. (b) Extraversion and Intraversion

10. (c) For most behaviourists, the structural unit of personality is the response. Each response is a behaviour, which is emitted to satisfy a specific need.

11. (a) Cardinal traits

12. (c) GAS - General Adaptation Syndrome

13. (d) Selye studied this issue by subjecting animals to a variety of stressors such as high temperature, X-rays and insulin injections, in the laboratory over a long period of time. He also observed patients with various injuries and illnesses in hospitals. Selye noticed a similar pattern of bodily response in all of them. He called this pattern the General Adaptation Syndrome (GAS).

14. (d) It consists of 'the three Cs', i.e. commitment, control, and challenge. Hardiness is a set of beliefs about oneself, the world, and how they interact.

15. (d) Coping is a dynamic situation-specific individual reaction to stress. There are three main types of coping, task-oriented, emotion-oriented, and avoidance-oriented coping.

16. (a) These are the personal stresses we endure as individuals, due to the happenings in our daily life, such as noisy surroundings, commuting, quarrelsome neighbours, electricity and water shortage, traffic snarls, and so on. Attending to various emergencies are daily hassles experienced by a housewife.

17. (a) Many people with schizophrenia develop delusions. A delusion is a false belief that is firmly held on inadequate grounds. It is not affected by rational argument, and has no basis in reality.

18. (c) Another type of anxiety disorder is panic disorder, which consists of recurrent anxiety attacks in which the person experiences intense terror.

19. (b) This model states that psychological disorders develop when a diathesis (biological predisposition to the disorder) is set off by a stressful situation.

20. (c) Very often people who have been caught in a natural disaster (such as tsunami) or have been victims of bomb blasts by terrorists, or been in a serious accident or in a war-related situation, experience post-traumatic stress disorder (PTSD).

21. (d) People who have phobias have irrational fears related to specific objects, people, or situations.

22. (b) Illness anxiety disorder involves persistent preoccupation about developing a serious illness and constantly worrying about this possibility.

23. (b) These disorders include problems associated with the use and abuse of alcohol, cocaine, tobacco and opiods among others, which alter the way people think, feel and behave.

24. (d) The terms conduct disorder and antisocial behaviour refer to age-inappropriate actions and attitudes that violate family expectations, societal norms, and the personal or property rights of others. The behaviours typical of conduct disorder include aggressive actions that cause or threaten harm to people or animals, nonaggressive conduct that causes property damage, major deceitfulness or theft, and serious rule violations.

25. (b) In bulimia nervosa, the individual may eat excessive amounts of food, then purge her/his body of food by using medicines such as laxatives or diuretics or by vomiting. The person often feels disgusted and ashamed when s/he binges and is relieved of tension and negative emotions after purging.

26. (b) Psychological factors are also emphasised by the cognitive model. This model states that abnormal functioning can result from cognitive problems. People may hold assumptions and attitudes about themselves that are irrational and inaccurate.

27. (a) Psychodynamic therapy is of the view that intrapsychic conflicts, i.e. the conflicts that are present within the psyche of the person, are the source of psychological problems. According to behaviour therapies, psychological problems arise due to faulty learning of behaviours and cognitions. The existential therapies postulate that the questions about the meaning of one's life and existence are the cause of psychological problems.

28. (d) Learning through exposure to information : Many attitudes are learned in a social context, but not necessarily in the physical presence of others. Today, with the huge amount of information that is being provided through various media, both positive and negative attitudes are being formed. By reading the biographies of selfactualised persons, an individual may develop a positive

attitude towards hard work and other aspects as the means of achieving success in life.

29. (b) The two-step concept was proposed by S.M. Mohsin, an Indian psychologist. According to him, attitude change takes place in the form of two steps. In the first step, the target of change identifies with the source. T

30. (b) In addition, one must also consider the direction and extent of attitude change. An attitude change may be congruent — it may change in the same direction as the existing attitude (for example, a positive attitude may become more positive, or a negative attitude may become more negative).

31. (a) Beliefs refer to the cognitive component of attitudes, and form the ground on which attitudes stand, such as belief in God, or belief in democracy as a political ideology.

32. (d) Learning attitudes by being rewarded or punished: If an individual is praised for showing a particular attitude, chances are high that s/he will develop that attitude further.

33. (d) Throughout the world, doing good to others and being helpful is described as a virtue. All religions teach us that we should help those who are in need. This behaviour is called helping or pro-social behaviour. Prosocial behaviour is very similar to 'altruism', which means doing something for or thinking about the welfare of others without any self-interest (in Latin 'alter' means 'other', the opposite of 'ego' which means 'self').

34. (b) Size of the group : Conformity is greater when the group is small than when the group is large.

35. (c) Behaviour of people in crowds is irrational and there is no interdependence among members.

36. (c) Tuckman suggested that groups pass through five developmental sequences. These are: forming, storming, norming, performing and adjourning.

37. (d) Social loafing is a reduction in individual effort when working on a collective task, i.e. one in which outputs are pooled with those of other group members. An example of such a task is the game of tug-of-war.

38. (b) How would you know that someone has been listening? Ask her/him to restate what you had said. The person in doing this does not repeat your exact words. S/he makes a summary of the ideas just received and provides you with a restatement of what s/he understands. This is called 'paraphrasing'.

39. (d) These factors include maternal deprivation (separation from the mother, or lack of warmth and stimulation during early years of life), faulty parent-child relationships (rejection, overprotection, over-permissiveness, faulty discipline, etc.), maladaptive family structures (inadequate or disturbed family), and severe stress.

40. (a) Intimate distance (upto 18 inches): The distance you maintain when you are talking privately to someone, or interacting with a very close friend or relative.

   Personal distance (18 inches to 4 feet): The distance you maintain when you are interacting one-to-one with a close friend, relative, or even with someone not very close to you in a work setting or other social situation.

41. (a) Psychoanalytics

42. (c) Eysenck personality questionnaire

43. (a) In the first phase, called performance proper, the subjects are shown the cards and are asked to tell what they see in each of them. In the second phase, called inquiry

44. (b)

45. (d) This test was developed by Morgan and Murray. It is a little more structured than the Inkblot test. The test consists of 30 black and white picture cards and one blank card. Each picture card depicts one or more people in a variety of situations. Each picture is printed on a card.

46. (c) In sympathy, one has compassion and pity towards the suffering of another but is not able to feel like the other person.

47. (c) The tokens are collected and exchanged for a reward such as an outing for the patient or a treat for the child. This is known as token economy.

48. (a) Modelling is the procedure wherein the client learns to behave in a certain way by observing the behaviour of a role model or the therapist who initially acts as the role model.

49. (b) Non-specific factors attributable to the client/ patient are motivation for change, expectation of improvement due to the treatment, etc. These are called patient variables.

50. (d) Unconditional positive regard indicates that the positive warmth of the therapist is not dependent on what the client reveals or does in the therapy sessions.

1. According to Freud, which element of personality does not care for moral values, society or other individuals?
   (a) Super ego
   (b) Ego
   (c) Id
   (d) Libido

2. Match List - I with List - II

List I	List II
A. Self-Efficacy	I. Cattell
B. Real Self	II. Maslow
C. Self-Report measure	III. Bandura
D. Self-Actualization	IV. Rogers

   Choose the correct answer from the options given below
   (a) A-I, B-II, C-III, D-IV
   (b) A-II, B-IV, C-III, D-I
   (c) A-IV, B-II, C-I, D-III
   (d) A-III, B-IV, C-I, D-II

3. Street Smartness' is a part of :
   (a) Multiple Intelligence
   (b) Contextual Intelligence
   (c) Experiential Intelligence
   (d) Componential Intelligence

4. The important ideas proposed by Carl Rogers and Abraham Maslow are :
   A. People have a tendency to maximise self concept through self actualisation.
   B. There is a collective unconscious consisting of archetypes
   C. Behaviour is goal directed and worthwhile people try to express capabilities, potentials and talents to the fullest possible extent.
   D. An atmosphere of unconditional positive regard must be created in order to ensure enhancement of one's self concept.
   E. Human beings display a wide range of variations in psychological attributes (and it is possible)
   Choose the correct answer from the options given below:
   (a) A, B, D only
   (b) B, C, E only
   (c) A, D, E only
   (d) A, C, D only

5. The clinical psychologist assessed persm B's personality using a test based on less structured stimuli. The test helped to assess his unconscious motives and feelings. Identify the test used by the psychologist.
   (a) Self report measure
   (b) Projective Technique
   (c) Behavioural Analysis
   (d) Psychometric test

6. In __________ a person defends against anxiety by adopting behaviours opposite to her/his hue feelings.
   (a) Projection
   (b) Reaction formation
   (c) Rationalisation
   (d) Regression

7. __________ has been found extremely useful in career guidance, vocational exploration and occupational testing.
   (a) Minnesota Multiphasic Personality Inventory
   (b) Eysenck Personality Questionnaire
   (c) Sixteen Personality factor Questionnaire
   (d) Sentence Completion Test

8. __________ refers to our ability to organise and monitor our own behaviour,
   (a) Self efficacy
   (b) Self esteem
   (c) Self concept
   (d) Self regulation

9. A child is going through a tough time and is facing problems in school. He decides to discuss the same with the school counsellor so that he can vent out Iris feelings. Identify the type of coping response in this.
   (a) Avoidance oriented
   (b) Emotion oriented
   (c) Task oriented
   (d) Relaxation

10. Social support in the form of assistance involving material aid such as money or goods, is known as __________ support.
   (a) Emotional
   (b) Positive
   (c) Tangible
   (d) Informational

11. Radhika wants to do everything perfectly. Every time this expectation leads to disappointment and stress. Thus, the source of her psychological stress is ________.

    (a) Frustration   (b) Conflict

    (c) Internal Pressure   (d) Social Pressure

12. Match List - I with List – II

List I	List II
A. Emotional effect	I. Increased heart rate, constriction of blood vessels
B. Physiological effect	II. Mood swing, increased psychological tension
C. Cognitive effect	III. Disrupted sleep pattern, increased absenteeism
D. Behavioural effect	IV. Poor concentration, reduced short term memory capacity

Choose the correct answer from the options given below :

    (a) A-III, B-II, C-I, D-IV

    (b) A-IV, B-I, C-III, D-II

    (c) A-II, B-I, C-IV, D-III

    (d) A-I, B-IV, C-III, D-II

13. Once the date sheet was announced, the students started paying attention and preparing for the examination. They made notes, took tests and attended coaching class neglecting their diet and sleep. As the examination approached students felt draining of bodily resources and falling sick indicates _________ stage of General Adaptations syndrome.

    (a) Exhaustion stage   (b) Alarm reaction stage

    (c) Resistance stage   (d) Adjourning stage

14. In which of the following disorders, children may fuss, scream, throw severe tantrums, or make suicidal gestures ?

    (a) Obsessive compulsive and related disorder

    (b) Dissociative disorder

    (c) Separation anxiety disorder

    (d) Phobia

15. Dominating and bullying other without provocation is __________ type of aggression.

    (a) Verbal aggression

    (b) Proactive aggression

    (c) Physical aggression

    (d) Hostile aggression

16. Match List - I with List - II

List I	List II
A. Alogia	I. Lack of motivation to do the task
B. Delusion	II. Perception without stimuli
C. Avolition	III. False Belief
D. Hallucination	IV. Poverty of speech

Choose the correct answer from the options given below :

    (a) A-II, B-I, C-III, D-IV

    (b) A-IV, B-III, C-I, D-II

    (c) A-I, B-II, C-IV, D-III

    (d) A-III, B-IV, C-II, D-I

17. Bulimia Nersosa is a/an _______

    (a) Depressive disorder

    (b) Eating disorder

    (c) Conduct disorder

    (d) Anxiety disorder

18. Manjeet is inattentive, hyperactive and mostly impulsive. He is most likely to be diagnosed with ________.

    (a) Specific Learning Disorder

    (b) Intellectual Deficiency

    (c) Autism Spectrum disorder

    (d) Attention deficit hyper activity disorder

19. Match List - I with List - II

List I	List II
A. Positive symptoms of schizophrenia	I. Pathological deficits
B. Negative symptoms of schizophrenia	II. Odd grimaces and gestures
C. Inappropriate affect	III. Bizarre additions
D. Psychomotor symptoms of schizophrenia	IV. Emotion that are unsuited to the situation

Choose the correct answer from the options given below

    (a) A-I, B-IV, C-III, D-II

    (b) A-II, B-III, C-I, D-IV

    (c) A-III, B-I, C-IV, D-II

    (d) A-IV, B-I, C-II, D-III

20. Rajini uses yoga and meditation to focus her attention. This is a form of therapy

   (a) Electro convulsive

   (b) Humanistic existential

   (c) Cognitive

   (d) Alternative

21. The chief benefit of humanistic therapy is which is __________ the process of gaining increasing understanding of oneself and one's aspirations, emotions and motives.

   (a) Emotional insight

   (b) Instituting adaptive behaviours

   (c) Cognitive restructuring

   (d) Personal Growth

22. Which of the following is not an ethical standard in Psychotherapy ?

   (a) Informed consent needs to be taken

   (b) Help to be provided by mindfulness based meditation

   (c) Confidentiality of the client should be maintained

   (d) Respect for human rights and dignity

23. When using the cognitive behaviour therapy, we follow some methods given below. Which one of the following is not used in this therapy ?

   A. Addressing the childhood travmas on the client

   B. Addressing the biological aspects through relaxation

   C. Addressing the psychological aspects through behaviour therapy

   D. Addressing the social aspects through environmental changes.

Choose the correct answer from the options given below :

   (a) A, C, D

   (b) A, B, C, D

   (c) B, C, D

   (d) A, B, D

24. An alcoholic is given a mild electric shock and asked to smell the alcohol. Repeatedly pairing the smell of alcohol with the pair of the shock leads to giving up of alcohol by the person. Identify the behavioural technique being used here.

   (a) Negative reinforcement

   (b) Token economy

   (c) Aversive condition

   (d) Modeling

25. Out of the following statements, identify the statement that holds tine for Albert Ellist Rational Emotive therapy.

   A. The client is taught to recognise the bodily process and the emotions that are bloclud out from awareness thus increasing self awareness and self acceptance

   B. Unwanted behaviour can be reduced and wanted behaviour can be increased simultaneously through differential reinforcement

   C. The first step in RET is the (ABC) antecedent belief consequence analysis.

   D In the process of RET, the irrational beliefs are refuted by the therapist through a process of non-directive questioning.

Choose the correct answer from the options given below :

   (a) C and D only

   (b) A and B only

   (c) B and D only

   (d) C and B only

26. Sherif's summer camp experiment was conducted in 4 phases. Arrange in correct sequence the phases given below :

   A. Intergroup competition

   B. Friendship formation

   C. Intergroup cooperation

   D. Ingroup formation

Choose the correct answer from the options given below :

   (a) C, A, B, D

   (b) B, D, A, C

   (c) A, B, C, D

   (d) D, A, B, C

27. __________ refers to togetherness, binding, or mutual attraction among group members

   (a) Group think

   (b) Status

   (c) Cohesiveness

   (d) Roles

28. Manish gives something free to Raj at saying that it is for promotion of the product. Soon afterwards he asks Rajat to buy a product sold by his company. This technique of compliance is known as __________.

   (a) Foot in the door technique

   (b) The deadline technique

   (c) The door in the face technique

   (d) No refusal technique

29. Match List - I with List - II

List I		List II
A. Secondary group	I.	'We' feeling, supposed to be similar are viewed favourably
B. In-group	II.	Pre existing fomation, boundaries are less permeable
C. Primary group	III.	Functions are explicitly stated, based on specific rates
D. Formal group	IV.	Joins by choice, easy to leave

Choose the correct answer from the options given below :

(a) A-IV, B-I, C-II, D-III

(b) A-II, B-I, C-IV, D-III

(c) A-III, B-II, C-I, D-IV

(d) A-I, B-IV, C-III, D-II

30. Which one of the following is not associated with the stages of group formation ?

(a) Forming (b) Alarming

(c) Storming (d) Performing

31. To understand interpersonal physical distance as given by Edward Hall, align the following from the least to the maximum distance.

A. Personal distance

B. Public distance

C. Social distance

D. Intimate distance

Choose the correct answer from the options given below :

(a) B, C, A, D (b) C, B, A, D

(c) A, C, D, B (d) D, A, C, B

32. The experience of crowding has the following features:

A. Increase in privacy

B. Feeling of loss of control over social interactions

C. Feeling of discomfort

D. Negative view of the space around the person

E. Increase in motivation

Choose the correct answer from the options given below :

(a) A, B, D only

(b) B, C, D only

(c) C, D, E only

(d) A, C, E only

33. Match List - I with List - II

List I		List II
A. Body language	I.	Repeat or summarise in one's own words
B. Paraphrase	II.	Behavioural expressions are consistent with what one values
C. Reception	III.	Non verbal actions
D. Authenticity	IV.	The initial step in the listening process

Choose the correct answer from the options given below :

(a) A-I, B-III, C-II, D-IV

(b) A-II, B-IV, C-I, D-III

(c) A-III, B-I, C-IV, D-II

(d) A-IV, B-I, C-II, D-III

34. J.P. Guilford classified the structure-of-intellect model into __________.

(a) Cognition, Memory and Perception

(b) Operations, Memory and Perception

(c) Operations, Contents and Products

(d) Operations, Contents and Memory

35. According to the PASS model, _________ allows us to think of possible courses of action, implement them to reach the target, and evaluate their effectiveness.

(a) Pl arming

(b) Arousal

(c) Simultaneous processing

(d) Successive processing

36. Persons high on __________ intelligence have finer sensibilities regarding their identity, human existence and meaning of life.

(a) Interpersonal

(b) Intrapersonal

(c) Spatial

(d) Linguistic

37. Atul is able to monitor Iris own and others emotions, discriminate amongst them and he uses this information to guide Iris thinking and actions. He exhibits _________.

(a) High Intelligence Quotient

(b) High Intelligence Quotient and Emotional Quotient

(c) High Emotional Intelligence

(d) High Emotional Intelligence but low Intelligence Quotient

38. ________ involves employing systematic, organized and objective procedures to record behavioural phenomena occurring naturally in real time.

(a) Psychological test

(b) Self Report

(c) Observation

(d) Case study

39. The IQ range for individuals with moderate intellectual deficiency is

(a) 55 to 70　　　　　(b) 35 to 50

(c) 90 to 110　　　　(d) 20 to 35

40. The instinctual life force that energises the id is called

(a) Ego　　　　　　　(b) Libido

(c) Superego　　　　(d) Defence mechanisms

Directions for Quesitons 41 to 45:

Please read the passage and answer the questions that follows.

In our day-to day life, we assign certain causes or reasons to a person's behaviour. This process is called attribution. Broadly, causes of a person are attributed to internal and external factors. Internal factors are related to situation. With reference to success and failure, Weiner has classified causes into internal/external and stable/unstable factors. In general, people attribute success to internal factors such as their ability and hard work. However, failure is attributed to external factors such as task difficulty and bad luck. Ability/fate and hard-work/task-difficulty are considered as stable and unstable factors respectively. Stable factors refer to those causes that do not change with time. It has been observed that people have a tendency to give greater weightage to internal factors than external one. Tills phenomenon is called the fundamental attribution error. This tendency is stronger in some cultures than in others. Research suggests that Indians tend to make more external attributions than Americans do.

41. Match List - I with List - II.

List – I (Characteristics)	List – II (Causal factors)
A. Task characteristics	I. Internal-stable
B. Hard work	II. External-stable
C. Fate	III. Unstable- Internal
D. Ability	IV. Unstable-External

Choose the correct answer from the options given below

(a) A-I, B-II, C-III, D-IV

(b) A-II, B-IV, C-III, D-I

(c) A-III, B-I, C-IV, D-II

(d) A-IV, B-III, C-II, D-I

42. As per Weiner, if person A gives greater weightage to internal factors, then which one of the following will hold tine for A ?

(a) The task characteristic

(b) A's intelligence

(c) A's luck

(d) Pleasant weather conditions

43. People generally attribute failure to :

(a) Personality

(b) Disposition

(c) External factors

(d) Internal factors

44. Fundamental attribution error is known as a tendency to give greater weightage to :

(a) external factors than internal factors

(b) stable factors than unstable factors

(c) internal factors then external factors

(d) unstable factors than stable factors

45. Weiner is famous for his work on :

(a) Attraction

(b) Aptitude

(c) Attribution

(d) Affection

Directions for Quesitons 46 to 50:

Please read the passage and answer the questions that follows.

A person's thinking or behaviour is classified as abnormal if it violates social nouns. Norms are expected behaviour in a group. Every culture has certain standards for accepting behaviour as per socially acceptable norms. For example - child marriage was a noun about hundred years ago. Those who did not many their girl child like everyone else were considered to be breaking the norm. The most obvious problem with defining abnormality using social norms is that there is no universal agreement over social norms. Another definition of abnormality states that a person is considered abnormal if he/she is unable to perform the behaviours necessary for day-to-day living eg. self care, holding a job, managing everyday tasks. We must understand that mental health issues are prevalent in all cultures as there is ignorance and fear about psychological disorders. It is believed that these

46. 'A person's thinking or behaviour is classified as abnormal if it isolates social norms'. This statement refers to the concept of ________ in Abnormal Psychology.

(a) Deviance　　　　　(b) Distress

(c) Dysfunction　　　　(d) Danger

47. Norms of societies grow from its history, values, institutions, habits, skills, technology, art etc. These are together referred as its __________.

(a) Community

(b) Social norms

(c) Culture

(d) Rules

48. 'It is believed that psychological disorders are something to be ashamed of'. This is because of a __________ attached to mental illness.

(a) Deviance

(b) Danger

(c) Distress

(d) Stigma

49. 'A person is considered to be abnormal if he/she is unable to perform the behaviours necessary for day to day living'. This explains abnormality due to __________.

(a) Deviance

(b) Distress

(c) Dysfunction

(d) Danger

50. The best criterion for determining the normality of behaviour is that it :

(a) follows the norms of a society

(b) fosters overall wellbeing

(c) is not distressing

(d) is not dangerous

Answer Keys

1. (c)	**2.** (d)	**3.** (b)	**4.** (d)	**5.** (b)	**6.** (b)	**7.** (c)	**8.** (d)	**9.** (d)	**10.** (c)
11. (c)	**12.** (c)	**13.** (a)	**14.** (c)	**15.** (b)	**16.** (b)	**17.** (b)	**18.** (d)	**19.** (c)	**20.** (d)
21. (d)	**22.** (b)	**23.** (c)	**24.** (c)	**25.** (a)	**26.** (b)	**27.** (c)	**28.** (c)	**29.** (a)	**30.** (b)
31. (d)	**32.** (b)	**33.** (c)	**34.** (c)	**35.** (a)	**36.** (b)	**37.** (c)	**38.** (c)	**39.** (b)	**40.** (b)
41. (d)	**42.** (c)	**43.** (c)	**44.** (c)	**45.** (c)	**46.** (b)	**47.** (a)	**48.** (c)	**49.** (d)	**50.** (c)

Explanations

1. (c) Id : It is the source of a person's instinctual energy. It deals with immediate gratification of primitive needs, sexual desires and aggressive impulses. It works on the pleasure principle, which assumes that people seek pleasure and try to avoid pain.

2. (d) Maslow has given a detailed account of psychologically healthy people in terms of their attainment of self-actualisation, a state in which people have reached their own fullest potential.

3. (b) Contextual or practical intelligence involves the ability to deal with environmental demands encountered on a daily basis. It may be called 'street smartness' or 'business sense'.

4. (d) Rogers suggests that each person also has a concept of ideal self. An ideal self is the self that a person would like to be. When there is a correspondence between the real self and ideal self, a person is generally happy. Discrepancy between the real self and ideal self often results in unhappiness and dissatisfaction. Rogers' basic principle is that people have a tendency to maximise self-concept through self-actualisation.

5. (b) rojective techniques were developed to assess unconscious motives and feelings. These techniques are based on the assumption that a less structured or unstructured stimulus or situation will allow the individual to project her/ his feelings, desires and needs on to that situation.

6. (b) In reaction formation, a person defends against anxiety by adopting behaviours opposite to her/ his true feelings.

7. (c) 16PF The test can be used with high school level students as well as with adults. It has been found extremely useful in career guidance, vocational exploration, and occupational testing.

8. (d) Self-regulation refers to our ability to organise and monitor our own behaviour

9. (d) Relaxation procedures are used to decrease the anxiety levels.

10. (c) Social support may be in the form of tangible support or assistance involving material aid, such as money, goods, services, etc.

11. (c) Internal pressures stem from beliefs based upon expectations from inside us to ourselves such as, 'I must do everything perfectly'. Such expectations can only lead to disappointment.

12. (c) Emotional Effects : Those who suffer from stress are far more likely to experience mood swings, and show erratic behaviour that may alienate them from family and friends.

13. (a) Exhaustion stage : Continued exposure to the same stressor or additional stressors drains the body of its resources and leads to the third stage of exhaustion.

14. (c) To avoid separation, children with SAD may fuss, scream, throw severe tantrums, or make suicidal gestures

15. (b) Proactive aggression (i.e. dominating and bullying others without provocation).

16. (b) People with schizophrenia may have hallucinations, i.e. perceptions that occur in the absence of external stimuli.

17. (b) Another group of disorders which are of special interest to young people are eating disorders. These include anorexia nervosa, bulimia nervosa, and binge eating.

18. (d) Hyperactivity also takes many forms. Children with ADHD are in constant motion. Sitting still through a lesson is impossible for them. The child may fidget, squirm, climb and run around the room aimlessly.

19. (c) Positive symptoms are 'pathological excesses' or 'bizarre additions' to a person's behaviour.

20. (d) Alternative therapies are so called, because they are alternative treatment possibilities to the conventional drug treatment or psychotherapy. There are many alternative therapies such as yoga, meditation, acupuncture, herbal remedies and so on. In the past 25 years, yoga and meditation have gained popularity as treatment programmes for psychological distress.

21. (d) The humanistic therapy values personal growth as the chief benefit.

22. (b) Confidentiality of the client should be maintained.

Other feature of Ethics in Psychology are :

- Alleviating personal distress and suffering should be the goal of all attempts of the therapist.

- Integrity of the practitioner-client relationship is important.

- Respect for human rights and dignity.

- Professional competence and skills are essential.

23. (c) The rationale is that the client's distress has its origins in the biological, psychological, and social realms. Hence, addressing the biological aspects through relaxation procedures, the psychological ones through behaviour therapy and cognitive therapy techniques and the social ones with environmental manipulations makes CBT a comprehensive technique which is easy to use, applicable to a variety of disorders, and has proven efficacy

24. (c) Aversive conditioning refers to repeated association of undesired response with an aversive consequence.

25. (a) The first step in RET is the antecedentbelief-consequence (ABC) analysis. Antecedent events, which caused the psychological distress, are noted. The client is also interviewed to find the irrational beliefs, which are distorting the present reality.

26. (b) The experiment consisted of four phases, viz. friendship formation, group formation, intergroup competition, and intergroup cooperation

27. (c) Cohesiveness refers to togetherness, binding, or mutual attraction among group members.

28. (c) The door-in-the-face technique : In this technique, you begin with a large request and when this is refused a later request for something smaller, the one that was actually desired, is made, which is usually granted by the person.

29. (a) A major difference between primary and secondary groups is that primary groups are pre-existing formations which are usually given to the individual whereas secondary groups are those which the individual joins by choice.

30. (b) Tuckman suggested that groups pass through five developmental sequences. These are: forming, storming, norming, performing and adjourning

31. (d) Edward Hall, an anthropologist, mentioned four kinds of interpersonal physical distance, depending on the situation: • Intimate distance (upto 18 inches) : The distance you maintain when you are talking privately to someone, or interacting with a very close friend or relative.

32. (b) The experience of crowding has the following features:

- Feeling of discomfort,

- Loss or decrease in privacy,

- Negative view of the space around the person, and

- Feeling of loss of control over social interaction.

33. (c) Reception The initial step in the listening process is the reception of a stimulus or message. A message could be auditory and/or visual. The hearing process is based on a complex set of physical interactions that take place involving the ear and the brain

34. (c) J.P. Guilford proposed the structureof-intellect model which classifies intellectual traits among three dimensions: operations, contents, and products.

35. (a) Planning : This is an essential feature of intelligence. After the information is attended to and processed, planning is activated. It allows us to think of the possible courses of action, implement them to reach a target, and evaluate their effectiveness.

36. (b) Intrapersonal (an ability to understand of one's own feelings, motives, and desires): This refers to the knowledge of one's internal strengths and limitations and using that knowledge to effectively relate to others. Persons high on this ability have finer sensibilities regarding their identity, human existence, and meaning of life.

37. (c) This concept was first introduced by Salovey and Mayer who considered emotional intelligence as "the ability to monitor one's own and other's emotions, to discriminate among them, and to use the information to guide one's thinking and actions".

38. (c) Observation involves employing systematic, organised, and objective procedures to record behavioural phenomena occurring naturally in real time.

39. (b) moderate (IQs 35–40 to approximately

40. (b) The instinctual life force that energises the id is called libido.

41. (d)

	Internal Factors	External Factors
Stable Factors	Ability	Fate
Unstable Factors	Effort, Hard Work	Task Characteristics

42. (c) In making attributions, there is an overall tendency for people to give greater weightage to internal or dispositional factors, than to external or situational factors. This is called the fundamental attribution error.

43. (c) In general, people attribute success to internal factors, such as their ability or hard work. They attribute failure to external factors, such as bad luck, the difficulty of the task, and so on.

44. (c) In making attributions, there is an overall tendency for people to give greater weightage to internal or dispositional factors, than to external or situational factors. This is called the fundamental attribution error.

45. (c) When people make attributions for success and failure, the causes they give can be classified into internal or external factors, and also into stable or unstable factors. Stable factors refer to those causes that do not change with time, while unstable factors are those that do change.

46. (b)

47. (a) That is, psychological disorders are deviant (different, extreme, unusual, even bizarre)

48. (c)

49. (d) Again it is commonly believed that psychological disorder is something to be ashamed of. The stigma attached to mental illness means that people are hesitant to consult a doctor or psychologist because they are ashamed of their problems.

50. (c) dysfunctional (interfering with the person's ability to carry out daily activities in a constructive way.

SOCIOLOGY

1. 'Death rate' of a country can be understood as a :
   (a) Individual phenomenon
   (b) Social phenomenon
   (c) Statistical phenomenon
   (d) Arithmetical phenomenon

2. Population momentum refers to a situation where :
   (a) there is a rise in birth rate
   (b) there is a decline in death rate
   (c) a large cohort of women of reproductive age will fuel population growth over the next generation, even if each woman has fewer children
   (d) women in reproductive age group decline and hence population growth also declines.

3. Population growth is linked to overall levels of economic development and society's a typical pattern of development related population growth. This theory can be understood as :
   (a) Malthusian theory of population growth
   (b) Population Explosion theory
   (c) Theory of Demographic Transition
   (d) Theory of Population growth

4. Which of the following has **not** influenced rural to urban migration?
   (a) decline of common property resources
   (b) rapid urbanisation
   (c) relative anonymity
   (d) agricultural growth

5. Which of the following is NOT part of the Malthusian Theory of population :
   (a) Negative Checks
   (b) Positive Checks
   (c) Geometric Progression
   (d) Arithmetic Progression

6. Which among these is not true about caste ?
   (a) Caste is not determined by birth
   (b) Caste is endogamous group
   (c) There is hierarchy within caste
   (d) Caste is traditionally linked to occupation

7. Match **List I** with **List II** :

List I: Social Scientists and Reformers	List II: Contributed to society
A. M.S. Srinivas	I. Satyashodhok Samaj
B. Savitri Bai Phule	II. Leader of lower caste movement in South India
C. Jotirao Phule	III. Sanskritisation
D. E.V. Ramasami Periyar	IV. First headmistress of the country's first school for girls in Pune

Choose the correct answer from the options given below :
   (a) A-III, B-IV, C-I, D-II
   (b) A-I, B-II, C-III, D-IV
   (c) A-II, B-III, C-I, D-IV
   (d) A-IV, B-II, C-III, D-I

8. Extended family may be understood as :
   A. set of sisters living together with their families
   B. two generations living together
   C. set of brothers living together with their families
   D. women headed family

Choose the correct answer from the options given below :
   (a) B, C, D only
   (b) A, B, D only
   (c) A, B, C only
   (d) A, C, D only

9. Choose a statement that is incorrect for Khasi Matriliny Society :
   (a) Despite Matriliny, men are the power holders in Khasi Society
   (b) It is a society where women exercise dominance
   (c) It generates role conflict for men
   (d) Men are defacto power holders

10. Which of the following is NOT a characteristic of Dominant Caste ?
   (a) These castes have large population
   (b) They enjoy political power
   (c) Their social status is relatively higher in caste hierarchy
   (d) They draw economic power from their employment in government jobs

11. Why did British intervene in the caste system of India?
   (a) Caste system in India was extremely complex and needed intervention.
   (b) Indians were not able to resolve the problem of caste system themselves.
   (c) Wanted to govern the country efficiently.
   (d) Had a deep respect for Indians and their culture.

12. The non-economic characters of the market are :
   A. symbol of inter-group social relations
   B. expression of hierarchy and social distance
   C. buying and selling of forest products
   D. indigenous banking system of 'hundi'

Choose the correct answer from the options given below :

(a) A and D only   (b) C and D only

(c) A and B only   (d) B and C only

13. Arrange the statements given below in such a manner that depicts the emergence of new markets and business groups in India during colonial era.

A. Raw materials and agricultural products were exported from India to England under colonial rule

B. India began to be linked to the world capitalist economy, at the same time new groups entered into trade and business.

C. During pre colonial era, India was a major supplier of manufactured goods to tire world market.

D. In contemporary times, some of the Marwari families in India control India's industry

Choose the correct answer from the options given below :

(a) C, B, D and A   (b) C, D, B and A

(c) B, D, C and A   (d) C, A, B and D

14. Social inclusion happens through :

(a) limited employment

(b) limited food supply

(c) limited educational qualification

(d) increased social, cultural and political rights

15. 'Social Stratification' has the following features :

A. Intergenerational

B. legitimised by belief and Ideology

C. leads to discrimination

D. helps in the equitable distribution of resources

Choose the **correct** answer from the options given below :

(a) A, C and D only   (b) A, B and C only

(c) B, C and D only   (d) A, B and D only

16. During the Covid-19 pandemic, there was lack of medical supplies in India. However, it was found that some people due to their good social network were able to get the medical supplies. This example reflects which kind of capital ?

(a) Educational Capital

(b) Social Capital

(c) Economic Capital

(d) Cultural Capital

17. Who wrote Analogy of Religion ?

(a) M.G. Ranade

(b) Sir Syyed A. Khan

(c) Jotiba Phule

(d) Bishop Joseph Butler

18. Some of the enduring - characteristics of state - nation in India is :

A. allow multiple and complementary identities

B. political stability through policies of cultural recognition

C. by following an assimilationist model

D. participatory democracy

Choose the correct answer from the options given below :

(a) A, B, C only   (b) A, B, D only

(c) B, C, D only   (d) A, C, D only

19. Regionalism in India can be understood with reference to :

(a) Religion   (b) Caste

(c) Class   (d) Ethnicity

20. Bachpan Bachao Aandolam is a NGO that works for the betterment of children. This example can be categorised under which type of society ?

(a) Civil society   (b) Stateless society

(c) Authoritarian society (d) State society

21. Bengalimatrimony.com can considered to be an expression of :

(a) community identity

(b) linguistic identity

(c) regional identity

(d) religious identity

22. Industrialisation and urbanisation in India did not happen quite the way it did in Britain because :

(a) We began industrialisation late

(b) Our industrialisation & urbanisation in modern period were governed by colonial interests

(c) Industrialisation and urbanisation in India were aimed at profit maximisation only

(d) Indian industrialists used unfair means to hire & forcibly keep labourers

23. The legacy of 19th century social reforms can be traced to the pre-colonial ideas of :

(a) Buddhist and Sufi movements

(b) Caste-based movements

(c) Western modernity

(d) Secularism

24. Sanskritization and urbanization are respectively the processes of :

(a) Social & Cultural change

(b) Cultural & Structural change

(c) Structural & Cultural change

(d) Social & Non-Social change

25. M.S.A. Rao describes different situations of impact of urban influences in India. Which of the following is part of the situations of urban impact given by Rao ?

A. When more people start taking up agricultural work

B. When an industrial town comes up in the midst of villages

C. When there is an increase in the growth of metropolitan cities

D. When villagers in sizeable numbers migrate to work in far off cities

Choose the correct answer from the options given below :

(a) B, C & D only

(b) A, B & C only

(c) A, C & D only

(d) A, B & D only

26. Shopping Malls reflect a feature of which one of the following processes :

(a) Secularisation

(b) Sanskritisation

(c) Colonialism

(d) Urbanisation

27. Out of the following select the social welfare responsibilities that Panchayat needs to perform :

A. Recording of Birth and Death Rates and construction of Roads

B. Construction of public buildings and promoting small cottage industries

C. Maintaining burial grounds and establishment of child welfare centres

D. Propagation of family planning and promotion of agricultural activities

Choose the correct answer from the options given below :

(a) A and B only   (b) B and C only

(c) D and A only   (d) C and D only

28. Match the categories with correct explanations:

List I: Categories	List II: Explanation
A. Panchayati Raj System	I. Interest groups, dominant groups
B. Political Party	II. Village courts, address violence-against women
C. FICCI, ASSOCHAM	III. Gram-Sabha, Local self-governance
D. Nyaya Panchayat	IV. Governmental power, formal groups

Choose the correct answer from the options given below :

(a) A-I, B-II, C-III, D-IV

(b) A-II, B-III, C-IV, D-I

(c) A-III, B-IV, C-I, D-II

(d) A-IV, B-I, C-II, D-III

29. The name of the famous sociologist who argued that the use of machinery actually deskills workers:

(a) E.P. Thompson   (b) Karl Marx

(c) Satish Saberwal   (d) Harry Braverman

30. Repetitive and exhausting work in Industrialisation gives rise to:

(a) Economic equality   (b) Leisure time

(c) Informalisation   (d) Alienation

31. In an automobile company, worker A is making seat of a car, worker B is making tyres of a car, worker C is making body of a car; worker D is painting the car. What would you call this process?

(a) Rationalisation   (b) Bureaucratisation

(c) Privatisation   (d) Assembly line

32. India has a small size of organised sector. Which of the following statements are not the social implications of this small size of organised sector?

(a) Very few people have the experience of working in a large firm

(b) Very few Indians have access to secure jobs

(c) People are left to the whims and fancies of the employer or contractor

(d) People have the experience of collectively fighting for proper wages and safe working conditions.

33. Match the industrial concepts given in List I with their characteristics in List II.

List I: Industrial concepts	List II: Characteristics
A. Bombay Textile Strike	I. Extended working hours
B. Flexi-time	II. Informal sector
C. Beedi workers	III. Datta Samant
D. Badli workers	IV. Contract work in organised sector

Choose the correct answer from the options given below :

(a) A-III, B-IV, C-I, D-II

(b) A-IV, B-I, C-III, D-II

(c) A-III, B-I, C-II, D-IV

(d) A-II, B-IV, C-I, D-III

34. Match the names of newspapers given in List I with the pioneers given in List II.

List I: Names of newspapers	List II: Eminent personalities (Pioneer)
A. Sambad-Kaumudi	I. B.R. Ambedkar
B. Mook Nayak	II. Ishwar Chandra Vidyasagar
C. Bombay Samachar	III. Raja Ram Mohan Roy
D. Shome Prakash	IV. Fardoonji Murzban

Choose the correct answer from the options given below :

(a) A-II, B-III, C-I, D-IV

(b) A-IV, B-III, C-II, D-I

(c) A-I, B-II, C-III, D-IV

(d) A-III, B-I, C-IV, D-II

35. The shift of Nike factory from Japan in 1960 to India in the 1990s is an example of :

(a) multinational expansion

(b) liberalisation of government policies

(c) globalisation and flexible labour

(d) privatisation

36. What are the features of globalization ?

A. Movement of population, MNCs

B. Opening up of economy, loss of livelihood

C. Globalisation of finance and communication

D. Restriction on import and export of goods

Choose the correct answer from the options given below :

(a) B, C, D only

(b) D, C, A only

(c) A, B, C only

(d) A, B, D only

37. Match the following movements with their appropriate examples :

List I: Category of Movements	List II: Examples
A. New Social Movement	I. Right to Information
B. Reformist Movement	II. Naxalite Movement
C. Redemptive Movement	III. Ezhawa Community
D. Revolutionary Movement	IV. Chipko Movement

Choose the correct answer from the options given below :

(a) A-IV, B-I, C-III, D-II

(b) A-III, B-II, C-I, D-IV

(c) A-II, B-IV, C-I, D-III

(d) A-IV, B-III, C-II, D-I

38. Which of the following are characteristic of Social Movements ?

A. Ideology, sustained action, social change

B. Organisation, leadership, campaigns

C. Collective action, spontaneity, protest

D. Ideology, organisations, leadership

Choose the correct answer from the options given below :

(a) A, B, D only

(b) A, B, C only

(c) B, C, D only

(d) A, C, D only

39. Chipko Movement is an example of which of the following:

(a) Ecological Movement

(b) Women's Movement

(c) Peasant Movement

(d) Tribal Movement

40. Which of the following is not a Dalit Movement?

(a) Satnami Movement

(b) Adi Dharma Movement

(c) Tebhaga Movement

(d) Mahar Movement

Directions for Quesitons 41 to 45:

Please read the passage and answer the questions that follows.

Another significant change in rural society that is linked to the commercialisation of agriculture has been the growth of migrant agricultural labour. As 'traditional' bonds of patronage between labourers or tenants and landlords broke down, and as the seasonal demand for agricultural labour increased in prosperous Green Revolution regions such as the Punjab, a pattern of seasonal migration emerged in which thousands of workers circulate between their home villages and more prosperous areas where there is more demand for labour and higher wages. Labourers migrate also due to the increasing inequalities in rural areas from the mid-1990s, which have forced many households to combine multiple occupations to sustain themselves. As a livelihood strategy, men migrate out periodically in search of work and better wages, while women and children are often left behind in their villages with elderly grandparents. Migrant workers come mainly from drought- prone and less productive regions, and they go to work for part of the year on farms in the Punjab and Haryana, or on brick kilns in U.P., or construction sites in cities such as New Delhi or Bangalore. These migrant workers have been termed 'footloose labour' by Jan Breman, but this does not imply freedom. Breman's (1985) study shows, to the contrary, that landless workers do not have many rights, for instance, they are usually not paid the minimum wage. It should be noted here that wealthy farmers often prefer to employ migrant workers for harvesting and other such intensive operations, rather than the local working class, because migrants are more easily exploited and can be paid lower wages. This preference has produced a peculiar pattern in some areas where the local landless labourers move out of the home villages in search of work during the peak agricultural seasons, while migrant workers are brought in from other areas to work on the local farms. This pattern is found especially in sugarcane growing areas. Migration and lack of job security have created very poor working and living conditions for these workers.

41. What kind of process is the above passage reflecting?

(a) Capitalisation of Agriculture

(b) Green Revolution

(c) Circulation of Labour

(d) Benami Transfer

42. Sugarcane workers in Maharashtra migrate to Karnataka for 5 months and after the work is over, they go back to their village. What does this process reflect ?

(a) Green Revolution

(b) Exploitation of Labour

(c) Seasonal Migration

(d) Breakdown of Traditional Bonds

43. Who coined the term 'foot loose labour'?

(a) Jan Breman

(b) Max Weber

(c) M.N. Srinivas

(d) E. Durkheim

44. Out of the following which factor is NOT responsible for the migration of worker?

(a) Break-down of Traditional Bonds

(b) Regional Inequalities

(c) Lack of drought

(d) Green Revolution

45. Why do wealthy farmers give preference to migrant workers over local working clan for harvesting and other intensive operations ?

(a) They fire more laborious

(b) There is an idea of unfamiliarity that makes the work easy.

(c) Highly skilled

(d) Can be easily exploited and work at lower wages

Directions for Quesitons 46 to 50:

Please read the passage and answer the questions that follows.

If capitalism became the dominant economic system, nation states became the dominant political form. Societies however are not always organised along the lines of nation-states. Nation state pertains to a particular type of state, characteristic of the modern world. A government has sovereign power within a defined territorial area and the people are citizens of a single nation. Nation-state are closely associated with the rise of nationalism. The principle of nationalism assumes that any set of people have a right to be free and exercise sovereign power. It is an important part of the rise of democratic ideas. Nationalism implied that the people of India have an equal right to be sovereign. Indian nationalist during the colonial rule declared 'Swaraj' as their birth - right and fought for both political and economic freedom.

46. Nation state is the.

(a) Nationalism   (b) Political state

(c) Society   (d) Sovereignty

47. Which one of the following is not a characteristic of nation-states?

(a) Territoriality   (b) Citizenship

(c) Capitalism   (d) Sovereignity

48. What did the Indian nationalists fight for :

(a) Political freedom   (b) Economic freedom

(c) Citizenship   (d) Swaraj

49. Nationalism does not iply :

(a) that people have an equal right

(b) that people are sovereign

(c) social exclusion of citizens

(d) freedom as birth-right

50. Match the concepts given in List - I with their characteristics given in List - II :

List I: Concepts	List II: Characteristics
A. Capitalism	I. capitalism, nation-state
B. Democracy	II. economic system, dominant system
C. Swaraj	III. equality, soverienity
D. Modernity	IV. political and economic freedom

Choose the correct answer from the options given below :

(a) A-III, B-I, C-IV, D-II

(b) A-II, B-III, C-IV, D-I

(c) A-I, B-II, C-III, D-IV

(d) A-II, B-IV, C-I, D-III

Answer Keys

1. (b)	**2.** (c)	**3.** (c)	**4.** (d)	**5.** (a)	**6.** (a)	**7.** (a)	**8.** (a)	**9.** (d)	**10.** (d)
11. (c)	**12.** (d)	**13.** (d)	**14.** (d)	**15.** (b)	**16.** (b)	**17.** (d)	**18.** (b)	**19.** (a)	**20.** (a)
21. (a)	**22.** (b)	**23.** (c)	**24.** (c)	**25.** (a)	**26.** (d)	**27.** (d)	**28.** (c)	**29.** (d)	**30.** (d)
31. (d)	**32.** (c)	**33.** (c)	**34.** (d)	**35.** (c)	**36.** (c)	**37.** (a)	**38.** (a)	**39.** (a)	**40.** (c)
41. (c)	**42.** (c)	**43.** (a)	**44.** (c)	**45.** (d)	**46.** (b)	**47.** (c)	**48.** (d)	**49.** (c)	**50.** (b)

Explanations

1. (b) Aggregate statistics – or the numerical characteristics that refer to a large collectivity consisting of millions of people – offer a concrete and strong argument for the existence of social phenomena. Even though country-level or state-level statistics like the number of deaths per 1,000 population – or the death rate – are made up by aggregating (or adding up) individual deaths, the death rate itself is a social phenomenon and must be explained at the social level.

2. (c) Population momentum refers to a situation, where a large cohort of women of reproductive age will fuel population growth over the next generation, even if each woman has fewer children than previous generations did.

3. (c) Another significant theory in demography is the theory of demographic transition. This suggests that population growth is linked to overall levels of economic development and that every society follows a typical pattern of developmentrelated population growth.

4. (d) This flow of rural-tourban migration has also been accelerated by the continuous decline of common property resources like ponds, forests and grazing lands. These common resources enabled poor people to survive in the villages although they owned little or no land.

5. (a) Malthus's theory of population growth – outlined in his Essay on Population (1798) – was a rather pessimistic one. He argued that human populations tend to grow at a much faster rate than the rate at which the means of human subsistence (specially food, but also clothing and other agriculture-based products) can grow. While population rises in geometric progression (i.e., like 2, 4, 8, 16, 32 etc.), agricultural production can only grow in arithmetic progression (i.e., like 2, 4, 6, 8, 10 etc.).

Unfortunately, humanity has only a limited ability to voluntarily reduce the growth of its population (through 'preventive checks' such as postponing marriage or practicing sexual abstinence or celibacy). Malthus believed therefore that 'positive checks' to population growth – in the form of famines and diseases – were inevitable because they were nature's way of dealing with the imbalance between food supply and increasing population.

6. (a) Caste is determined by birth – a child is "born into" the caste of its parents. Caste is never a matter of choice. Membership in a caste involves strict rules about marriage. Caste groups are "endogamous", i.e. marriage is restricted to members of the group. Caste involves a system consisting of many castes arranged in a hierarchy of rank and status.

7. (a) • Mysore Narasimhachar Srinivas was one of India's foremost sociologists and social anthropologists. He was known for his works on the caste system and terms such as 'sanskritisation' and 'dominant caste'.

• Jotirao Govindrao Phule denounced the injustice of the caste system and scorned its rules of purity and pollution. In 1873 he founded the Satyashodhak Samaj (Truth Seekers Society).

• Savitri Bai Phule was the first headmistress of the country's first school for girls in Pune. She devoted her life to educating Shudras and Ati-Shudras.

• Periyar (E.V. Ramasami Naickar) is known as a rationalist and the leader of the lower caste movement in South India.

8. (a) A family can be defined as nuclear or extended. It can be male-headed or female-headed. The line of descent can be matrilineal or patrilineal.An extended family (commonly known as the 'joint family') can take different forms, but has more than one couple, and often more than two generations, living together. This could be a set of brothers with their individual families, or an elderly couple with their sons and grandsons and their respective families.

9. (d) Khasi matriliny generates intense role conflict for men. They are torn between their responsibilities to their natal house on the one hand, and to their wife and children on the other. In a way, the strain generated by such role conflict affects Khasi women more intensely

10. (d) 'Dominant caste' is a term used to refer to those castes which had a large population and were granted landrights by the partial land reforms effected after Independence. Their large numbers also gave them political power in the era of electoral democracy based on universal adult franchise.

11. (c) Initially, the British administrators began by trying to understand the complexities of caste in an effort to learn how to govern the country efficiently.

12. (d) And while various kinds of non-market exchange systems (such as the 'jajmani system') did exist in many villages and regions, even during the precolonial period villages were incorporated into wider networks of exchange through which agricultural products and other goods circulated, an important instrument of exchange and credit was the hundi, or bill of exchange (like a credit note), which allowed merchants to engage in long-distance trade. Because trade took place primarily within the caste and kinship networks of these communities, a merchant in one part of the country could issue a hundi that would be honoured by a merchant in another place.

13. (d) A well-known example is the demise of the handloom industry due to the flooding of the market with cheap manufactured textiles from England. Although pre-colonial India already had a complex monetised economy, most historians consider the colonial period to be the turning point. In the colonial era India began to be more fully linked to the world capitalist economy. Before being colonised by the British, India was a major supplier of manufactured goods to the world market. After colonisation, she became a source of raw materials and agricultural products and a consumer of manufactured goods, both largely for the benefit of industrialising England. In the late colonial period and after Independence, some Marwari families transformed themselves into modern industrialists, and even today

Marwaris control more of India's industry than any other community.

14. (d) Social inclusion can happen with the increased social, cultural and political rights

15. (b) Social stratification persists over generations. It is closely linked to the family and to the inheritance of social resources from one generation to the next.

    Social resources are unequally distributed to various social categories regardless of people's innate individual abilities.

16. (b) In every society, some people have a greater share of valued resources – money, property, education, health, and power – than others. These social resources can be divided into three forms of capital – economic capital in the form of material assets and income; cultural capital such as educational qualifications and status; and social capital in the form of networks of contacts and social associations.

17. (d) Ranade used the writings of scholars such as Bishop Joseph Butler whose Analogy of Religion and Three Sermons on Human Nature dominated the moral philosophy syllabus of Bombay University in the 1860s.

18. (b) An alternative to the nation-state, then, is the "state nation", where various "nations"— be they ethnic, religious, linguistic or indigenous identities— can co-exist peacefully and cooperatively in a single state polity. Case studies and analyses demonstrate that enduring democracies can be established in polities that are multicultural. Explicit efforts are required to end the cultural exclusion of diverse groups ... and to build multiple and complementary identities. Such responsive policies provide incentives to build a feeling of unity in diversity — a "we" feeling. Citizens can find the institutional and political space to identify with both their country and their other cultural identities, to build their trust in common institutions and to participate in and support democratic politics. All of these are key factors in consolidating and deepening democracies and building enduring "state-nations".

19. (a) Regionalism in India is rooted in India's diversity of languages, cultures, tribes, and religions.

20. (a) Civil society is the name given to the broad arena which lies beyond the private domain of the family, but outside the domain of both state and market. Civil society is the non-state and non-

market part of the public domain in which individuals get together voluntarily to create institutions and organisations. It is the sphere of active citizenship: here, individuals take up social issues, try to influence the state or make demands on it, pursue their collective interests or seek support for a variety of causes. It includes political parties, media institutions, trade unions, non-governmental organisations (NGOs), religious organisations, and other kinds of collective entities.

21. (a) Our community provides us the language (our mother tongue) and the cultural values through which we comprehend the world. It also anchors our self-identity.

22. (b) The industrialisation and urbanisation did not happen in India quite the way it did in Britain. More importantly, this is not because we began industrialisation late, but because our early industrialisation and urbanisation in the modern period were governed by colonial interests.

23. (c) The 19th century social reform attempts was the modern context and mix of ideas. It was a creative combination of modern ideas of western liberalism and a new look on traditional literature.

24. (c) India's structural and cultural diversity is self-evident. This diversity shapes the different ways that modernisation or westernisation, sanskritisation or secularisation effects or does not effect different groups of people. The following pages seek to capture these differences.

25. (a) Writing on the different kinds of urbanisation witnesses in the first two decades after independence sociologist M.S.A. Rao argued that in India many villages all over India are becoming increasingly subject to the impact of urban influences.

- A considerable number of emigrants reside not only in Indian cities but also in overseas towns.
- The second kind of urban impact is to be seen in villages which are situated near an industrial town.
- The growth of metropolitan cities accounts for the third type of urban impact on the surrounding villages

26. (d) Industrialisation and urbanisation transformed the lives of people. Factories replaced fields as places of work for some. Cities replaced villages as places to live for many. Living and working arrangements or structures changed. Changes also took place in culture, ways of life, norms, values, fashions and even body language. Shopping malls is an example of urbanization

27. (d) Social welfare responsibilities of the Panchayats include the maintenance of burning and burial grounds, recording statistics of births and deaths, establishment of child welfare and maternity centres, control of cattle pounds, propagation of family planning and promotion of agricultural activities.

28. (c) Panchayati Raj Institution: Panchayati Raj translates literally to 'Governance by five individuals'. The idea is to ensure at the village or grass root level a functioning and vibrant democracy. While the idea of grassroot democracy is not an alien import to our country, in a society where there are sharp inequalities democratic participation is hindered on grounds of gender, caste and class.

Political Party: A political party may be defined as an organisation oriented towards achieving legitimate control of government through an electoral process. Political Party is an organisation established with the aim of achieving governmental power and using that power to pursue a specific programme

FICCI, ASSOCHAM: Industrialists form associations / interest groups such as Federation of Indian Chambers and Commerce (FICCI) and Association of Chambers of Commerce (ASSOCHAM).

Nyay Panchayat: They possess the authority to hear some petty, civil and criminal cases. They can impose fines but cannot award a sentence. They have been particularly effective in punishing men who harass women for dowry and perpetrate violence against them.

29. (d) The famous sociologist, Harry Braverman, argues that the use of machinery actually deskills workers.

30. (d) People often do not see the end result of their work because they are producing only one small part of a product. The work is often repetitive and exhausting. Yet, even this is better than having no work at all, i.e., being unemployed. Marx called this situation alienation.

31. (d) Production was further speeded up by the introduction of the assembly line. Each worker sat along a conveyor belt and assembled only one part of the final product. The speed of work could be set by adjusting the speed of the conveyor belt.

32. (c) It means that very few people have the experience of employment in large firms where they get to meet people from other regions and backgrounds. Very few Indians have access to secure jobs with benefits. Of those who do, two-thirds work for the government the unorganised or informal sector workers do not have the experience of collectively fighting for proper wages and safe working conditions.

33. (c) • The Bombay Textile strike of 1982, which was led by the trade union leader, Dr. Datta Samant, and affected nearly a quarter of a million workers and their families.

• Extended working hours are legitimised by the common management practice of 'flexi-time', which in theory gives an employee freedom to choose his or her working hours (within limits) but, which in practice, means that they have to work as long as necessary to finish the task at hand.

• Home-based work is an important part of the economy. This includes the manufacture of lace, zari or brocade, carpets, bidis, agarbattis and many such products.

34. (d) Though a few newspapers had been started by people before Raja Rammohun Roy, his Sambad-Kaumudi in Bengali published in 1821, and Mirat-Ul-Akbar in Persian published in 1822, were the first publications in India with a distinct nationalist and democratic approach. Ishwar Chandra Vidyasagar started the Shome Prakash in Bengali in 1858. Fardoonji Murzban was the pioneer of the Gujarati Press in Bombay. It was as early as 1822 that he started the Bombay Samachar as a daily.

35. (c) Nike grew enormously from its inception in the 1960s. Nike grew as an importer of shoes. The founder Phil Knight imported shoes from Japan and sold them at athletics meetings. Since the 1990s we in India produce Nike. However, if labour is cheaper elsewhere production centres will move somewhere else.

36. (c) Features of globalization:

Globalisation involves a stretching of social and economic relationships throughout the world. This stretching is pushed by certain economic policies. Very broadly this process in India is termed liberalisation. The term liberalisation refers to a range of policy decisions that the Indian state took since 1991 to open up the Indian economy to the world market.

Globalisation of finance: It should also be noted that for the first time, mainly due to the information technology revolution, there has been a globalisation of finance.

37. (a) A redemptive social movement aims to bring about a change in the personal consciousness and actions of its individual members. For instance, people in the Ezhava community in Kerala were led by Narayana Guru to change their social practices.

Reformist social movements strive to change the existing social and political arrangements through gradual, incremental steps. The 1960s movement for the reorganisation of Indian states on the basis of language and the recent Right to Information campaign are examples of reformist movements.

Revolutionary social movements attempt to radically transform social relations, often by capturing state power. The Bolshevik revolution in Russia that deposed the Tsar to create a communist state and the Naxalite movement in India.

The Chipko Movement, an example of the new social and ecological movement, in the Himalayan foothills is a good example of such intermingled interests and ideologies.

38. (a) A social movement requires sustained collective action over time. Collective action must be marked by some degree of organisation. This organisation may include a leadership and a structure that defines how members relate to each other, make decisions and carry them out. Those participating in a social movement also have shared objectives and ideologies.

39. (a) The Chipko Movement, an example of the ecological movement, in the Himalayan foothills is a good example of such intermingled interests and ideologies.

40. (c) Some Dalit movements are - Satnami Movement of the Chamars in the Chattisgarh plains in eastern MP, Adi Dharma Movement in Punjab, the Mahar Movement in Maharashtra, the socio-political mobilisation among the Jatavas of Agra and the Anti Brahman Movement in south India.

41. (c) The above passage is on Circulation of labor

42. (c) As a livelihood strategy, men migrate out periodically in search of work and better wages.

43. (a) These migrant workers have been termed 'footloose labour' by Jan Breman, but this does not imply freedom.

44. (c) Labourers migrate also due to the increasing inequalities in rural areas from the mid-1990s, which have forced many households to combine multiple occupations to sustain themselves.

45. (d) It should be noted here that wealthy farmers often prefer to employ migrant workers for harvesting and other such intensive operations, rather than the local working class, because migrants are more easily exploited and can be paid lower wages.

46. (b) If capitalism became the dominant economic system, nation states became the dominant political form.

47. (c) A government has sovereign power within a defined territorial area, and the people are citizens of a single nation.

48. (d) Indian nationalist leaders were quick to grasp this irony. They declared that freedom or swaraj was their birth- right and fought for both political and economic freedom.

49. (c) swaraj was their birth- right and fought for both political and economic freedom.

50. (b) Capitalism became the dominant economic system, swaraj was both political and economic freedom.

1. Life expectancy refers to:-
   - (a) The estimated number of years that an average person is expected to survive
   - (b) Total number of live births that a hypothetical woman would have if she lived through the reproductive age
   - (c) Difference between birth rate and death rate
   - (d) The number of live births per 1000 women in the child bearing age group

2. A situation where a large cohort of women of reproductive age will fuel population growth over the next generation, even, if each woman has fewer children than previous generation did is called:
   - (a) Fertility Rate
   - (b) Total Fertility Rate
   - (c) Population Momentum
   - (d) Population Growth

3. The type of demography that enquires into the wider causes and consequences of social Structures and processes on population is called:
   - (a) Social Demography
   - (b) Formal Demography
   - (c) Arithmetic Progression
   - (d) Geometric Progression

4. Famines and diseases are nature's way of dealing with the imbalance of food supply vis-a-vis increase in population. Malthus identified this as :
   - (a) Preventive checks
   - (b) Positive checks
   - (c) Negative checks
   - (d) Promotive checks

5. Sex ratio refers to the :
   - (a) Number of females per 100 males in a given area at a specified time period,
   - (b) Number of males per 1000 females in a given area at a specified time period.
   - (c) Number of females per 1000 males in a given area at a specified time period.
   - (d) Number of females per 1000 males in a given area at a non-specified time period.

6. Match List I with List II

List I	List II
A. Jatavas	I. Muslim Community
B. Multani Lohars	II. Meghalaya
C. Khasis	III. Karnataka
D. Vokkaligas	IV Uttar Pradesh

Choose the correct answer from the options given below:
   - (a) A-IV, B-I, C-III, D-II
   - (b) A-IV, B-I, C-II, D-III
   - (c) A-IV, B-III, C-II, D-I
   - (d) A-IV, B-II, C-III, D-I

7. Match **List I** with **List II**:

List I : **Contribution**	List II : **Important Personalities**
A. Brahmo Samaj	I. M. G. Ranade
B. Widow remarriage	II. Raja Ram Mohan Roy
C. Country's first school for girls	III. Jyotiba Phule
D. Anti Caste Movement	IV. Savitri Bai Phule

Choose the correct answer from the options green below:
   - (a) A-II, B-I, C-III, D-IV
   - (b) A-I, B-II, C-IV, D-III
   - (c) A-II, B-I, C-IV, D-III
   - (d) A-IV, B-I, C-III, D-II

8. The legal provisions against violence and humiliation to Dalits and Adivasis strengthened by :
   - (a) Government of India Act, 1935
   - (b) Scheduled Castes and Tribes Act, 1989
   - (c) 93rd Constitutional Amendment, 2006
   - (d) Article 17, Constitution of India 1950

9. Which of the following is not the characteristic of Caste?
   - (a) Social and Religious hierarchy
   - (b) Segmental Division of Society
   - (c) Unrestricted Choice of Occupation
   - (d) Restrictions on feeding and Social Intercourse

10. The terms 'Matrilineal' and 'Patrilineal' are associated with:
   - (a) Residence of family
   - (b) Line of descent
   - (c) Nature of marriage rules
   - (d) Structure of family

11. Who wrote the book "The Wealth of Nations"?
   - (a) John Smith
   - (b) David Ricardo
   - (c) Adam Smith
   - (d) Emile Durkheim

12. Liberalisation can be understood as :
   - (a) Privatisation and Marketisation
   - (b) Government regulations for industry
   - (c) Promoting government investment
   - (d) Increasing import duties on goods

13. 'Other Backward Class' refers to:

    (a) Socially and educationally backward class

    (b) Part of SC, ST

    (c) Dominant Caste

    (d) Economically and politically powerful classes

14. Match List I with List II

List I : Concept	List II : Characteristics
A. Third sender	I. Separation of races
B. Apartheid	II. Social category of persons who are neither male nor female
C. Adivasis	III. Conversion of gender status of body into opposite gender by choice
D. Transgender	IV. Indigenous population, identity struggles

Choose the correct answer from the options given below:

    (a) A-II, B-I, C-IV, D-III

    (b) A-I, B-II, C-III, D-IV

    (c) A-IV, B-III, C-I, D-II

    (d) A-IV, B-II, C-I, D-III

15. The term that literally means 'pre-judgement', that is, an opinion formed in advance of any familiarity with the subject, before considering any available evidence is:

    (a) Stratification   (b) Discrimination

    (c) Prejudice   (d) Stereotypes

16. Match List I with List II

List I : Books	List II : Authors
A. Stree Punish Tulana	I. M. G. Ranade
B. Three Sermons on Human nature	II. Taiabai Sliinde
C. Sultana's Dream	III. Bishop Joseph Butler
D. The texts of the Hindu law	IV. Begum Rukkaiyah Hossain

Choose the correct answer from the options given below:

    (a) A-III, B-II, C-I, D-IV   (b) A-II, B-III, C-IV, D-I

    (c) A-IV, B-III, C-II, D-I   (d) A-II, B-I, C-III, D-IV

17. Indian nationalism is inclusive because it recognizes ____________.

    (a) Diversity

    (b) Majority groups

    (c) Regionalism

    (d) Has one national language

18. Which of the following is NOT correct?

    (a) There is separation of religious and political authority' in Western Secularism

    (b) In Indian Context. Secularism goes hand in hand with Communalism

    (c) Secular Indian state respect all religion

    (d) A Secular state does not favour any religion

19. Community Identity is based on:

    (a) Birth and belongingness

    (b) Qualification and achievements

    (c) Choice and competency

    (d) Competency and negotiation

20. Identify the correct statement:

    (a) During emergency, people experienced authoritarian rule

    (b) During elections, immediately after the emergency, people voted overwhelmingly for Congress party

    (c) The Civil liberties of people remain unaffected during the emergency

    (d) Press was given freedom of speech during emergency

21. Which of the following is not Sanskritisation?

    (a) Exaggerate social mobility

    (b) Improve positional status for individuals

    (c) Rests on purity and pollution

    (d) Dalit Culture eroded

22. Colonialism had a deep impact on structure of the Indian Society. Which of the following is not true regarding colonialism in India?

    (a) Britishers interfered with Indian markets to ensure greater profits

    (b) They altered the way of production

    (c) They implemented Forest Act which changed the lives of pastoralists

    (d) They benefited from continuous flow of tribute without interference in economic base

23. Cities play a key role in economic systems of the empires. Which of the following is not one of them?

    (a) Goods can be cheaply imported

    (b) Concrete expression of Global Capitalism

    (c) Link between margins of Colonized India and Britain

    (d) To maintain the traditional values

24. The first society to undergo industrialization was ________

    (a) Germany   (b) America (USA)

    (c) Britain   (d) India

25. A process of decline in the influence of religions is cailed:-

(a) Communalism   (b) Modernization

(c) Regionalism   (d) Secularization

26. Which of the following Statements is not power and responsibility delegated to the Panchayats?

(a) To prepare plans and schemes for economic development

(b) To promote skills that will enhance social justice

(c) To levy, collect and appropriate taxes, duties, tolls and fees

(d) To make sure that endogamy is practiced amongst rural youth

27. The Panchayat that has the authority' to hear some petty, civil and criminal cases is:-

(a) Zila Panchayat   (b) Gram Panchayat

(c) Nvava Panchayat   (d) Gram Sabhas

28. Which of the following is not a change due to green revolution?

(a) Shift from payment in kind to payment in cash

(b) Increasing bonded labour

(c) Rise of rural elites

(d) Commercialization of Agriculture

29. Commercialization of agriculture does not lead to:

(a) Regional inequality

(b) Integration of rural to wider economy

(c) Development of rural infrastructure

(d) Increase in organic farming

30. Washermen, Potters, Goldsmiths, Oil-pressures are known as:

(a) Dalits   (b) Service Castes

(c) Labourers   (d) Vaishyas

31. Choose the correct option:

Farmers suicide can be linked to 'agrarian distress' caused by structural changes in agriculture. These include:

A. Liberalization policies

B. Declining State Support

C. High Cost inputs

D. Community involvement increased in agricultural operations

E. Changing Crop pattern

Choose the correct answer from die options given below:

(a) A, C, D, E   (b) A, B, C, E

(c) A, B, D, E   (d) B, C, D, E

32. Which of the following statement is NOT true about the second phase of green revolution?

(a) Increasing dependence on market

(b) Farmers switched to Multi-crop system from Mono-crop system

(c) Green revolution resulted in increased regional inequalities

(d) Increased risks for farmers

33. Match the Concepts/ Sociologists given in List I with their Characteristics given below in List II

List I : Concepts/Sociologists		List II : Characteristics
A. Alienation	I.	Work broken into small repetitive elements to increase efficiency
B. Convergence thesis	II.	When workers do not enjoy work and task becomes repetitive and exhausting
C. Scientific Management	III.	All countries follow same path to modernization
D. Harry Braverman	IV.	Machinery actually de skills workers

Choose the correct answer from the options given below:

(a) A-III, B-II, C-IV, D-I

(b) A-II, B-III, C-I, D-IV

(c) A-I, B-IV, C-II, D-III

(d) A-I, B-II, C-III, D-IV

34. Arrange in sequence the process of Bidi making,

A. Dampening the tender leaves

B. Contractor sells bidi to manufacturer

C. Filling tobacco evenly and trying them with thread.

D. Manufacturer sells to distributor.

E. Villagers picks up tender leaves and sell them to forest department

Choose the correct answer from the options given below:

(a) E, C A, B, D   (b) E, A, C, B, D

(c) E, B, C, A, D   (d) A, C, B, D, E

35. When government sells its share to several public sector companies. This process is known as ______

(a) Deinvestment   (b) Uninvestment

(c) Laissez-faire   (d) Disinvestment

36. Retail chains are a threat to Indian market because-
    (a) They promote the policy of liberalization
    (b) They provide more job opportunity
    (c) Small local chains (grocery stores) will be destroyed
    (d) Retail sector is attractive

37. Match the Industrial Outcomes given in List I with their Characteristics given below m List II

List I : Industrial Outcomes	List II : Characteristics
A. Engineers using a software for draughting	I. Occupational hazard
B. Trade Union	II. De-skilling of workers
C. Silicosis in miners	III. Knowledge economy
D. Growth of IT sector	IV. Bargaining power of workers

    Choose the correct answer from the options green below:
    (a) A-I, B-II, C-III, D-IV
    (b) A-III, B-I, C-II, D-III
    (c) A-II, B-IV, C-I, D-III
    (d) A-IV, B-II, C-III, D-I

38. Name the branch of management theory that seeks to increase productivity and competitiveness through the creation of a unique organizational culture involving all members of a firm.
    (a) Culture of Consumption
    (b) Corporate Culture
    (c) Knowledge economy
    (d) Competitive Culture

39. Match the (Concepts) given in List I with their Characteristics given below in List II

List I : Industrial Outcomes	List II : Characteristics
A. Globalization	I. Economic Globalisation
B. Electric Economy	II. Growing interdependence between people, regions and countries
C. Liberalisation	III. Growth in the usage of cell phones
D. Cellular Telephone	IV. Steady removal of the rules that regulates Indian trade and finance regulations

    Choose the correct answer from the options given below:
    (a) A-III, B-IV, C-I, D-II
    (b) A-IV, B-III, C-II, D-I
    (c) A-I, B-II, C-III, D-IV
    (d) A-II, B-I, C-IV, D-III

40. In 1957, All India Radio acquired hugely popular channel which grew to become a money-spinning channel for AIR. The name of the channel was:
    (a) Hum Log
    (b) Vividh Bharati
    (c) Doordarshan
    (d) Bunivaad

Directions for Quesitons 41 to 45:

Please read the passage and answer the questions that follows.

Jharkhand is one of the newly formed states of India carved out of South Bihar in the year 2000. Behind the formation of this state lies more than a century of resistance. The social movement for Jharkhand had a charismatic leader in Birsa Munda. an adivasi who led a major uprising against the British. After his death Birsa became an important icon of the movement literate adivasis began to research and write about him. They disseminated information about tribal customs and cultural practices. This helped create a unified ethnic consciousness and a shared identity as Jharkhandis.

41. Name the leader who headed the social movement for Jharkhand state.
    (a) Kalidas
    (b) Gunda Dhar
    (c) Birsa Munda
    (d) Mahatma Gandhi

42. Choose the incorrect feature of a social movement.
    (a) Sustained Collective Action
    (b) Shared objectives and ideologies
    (c) Spontaneous and disorganized
    (d) Leadership

43. Tribal movements are considered to be a part of New Social Movement. What comprises of New Social Movement?
    (a) Old issues of economic inequality
    (b) Recognisation of power relatives
    (c) Central role of political parties
    (d) Quality life issues, identity, environment

44. Adivasis shared a common hatred towards ______
    A. Dikus
    B. Migrant traders
    C. Moneylenders
    D. Christian missionaries
    Choose the correct answer from the options given below:
    (a) B, C and D Only
    (b) C, D and A Only
    (c) A, B and C Only
    (d) A, B and D Only

45. Tribal movements help in creating, among Jharkhandis, a sense of
    (a) Ethnic consciousness, shared identity
    (b) Marginalization, injustice
    (c) Tribal customs and cultural practices
    (d) Poverty, insecurity

Directions for Quesitons 46 to 50:

Please read the passage and answer the questions that follows.

The industry began in India in 1851. Most of the tea gardens were situated in Assam. Since Assam was sparsely populated and the tea plantations were often located on uninhabited hillsides, the bulk of the sorely needed labour had to be imported from other provinces. But to bring thousands of people every year from their far-off homes into strange lands, possessing an unhealthy climate required the provision of financial and other incentives which the tea planters were unwilling to offer. Instead they took recourse to fraud coercion and persuaded the government to pass regressive penal laws. Thus the recruitment of labourers for tea gardens of Assam was carried on by contractor under the provisions of transport of Native Labourers Act (No 111) of 1863 of Bengal as amended in 1865, 1870 and 1873

46. The industry developed during the ________.

    (a) Pre-colonial period

    (b) Colonial period

    (c) Post-independence period

    (d) Vedic period

47. Tea industry during colonial times was ________.

    (a) Labour intensive

    (b) Machinery intensive

    (c) Financially well paid jobs for labourers

    (d) Based on democratic set up

48. Which of these reasons is **NOT** valid for the questions given below:

The tea plantations was based on migrant labourers because:

    (a) The plantations were based in sparsely populated areas

    (b) Offered high wages to workers

    (c) Work was labour intensive in nature

    (d) Plantation was located in uninhabited hillsides

49. Transport of Native Labourers Act (No. 111) of 1863 was not helpful for:

    (a) Tea plantation owners

    (b) Contractors

    (c) Colonial government

    (d) Labourers

50. Choose the right/correct answer:

Transport of Native Labourers Act (No. 111) of 1863 of Bengal as amended in the years ________.

    (a) 1947, 1983, 1985

    (b) 1863, 1865, 1873

    (c) 1865, 1870, 1873

    (d) 1965, 1870, 1873

Answer Keys

1. (a)	**2.** (c)	**3.** (a)	**4.** (b)	**5.** (c)	**6.** (b)	**7.** (b)	**8.** (a)	**9.** (a)	**10.** (b)
11. (c)	**12.** (a)	**13.** (a)	**14.** (a)	**15.** (c)	**16.** (b)	**17.** (a)	**18.** (b)	**19.** (a)	**20.** (a)
21. (c)	**22.** (d)	**23.** (d)	**24.** (c)	**25.** (d)	**26.** (d)	**27.** (c)	**28.** (b)	**29.** (d)	**30.** (b)
31. (b)	**32.** (b)	**33.** (b)	**34.** (b)	**35.** (a)	**36.** (c)	**37.** (c)	**38.** (b)	**39.** (d)	**40.** (b)
41. (c)	**42.** (c)	**43.** (d)	**44.** (c)	**45.** (a)	**46.** (b)	**47.** (a)	**48.** (b)	**49.** (d)	**50.** (c)

Explanations

1. (a) Life Expectancy refers to the estimated number of years that an average person is expected to survive.

2. (c) Population momentum refers to a situation, where a large cohort of women of reproductive age will fuel population growth over the next generation, even if each woman has fewer children than previous generations did.

Indian Society – Chapter 2 – Demographic Structure of India; India's Demographic Transition

3. (a) Population studies or social demography, on the other hand, enquires into the wider causes and consequences of population structures and change.

4. (b) Malthus believed therefore that 'positive checks' to population growth – in the form of famines and diseases – were inevitable because they were nature's way of dealing with the imbalance between food supply and increasing population.

5. (c) The sex ratio refers to the number of females per 1000 males in a given area at a specified time period.

6. (b) Examples of such dominant castes include the Yadavs of Bihar and Uttar Pradesh, the Vokkaligas of Karnataka, the Reddys and Khammas of Andhra Pradesh, the Marathas of Maharashtra, the Jats of Punjab, Haryana and Western Uttar Pradesh and the Patidars of Gujarat.

7. (b) Jotirao Govindrao Phule denounced the injustice of the caste system and scorned its rules of purity and pollution. In 1873 he founded the Satyashodhak Samaj (Truth Seekers Society), which was devoted to securing human rights and social justice for low-caste people.

Savitri Bai Phule was the first headmistress of the country's first school for girls in Pune. She devoted her life to educating Shudras and Ati-Shudras. She started a night school for agriculturists and labourers. She died while serving plague patients.

8. (a) The Government of India Act of 1935 was passed which gave legal recognition to the lists or 'schedules' of castes and tribes marked out for special treatment by the state. This is how the terms 'Scheduled Tribes' and the 'Scheduled Castes' came into being.

9. (a) Caste involves a system consisting of many castes arranged in a hierarchy of rank and status.

Castes also involve sub-divisions within themselves, i.e., castes almost always have sub-castes and sometimes sub-castes may also have subsub-castes. This is referred to as a segmental organisation.

Caste membership also involves rules about food and food-sharing.

10. (b) The line of descent can be matrilineal or patrilineal.

11. (c) The most famous of the early political economists was Adam Smith, who in his book, The Wealth of Nations, attempted to understand the market economy that was just emerging at that time.

12. (a) Liberalisation includes a range of policies such as the privatisation of public sector enterprises. Another word for such changes is marketisation, or the use of markets or market-based processes (rather than government regulations or policies) to solve social, political, or economic problems.

13. (a) Other Backward Classes were described as the 'socially and educationally backward classes'.

14. (a) To ensure their political control, the White European minority developed the policy of apartheid, or separation of the races.

Trans Gender – In general 'male body' and 'female body' as social unit are unchanging identity but due to so many researches in the field of physiology, the notion of the body is now liked with 'choice structure'.

Third Gender – Third gender refers to that social category of persons who are neither male nor female.

Adivasis are indigenous population who fought for their identities.

15. (c) Prejudices refer to pre-conceived opinions or attitudes held by members of one group towards another. The word literally means 'pre-judgement', that is, an opinion formed in advance of any familiarity with the subject, before considering any available evidence.

16. (b) Stree Purush Tulana (or Comparison of Men and Women) was written by a Maharashtrian housewife, Tarabai Shinde, as a protest against the double standards of a male dominated society.

Begum Rokeya Sakhawat Hossain was born in a well-to-do Bengali Muslim family, and was lucky to have a husband who was very liberal in outlook and encouraged her education first in Urdu and later in Bengali and English. She was already a successful author in Urdu and Bengali when she wrote Sultana's Dream to test her abilities in English.

Ranade used the writings of scholars such as Bishop Joseph Butler whose Analogy of Religion and Three Sermons on Human Nature dominated the moral philosophy syllabus of Bombay University in the 1860s. At the same time, M.G. Ranade's writings entitled the The Texts of the Hindu Law on the Lawfulness of the Remarriage of Widows and Vedic Authorities for Widow Marriage elaborated the shastric sanction for remarriage of widows.

17. (a) In Indian nationalism, the dominant trend was marked by an inclusive and democratic vision. Inclusive because it recognised diversity and plurality.

18. (b) The separation of religious and political authority marked a major turning point in the social history of the west. This separation was related to the process of "secularisation", or the progressive retreat of religion from public life, as it was converted from a mandatory obligation to a voluntary personal practice. Secularisation in turn was related to the arrival of modernity and the rise of science and rationality as alternatives to religious ways of understanding the world. The Indian meanings of secular and secularism include the western sense but also involve others.

19. (a) Community identity is based on birth and 'belonging' rather than on some form of acquired qualifications or 'accomplishment'. It is what we 'are' rather than what we have 'become'.

20. (a) The Indian people had a brief experience of authoritarian rule during the 'Emergency' enforced between June 1975 and January 1977. Parliament was suspended and new laws were made directly by the government. Civil liberties were revoked and a large number of politically active people were arrested and jailed without trial. Censorship was imposed on the media and government officials could be dismissed without normal procedures.

21. (c) Sanskritisation as a concept has been criticised at different levels. One, it has been criticised for exaggerating social mobility or the scope of 'lower castes' to move up the social ladder. For it leads to no structural change but only positional change of some individuals. 'Sanskritisation' seems to justify a model that rests on inequality and exclusion. It appears to suggest that to believe in pollution and purity of groups of people is justifiable or all right. The effect of such a trend is that the key characteristics of dalit culture and society are eroded.

22. (d) There is a vital difference between the empire building of pre-capitalist times and that of capitalist times. Pre-colonial rulers simply took the tribute that was skimmed off the economic surplus that was produced traditionally in the subjugated areas.

23. (d) Cities had a key role in the economic system of empires. Coastal cities such as Mumbai, Kolkata and Chennai were favoured. From here primary commodities could be easily exported and manufactured goods could be cheaply imported. Colonial cities were the prime link between the economic centre or core in Britain and periphery or margins in colonised India. Cities in this sense were the concrete expression of global capitalism.

24. (c) The Britain, the first society to undergo industrialisation, was also the earliest to move from being rural to a predominantly urban country.

25. (d) In the modern west, secularisation has usually meant a process of decline in the influence of religion.

26. (d) The following powers and responsibility were delegated to the Panchayats:

- to prepare plans and schemes for economic development
- to promote schemes that will enhance social justice
- to levy, collect and appropriate taxes, duties, tolls and fees
- help in the devolution of governmental responsibilities, especially that of finances to local authorities

27. (c) Nyaya Panchayats have been constituted in some states. They possess the authority to hear some petty, civil and criminal cases.

28. (b) Impact of Green Revolution:

- an increase in the use of agricultural labour as cultivation became more intensive;
- a shift from payment in kind (grain) to payment in cash;
- a loosening of traditional bonds or hereditary relationships between farmers or landowners and agricultural workers (known as bonded labour) and
- the rise of a class of 'free' wage labourers.

29. (d) In the first phase of the Green Revolution, in the 1960s and 1970s, the introduction of new technology seemed to be increasing inequalities in rural society. Increasing commercialisation and dependence on the market in these areas (for instance, where cotton cultivation has been promoted) has increased rather than reduced livelihood insecurity, as farmers who once grew food for consumption now depend on the market for the incomes.

30. (b) Rural life also supported many other specialists and crafts persons as storytellers, astrologers, priests, water-distributors, and oil-pressers. The diversity of occupations in rural India was reflected in the caste system, which in most regions included specialist and 'service' castes such as Dry Cleaners, Potters, and Goldsmiths.

31. (b) Many farmers, who have committed suicide were marginal farmers, who were attempting to increase their productivity, primarily by practising Green Revolution methods. However, undertaking such production meant facing several risks: the cost of production has increased tremendously due to a decrease in agricultural subsidies, the markets are not stable, and many farmers borrow heavily in order to invest in expensive inputs and improve their production. The loss of either the crop (due to spread of disease or pests, excessive rainfall, or drought), and in some cases, lack of an adequate support or market price means that farmers are unable to bear the debt burden or sustain their families.

32. (b) The second phase of the Green Revolution which began in 1980s, farmers living in the dry and semi-arid regions of India began following Green Revolution cultivation practices. In these areas there has been a significant shift from dry to wet (irrigated) cultivation, along with changes in the cropping pattern and type of crops grown. Increasing commercialisation and dependence on the market in these areas (for instance, where cotton cultivation has been promoted) has increased rather than reduced livelihood insecurity, as farmers who once grew food for consumption now depend on the market for the incomes. In marketoriented cultivation, especially where a single crop is grown, a fall in prices or a bad crop can spell financial ruin for farmers. In most of the Green Revolution areas, farmers have switched from a multi-crop system, which allowed them to spread risks, to a mono-crop regime, which means that there is nothing to fall back on in case of crop failure.

33. (b) Marx called this situation alienation, when people do not enjoy work, and see it as something they have to do only in order to survive, and even that survival depends on whether the technology has room for any human labour.

According to the convergence thesis put forward by modernisation theorist Clark Kerr, an industrialised India of the 21st century shares more features with China or the United States in the 21st century than it shares with 19th century India.

Another way of increasing output is by organising work. An American called Frederick Winslow Taylor invented a new system in the 1890s, which he called 'Scientific Management'. It is also known as Taylorism or industrial engineering. Under his system, all work was broken down into its smallest repetitive elements, and divided between workers.

The famous sociologist, Harry Braverman, argues that the use of machinery actually deskills workers. For example, whereas earlier architects and engineers had to be skilled draughtsmen, now the computer does a lot of the work for them.

34. (b) The process of bidi making:

1. The process of making bidis starts in forested villages where villagers pluck tendu leaves and sell it to the forest department or a private contractor who in turn sells it to the forest department. On average a person can collect 100 bundles (of 50 leaves each) a day.

2. The government then auctions the leaves to bidi factory owners who give it to the contractors.

3. The contractor in turn supplies tobacco and leaves to home-based workers. These workers, mostly women, roll the bidis – first dampening the leaves, then cutting them, filling in tobacco evenly and then tying them with thread.

4. The contractor picks up these bidis and sells them to the manufacturer who roasts them, and puts on his own brand label.

5. The manufacturer then sells them to a distributor who distributes the packed bidis to wholesalers who in turn sell to your neighbourhood pan shops.

35. (a) The government is trying to sell its share in several public sector companies, a process which is known as disinvestment.

36. (c) India's retail sector is attractive not only because of its fast growth, but because family-run street corner stores have 97% of the nation's business. But this industry trait is precisely why the government makes it hard for foreigners to enter the market. Politicians frequently argue that global retailers would destroy thousands of small local players and fledgling domestic chains.

37. (c) Occupational hazard: Many workers develop breathing problems and diseases like tuberculosis and silicosis.

The phrase 'knowledge economy' is use to describe the growth of IT sector in India.

The famous sociologist, Harry Braverman, argues that the use of machinery actually deskills workers. For example, whereas earlier architects and engineers had to be skilled draughtsmen, now the computer does a lot of the work for them.

38. (b) Corporate culture is a branch of management theory that seeks to increase productivity and competitiveness though the creation of a unique organisational culture involving all members of a firm.

39. (d) Globalisation refers to the growing interdependence between different people, regions and countries in the world as social and economic relationships come to stretch world-wide.

The 'electronic economy' is another factor that underpins economic globalisation.

Globalisation involves a stretching of social and economic relationships throughout the world. This stretching is pushed by certain economic policies. Very broadly this process in India is termed liberalisation.

Cellular telephony has also grown enormously and cell phones are a part of the self for most urban-based middle class youth. There has been a tremendous growth in the usage of cell phones and a marked change in how its use is seen.

40. (b) In 1957 AIR acquired the hugely popular channel Vividh Bharati, which soon began to carry sponsored programmes and advertisements and grew to become a money-spinning channel for AIR.

41. (c) The social movement for Jharkhand had a charismatic leader in Birsa Munda, an adivasi who led a major uprising against the British.

42. (c) A social movement requires sustained collective action over time. Such action is often directed against the state and takes the form of demanding changes in state policy or practice. Spontaneous, disorganised protest cannot be called a social movement either. Collective action must be marked by some degree of organisation. This organisation may include a leadership and a structure that defines how members relate to each other, make decisions and carry them out. Those participating in a social movement also have shared objectives and ideologies

43. (d) It was difficult to classify the members of these so-called 'new social movements' as belonging to the same class or even nation. Rather than a shared class identity, participants felt that they shared identities as students, women, blacks, or environmentalists.

44. (c) Adivasis shared a common hatred of dikus – migrant traders and moneylenders who had settled in the area and grabbed its wealth, impoverishing the original residents.

45. (a) Literate adivasis in Jharkhand began to research and write about their history and myths. They documented and disseminated information about tribal customs and cultural practices. This helped create a unified ethnic consciousness and a shared identity as Jharkhandis.

46. (b) During the time of colonial government industry was developed in India.

47. (a) Tea industry was labor intensive.

48. (b) In 1903, the industry employed 4,79,000 permanent and 93,000 temporary employees. Since Assam was sparsely populated and the tea plantations were often located on uninhabited hillsides, bulk of the sorely needed labour had to be imported from other provinces.

49. (d) The recruitment of labourers for tea gardens of Assam was carried on for years mostly by contractors under the provisions of the Transport of Native Labourers Act (No. III) of 1863 of Bengal.

50. (c) The Transport of Native Labourers Act (No. III) of 1863 of Bengal as amended in 1865, 1870 and 1873.

www.ingramcontent.com/pod-product-compliance
Lightning Source LLC
LaVergne TN
LVHW080606200726
843509LV00007B/255